THE WILD WORD

THE WILD WORD

Animals in the Gospels

JAEDA CHARLOTTE CALAWAY

McGill-Queen's University Press
Montreal & Kingston • London • Chicago

ISBN 978-0-2280-2471-2 (paper)
ISBN 978-0-2280-2512-2 (ePDF)
ISBN 978-0-2280-2513-9 (ePUB)

Legal deposit second quarter 2025
Bibliothèque et Archives nationales du Québec

Printed in Canada on acid-free paper that is 100% ancient-forest-free, containing 100% sustainable, recycled fibre, and processed chlorine-free.

McGill-Queen's University Press in Montreal is on land which long served as a site of meeting and exchange amongst Indigenous Peoples, including the Haudenosaunee and Anishinabeg nations. In Kingston it is situated on the territory of the Haudenosaunee and Anishinaabek. We acknowledge and thank the diverse Indigenous Peoples whose footsteps have marked these territories on which peoples of the world now gather.

Library and Archives Canada Cataloguing in Publication

Title: The wild word : animals in the Gospels / Jaeda Charlotte Calaway.
Other titles: Animals in the Gospels
Names: Calaway, Jaeda Charlotte, author.
Description: Includes bibliographical references and index.
Identifiers: Canadiana (print) 20250126389 | Canadiana (ebook) 20250126419 | ISBN 9780228024712 (paper) | ISBN 9780228025122 (EPDF) | ISBN 9780228025139 (EPUB)
Subjects: LCSH: Bible. Gospels—Criticism, interpretation, etc. | LCSH: Animals in the Bible. | LCSH: Human-animal relationships—Religious aspects—Christianity.
Classification: LCC BS663 .C35 2025 | DDC 220.8/59—dc23

This book was designed and typeset by True to Type in 10½/14 Bembo.
Copyediting by Lesley Trites.

McGill-Queen's University Press
Suite 1720, 1010 Sherbrooke St West, Montreal, QC, H3A 2R7

Authorized safety representative in the EU: Mare Nostrum Group BV, Mauritskade 21D, 1091 GC Amsterdam, the Netherlands, gpsr@mare-nostrum.co.uk

To the beasts, the critters, the living ones; to those who crawl, slither, scurry, swim, hop, and fly; to those who growl, bark, meow, purr, buzz, chirp, and sing; I see your face.

Contents

Acknowledgments

This project began in the classroom. I taught a course at Illinois College on religion, agriculture, and ecology. As I worked through how different religious perspectives, practices, and traditions impacted land use, farming practices, eating practices, and the treatment of animals, I noticed students became the most interested when we talked about animals. I began to spend more time on various kinds of human-animal interactions, including raising, sacrificing, and eating animals both inside and outside the classroom. When COVID-19 lockdowns hit, I would spend time outside with my kids and look at the various critters around our house, including birds, stray cats, spiders, wasps, bees, butterflies, moths, squirrels, slugs, snails, and more, in what I called "backyard ecology." I became increasingly sensitized to the taken-for-granted animals that surround us all the time. In the process, I turned to the gospels, both canonical (domesticated) and extracanonical (feral), and began noting every explicit and, with more difficulty, implicit mention of animals throughout. I began to categorize these mentions in various ways, and the product is this book.

In addition to in the classroom, I had the opportunity to present some of this material at professional meetings before and during COVID-19 lockdowns. I presented a version of "Jesus and the Ancient Abattoir" at the Central States Society of Biblical Literature (SBL) in the spring of 2020, a week before my state shut everything down. I presented a version of "Reshaping Gospel Animality in the Filmic Imagination" to the Bible and Film group at the virtual SBL conference in November of 2020. I want to thank all the participants at these conferences for their feedback and early encouragement in this area of research, particularly questions and feedback from Mark Given on discussions of theorizing animality and Adam Porter for discussions on film criticism. I want to thank Celia Deutsch, who gave feedback on early versions of these chapters as she has generously done for all of my book manuscripts since I was a graduate student. My former colleague in sociology at Illinois College, Paul Fuller, also read very early versions of most of this manuscript, including when some portions were merely in outline form. We have had many conversations about theory, especially social theories, from travelling to Greece together to chatting on the porch while our kids played together.

Other friends expressed interest, gave support, and read earlier versions of the entire manuscript, including Skyler McGee and Heather Leonard. Skyler, especially, has a spirit much like St Francis of Assisi, having an extraordinary sensitivity to nonhuman animals. She and I regularly chatted about this project – as well as her art projects – while dropping off and picking up our kids from school.

A version of "Into Gospel Wilds: Divine, Demonic, and Animal" was previously published by the journal *Bible & Critical Theory* in 2024. I want to thank Rhiannon Graybill and Rob Seesengood for shepherding this chapter through the publication process for their journal. I want to thank the anonymous reviewers who helped me reframe that article and now chapter.

I want to thank the publication team at McGill-Queen's University Press. As with my previous book, Kyla Madden has done an extraordinary job shepherding this manuscript through the publication project. I chatted with Kyla for well over an hour at the Society of Biblical Literature / American Academy of Religion meeting in Denver in 2022, discussing a wide variety of topics, including this book. I want to thank my three anonymous reviewers for their support, their encouraging comments, and even their critical comments, all of which gave me a push to make this manuscript better than the one I originally submitted. Thank you to Lesley Trites for her attention to the mechanics of my prose. And to everyone on the publication team who worked on everything from the title and book cover to marketing.

More than any other book I have written, this is a personal book. My students, colleagues, friends, and family have all shaped me in ways that have become apparent in this book more so than any other. As I wrote this book, I regularly had memories of my mother Rebecca Jane Calaway indulging my fascination with pets as a child, when I had dogs, birds, and a rabbit, and who, to this day, sends me pictures of wild birds she sees; of my father feeding our dog Inky peanut butter while watching St Louis Cardinals games and also taking me out into the woods to explore, go fishing, and, yes, even hunt; of my kids who have grown to love animals; of my spouse Stacy Camacho's embrace of my miniature pinscher, Daphne, and their love of cats. I could not have written this manuscript without continual inspiration from and daily interaction with my partner – Stacy Camacho – and my kids – Ben, Xander, and Felix. And of course, to all the companion species who have wandered in and out of my life: Inky, Cuddles, Miss Lacey, Chirp Chirp, Pat, Daphne, Liz, Rainbow, and Beer. Unlike Levinas's uncertainty, when I look into your eyes, I see your face.

Abbreviations

1 Clem.	*1 Clement*
1 Cor.	1 Corinthians
1 Kgs.	1 Kings
1 Pet.	1 Peter
1 Sam.	1 Samuel
1 Tim.	1 Timothy
1QH[a]	*Thanksgiving Hymns*
1QS	*Community Rule*
2 Clem.	*2 Clement*
2 Kgs.	2 Kings
2 Macc.	2 Maccabees
2 Pet.	2 Peter
2 Sam.	2 Samuel
4Q266	*Damascus Document*
4Q429	*Hodayot*
4QMMT	*Miqsat Ma'ase ha-Torah*
11QT	*Temple Scroll*
Acts	Acts of the Apostles
Aristotle, *Nic.*	Aristotle, *Nicomachean Ethics*
b. 'AZ	*Bavli (Babylonian Talmud), 'Avodah Zarah*
b. B. Bat.	*Bavli, Baba Batra*
b. Ber.	*Bavli, Berakot*

b. Hul.	*Bavli, Hullin*
b. Meg.	*Bavli, Megillah*
b. Sanh.	*Bavli, Sanhedrin*
Barn.	*Epistle of Barnabas*
CD	*Damascus Document*
Dan.	Daniel
Deut.	Deuteronomy
Exod.	Exodus
Exod. Rab.	*Exodus Rabbah*
Ezek.	Ezekiel
Gen.	Genesis
Gen. Rab.	*Genesis Rabbah*
Hos.	Hosea
Isa.	Isaiah
Jer.	Jeremiah
Josephus, *Ant.*	*Antiquities of the Jews*
Josephus, *War*	*Jewish War*
Judg.	Judges
Lam.	Lamentations
Lev.	Leviticus
Lev. Rab.	*Leviticus Rabbah*
LXX	Septuagint
m. Avot	*Mishnah, Avot*
m. ʿAZ	*Mishnah, Avodah Zarah*
m. Bek.	*Mishnah, Bekhorot*
m. Ber.	*Mishnah, Berakot*
m. ʿEd.	*Mishnah, ʿEduyot*
m. Hul.	*Mishnah, Hullin*
m. Sanh.	*Mishnah, Sanhedrin*
m. Ter.	*Mishnah, Terumot*
Mal.	Malachi
Matt.	Matthew
Mid. Ps.	*Midrash Psalms / Tehillim*
NRSV	New Revised Standard Version

Num.	Numbers
Num. Rab.	*Numbers Rabbah*
P. Oxy.	Papyrus Oxyrynchus
Phil.	Philippians
Philo, *Spec. Laws*	Philo of Alexandria, *On the Special Laws*
PRE	*Pirqe Rabbi Eliezer*
Prov.	Proverbs
Ps.	Psalms
Ps. Sol.	Psalms of Solomon
Pseudo-Jonathan	*Targum Pseudo-Jonathan*
Rep.	Plato, *Republic*
Rev.	Revelation
Sir.	Sirach / Ecclesiasticus
t. Sanh.	*Tosefta, Sanhedrin*
t. Ter.	*Tosefta, Terumah*
T. Abr.	*Testament of Abraham*
T. Jud.	*Testament of Judah*
T. Levi	*Testament of Levi*
Tanh.	*Midrash Tanhuma*
y. Shab.	*Yerushalmi* (Palestinian Talmud), *Shabbat*
Zech.	Zechariah

THE WILD WORD

Introduction to Gospel Beasts

Ask the beasts and they will teach you; the birds of the air and they will tell you; ask the plants of the earth, and they will teach you; and the fish of the sea will declare to you.

Job 12:7–8 (adapted)[1]

Caring means becoming subject to the unsettling obligation of curiosity, which requires knowing more at the end of the day than at the beginning.

Haraway, *When Species Meet*

For, on the one hand, the relationships between animals are the object not only of science but also of dreams, symbolism, art and poetry, practice and practical use. And on the other hand, the relationships between animals are bound up with the relationships between man and animal, man and woman, man and child, man and the elements, man and the physical and microphysical universe.

Gilles Deleuze and Félix Guattari, *A Thousand Plateaus*

As I was pulling into the driveway when coming home from taking my eldest child to school, I was met by my neighbour's indoor/outdoor black-and-white cat. She did not move with the approach of my car but was staring at something in the street. I looked at what she was looking at and saw a feral calico – whom my kids have affectionately named "mommy cat" because she briefly kept a litter of kittens in our mud room – trying to capture a small bird. The bird was fighting with all its might, pecking at mommy cat's face while mommy cat tried to subdue it. Another neighbour, leaving at the same time, got out of his truck and helpfully moved the black-and-white cat out of the way so I could get in. After I got out of my car, my neighbour did something unexpected: he walked into the street and saved the bird from mommy cat. He tried to find a spot for the injured bird to rest and gather its strength away from the reach of mommy cat. He finally put it in the crook of a branch in a skinny tree in his front yard. Mommy cat moved on and tried to chase a less-injured bird. The black-and-white cat circled and watched. The neighbour left. I stood there speechless. I walked over to the tree, looked at the bird, and saw its left wing was damaged. It stood motionless in the crook, but with feathers ruffled. Probably in shock.

I began to wonder: Why did my neighbour do that? What motivated him to save a wild bird from a feral cat? Did he have some deep-seated religious, philosophical, or ethical purpose? Was he simply sensitive to the suffering of animals? Why did I not think to do the same thing? Why did I not act? Did I feel that the bird was finished anyway and would probably die within the day? That saving it would prolong its suffering? Or did I feel that this is just what cats do, that they capture birds, mice, and other small critters? Should I have intervened in this instinctual process on behalf of the bird? Or, since the bird was a native species and the cat an invasive species, maybe an even greater intervention than what my neighbour gave was preferred.[2] When is it right to intervene and when to let things take their course?[3] And, finally, what was the domesticated black-and-white cat doing in all of this? What did she see when she watched? What was she waiting for? I was already entangled with a series of overlapping interactions between animals: between at least two birds, two cats, and my neighbour. I have become curious about such entanglements among animals, including humans, whether domesticated, feral, or wild, and such curiosity has led me on a recursive search for animals and animal-human interactions in my own intellectual playground: biblical literature – in this case, the gospels.

THE OBLIGATION OF CURIOSITY: WHY ANIMALS IN THE GOSPELS?

In my day job I teach information literacy, and I put that quotation from Donna Haraway on my syllabus for every class: caring and curiosity come with an obligation. For Haraway that obligation is knowing something at the end of the day that you didn't know at the beginning. When we poke and prod into the gospels, what will we know? What in our situated histories are we capable of knowing? What is at stake in this knowing?

I am a biblical studies scholar, so I am more likely to study the biblical texts first. But there are reasons why someone who is not a biblical studies scholar should also consider the following pages: for better or worse, the reading and retelling of the stories of Jesus in the canonized gospels have shaped us and our society in ways that, for example, reading Ovid's *Metamorphoses* with its ample animalizations has not, because the gospel stories of Jesus are not usually told for their entertainment value but shape normative behaviours in Christian-majority societies. As such, according to religious studies scholar Laura Hobgood-Oster, one must study the animals in Christian stories, rituals, and recountings "to acknowledge the impact of Christianity on animals."[4]

When I was a teenager in a church youth group, I wore a purple band around my wrist that read "WWJD," an abbreviation of "What Would Jesus Do?" While others wore different colours, I was not alone in this practice. We were taught when coming upon any decision to think of what Jesus would do in that situation, even though we did not always follow through. Even modern critics of Christianity regularly give Jesus himself an ethical pass; therefore, when I talk about the gospels, there is more at stake in the conversation than with other literature I am conversant with, even more at stake than when I talk about other biblical texts, such as Hebrews.[5] Modern retellings and interpretations of gospel stories, whether in fragments or in their narrative wholes, have shaped many people, whether Christian or not, and, in turn, our readings of the gospel stories have been shaped by our own life experiences, backgrounds, and expertise.

TRACKING GOSPEL BEASTS

I am shaped by my own entanglements with animals, including human animals, my ranging life experiences, and my expertise as a biblical studies scholar. I began my research with a simple question: How do the (mostly) canonized gospels represent animals? With that question I gathered all the references to animals in the gospels I could find and collated them into topical categories: eating, wearing, working, sacrificing, animalizing humans, and wildness in its animalistic, demonic, and divine entanglements. Some cases fit more than one category (eating an animal that is wild or eating an animal that is otherwise a working animal). Some things are going to be left out, like the rooster crowing at Peter's denial of Jesus (Matt. 26:34; Mark 14:68–72). I could have organized things differently: by domesticated, feral, or wild; by type of "form," such as parable, miracle story, or apophthegm; or by flying animals, land animals, and sea animals, as the priestly creation story does in Genesis 1. That is, this analysis could have been otherwise, and I welcome seeing others follow different approaches. Next, with my topical groupings, I considered multiple frameworks of analysis including historical, ecological, animal ethics, posthumanism, or queer theory.[6] This process led me to the more complex, more reflective question that has driven the final form of this project: What human-animal-spirit entanglements can one find in the ancient gospels?

While I tried to consider animals as living, eating, and excreting animals in themselves, the gospels resisted my intentions. What we have in the gospels with few exceptions are animal-human entanglements or intra-actions. I am using the language of Karen Barad, a theoretical physicist who specializes in quantum mechanics. Their theory is called "agential realism." Central to "agential realism" is their concept of "intra-action," which they define as "the mutual constitution of entangled agencies."[7] They write, "Individuals do not preexist their interactions; rather, individuals emerge through and as part of their entangled intra-relating."[8] Similarly, the philosopher Alphonso Lingis writes, "There is perhaps no species of life that does not live in symbiosis with another species."[9] Whether humans are eating, wearing, working, or sacrificing animals, such animals end up signifying, creating, and reinforcing complex social relationships among humans as well as human intra-actions with other animals and other nonhuman actors, such as demonic and divine entities. These asymmetrical intra-actions enable our continued existence and our mutual becoming. Animals attract extended symbolic importance as they are used to animalize humans, creating in-group and out-group animalizations, and extend to the spirit realm, creating queer assemblages with demonic and divine forces. So animals in the gospels rarely get to be just animals but exist in relation to and signify fraught entanglements between animals, humans, demons, and the divine.

ASK THE BEASTS: FINDING THE RIGHT WORDS

We, however, have a terminological problem.[10] What words do we use? We usually speak of "animals" as distinct from humans. Jacques Derrida, who has written on animals in philosophical inquiries, writes, "The animal, what a word! The animal is a word, it is an appellation that men have instituted, a name they have given themselves the right and the authority to give to the living other."[11] Even so, our modern assumptions of what this word designates does not always translate the assumptions, connotations, or linguistic echoes of the ancient terms in Hebrew and Greek that we find in the biblical and related stories.[12] The Hebrew and Greek of the biblical texts under consideration do not have the same lexical range as our word "animal," nor do the Hebrew and Greek have precisely the same lexical range of each other, although they have significant overlap.

"Animals" are rarely spoken about in such broad strokes; biblical sources, if speaking broadly at all, will mention birds in general, land animals in general, or fish in general. The rough ancient equivalents that are currently translated as "animal," moreover, typically refer to land animals as distinct from birds or fish. As such, the archaic word "beast" or the colloquial "critter" may be preferred translations, since these references usually more precisely designate land animals.[13] Usually, a particular animal species is invoked: a horse, a donkey, or a dove.

One word, however, is used to include all living beings that either move on land, swim in water, or fly in the sky, especially in Genesis: "living souls" (*nefesh chayyah*).[14] There are "swarms of living souls (*nefesh chayyah*)" (Gen. 1:20; also terminology in v. 21) that come from the waters, as well as "living souls (*nefesh chayyah*)" (Gen. 1:24) from the earth. I am rendering the phrase literally; most translations use "living things" or "living creatures," but this hides the fact that the same term rendered as "soul" for humans is being used for nonhuman animals as well in the Hebrew text. "Living things" creates an additional separation from humans, who are not referred to as "things" by translators. "Living creatures" emphasizes their created status – which is technically true – but does not accurately render the meaning here. "Soul" has some additional problems from a post-Hellenic philosophical perspective as something distinct from the body, but it does come closer to the "animating force" of the term.

This terminology has some significant resonances. It strongly correlates with the creation of Adam in Genesis 2:7. There, God breathes into Adam the "breath of life" (*nishmat chayyim*) and Adam becomes a "living soul" (*l'nefesh chayyah*) – the same term used for "living souls" in Genesis 1. The same term is used for the "living soul" God makes for Adam in Genesis 2:19 in the naming of the animals. Humans and other animals are all "living souls." Further binding humans and other animals together is how they are made in the second creation account: God makes both from the ground (Adam in 2:7; the other "living souls" in 2:19).

Ezekiel uses similar terminology for the heavenly beings, later identified as Cherubim (Ezek. 10), in Ezekiel 1, calling them "living ones" (*chayyot*), though not "living souls" – there is no *nefesh* (e.g., Ezek. 1:5, 13, 15, 19–22). Ezekiel does, however, speak of the "spirit of the living creatures (*ruach hachayyah*)" residing in the wheels of the throne-chariot (1:20; cf. 1:21).

Ultimately, however, these living creatures become differentiated: when differentiated, the term "living ones" (*hachayyah*) is reserved for what we typically think of as "wild ones," as opposed to "domesticated animals" (*hab'hemah*). This complicates our terminology even more, since different societies align domesticated/wild differently and the line between them can get blurry. This latter term, *hab'hemah*, which typically refers to what we think of as "domesticated animals," and which I will render with either "beasts" or "critters," literally means "mute" or "dumb."[15]

Genesis 1:24–5 is a good test case here. At first God makes all land "living souls" (*nefesh chayyah*), then differentiates the domesticated animals or cattle (*b'hemah*) and the "wild" animals (*chayyah*). Here, the shortened form without the "nefesh" becomes a shorthand for "wild animal," while domesticated animals, "beasts," become marked with a separate term. Does this indicate that the "living ones" of Ezekiel 1 are also "wild"? This same differentiation occurs in the flood story (Gen. 7:14). But wild creatures could be "field beasts" as well, so one can find some lexical overlaps. And there are "wild beasts," such as the monstrous "Behemoth" or "super beast" (*b'hemoth*) of Job 40:15–24. Yet Job also reinforces that *b'hemoth* are land animals when Job differentiates them from birds and fish in his famous request: "Ask the beasts" (Job 12:7–8). *B'hemah*, therefore, cannot be translated generically as "animals," since biblical usage restricts it to land animals and usually, but not always, domesticated land animals.

The Greek lexicon has overlapping but inexact equivalents. A generic word for animal, *zoë* means life in general (much like the Hebrew *chayyah*) and is the translation of the meaning of Eve's name in Greek. *To zoön* can refer to a living creature in general or specifically an animal. It is where we get the word "zoo." But a different word is used for "wild animal," such as *to therion* (see Mark 1:13). For comparison, we can look at the Greek translation of the same Hebrew passages to see how the translator(s) dealt with the semantic overlaps and divergences.

Revisiting the creation stories, the Septuagint (LXX) renders the *nefesh chayyah* of "living souls" literally as *psuchon zoson* (Gen. 1:20, 21; *psuchen zosan* in 1:24). The "wild animals" in v. 25 are differentiated, however, with *theria*, differentiating as one must in Greek, yet the Septuagint also introduces a different term for domesticated animals (*ta ktene*) to mirror the wild animals, which is repeated in the flood story (7:14). This term can also be used to differentiate land animals from birds and fish (cf. 1 Cor. 15:49). A new term is introduced for *b'hemah* in 1:25: *tetrapoda* – literally, a "tetrapod" or "four-legged one." Adam, too, is a "living soul" (*psuchen zosan*), yet the verse speaks of *theria* of the ground to refer to all groundlings in 2:19, while referring to all creatures as *psuchen zosan*.

Both the Hebrew text and the Greek versions of the Genesis stories agree that the most generic term for animate creatures is "living soul." From there, some differentiations occur along shifting domesticated/wild dividing lines. So in Hebrew, the generic word for animals and all living non-plant creatures also specifically connotes wild animals, whereas a separate word indicates domesticated land animals ("beasts"). In Greek, there is a general word for all living non-plant creatures, but a different word for "wild" animals or "beasts" otherwise hostile to humans. A "living soul" could include humans; a *therion* is distinctively nonhuman if not inhuman – it could even denote something monstrous or fearsome. A *chayyah*, by contrast, also includes humans, but a domesticated beast (*b'hemah*) excludes humans, not as anti-human, but under human control. While Hebrew aligns the wild with the generic term for "living soul," Greek can differentiate both domesticated and wild from the generic terminology.

Overall, this set of basic terms indicates that, while there are variable lines of demarcation between types of created beings (humans, other animals, and angelic beings), the clearest differentiation appears to be between created living beings (humans, other animals, heavenly beings, etc.) and uncreated beings (God/s).

HOW TO READ A CAT: BEASTLY FRAMEWORKS

Nonetheless, most modern researchers tend to prefer the word "animal." So when I started this project, I put the search terms "animals" and "bible" into the databases of the Schewe Library of Illinois College, and the overwhelming number of books that populated the search were children's books, mostly having to do with Noah's ark. Paradoxically, the story of the greatest destruction of animals and humans in the biblical narrative is thought ripe for children's entertainment because there are animals there! Some of these stories, amusingly, include dinosaurs, dragons, or unicorns who forgot it was the day to get on the boat.[16]

Turning to the fewer scholarly treatments that got caught up in the search, there were at least three ways in which scholars have considered animals and animality in the New Testament, biblical literature, or adjacent fields: biological taxonomy, ecological and animal ethics, and posthumanist studies.

First, in the late nineteenth and early twentieth century, the primary category of thinking through biblical animals was through natural history, often relying on the classificatory work of the natural sciences as biologists, geologists, and others brought their areas of study to bear on sacred writ.[17] There are, to be sure, continued collections of zoology in the Bible, from Wikipedia's alphabetical listing of all the names of animals in the Bible to the scholarly reference work by Edwin Firmage on "zoology" in the *Anchor Bible Dictionary*, which, using archaeological and comparative anthropological evidence, creates a profile of every animal with an anthropocentric focus on "those features which made it useful to humans."[18] One rarely sees these studies cited directly by biblical scholarship, yet the impact of natural history, biology, and the classificatory and taxonomic framework on biblical animals appear in other ways as well.

The insights of natural scientists wend their way through ecological studies and animal studies, which, in turn, have more directly impacted biblical studies in recent decades. Before the rise of animal rights movements, for example, Charles Darwin noted in *Descent of Man* that "lower animals, like man, manifestly feel pleasure and pain, happiness and misery."[19] He does not limit the similarity between humans and animals to sensory stimuli but also includes emotions, something long ignored in the sciences until relatively recently. He does, however, situate humans as uniquely able to empathize with all other sentient beings: "Sympathy beyond the confines of man, that is humanity to the lower animals, seems to be one of the latest moral acquisitions … This virtue, one of the noblest with which man is endowed, seems to arise incidentally from our sympathies becoming more tender and more widely diffused, until they are extended to all sentient beings."[20] This point has been proven wrong, as one finds several animals that cooperate with and help different species. Finally, after discussing senses and emotions, he turns to the mind, arguing that the difference between human and animal cognition is one of degree and not kind.[21]

Darwin's emphasis on human sympathy for all sentient beings and on the similarity between humans' and other animals' bodily structures,[22] happiness and pain, emotions, and cognition has resonated more recently with animal rights thinkers and, closer to my field, affect theorists who study religion.[23] Moreover, while much of the Christian tradition has been stuck in an apologetic mode, more recently, the ecofeminist theologian Elizabeth Johnson has directly engaged Darwin's writings in a creative dialogue with the Christian theological tradition, especially the Niceno-Constantinopolitan Creed, with beauty, clarity, and insight.[24] Her engagement, moreover, also shifts the analytical register from biological evolution to ethical considerations; in her case, the ecological and theological value of care.

This flows directly into the second way of reading about animals in the Bible: ethical considerations at the intersections of ecological, animal rights, and ecofeminist works. Ecological readings predominantly respond to the critique of (Western) Christianity's anthropocentrism roughly sixty years ago by Lynne White Jr's essay "The Historical

Roots of Our Ecological Crisis."[25] A somewhat naive rejoinder was broached by *The Green Bible*, which tried to defend the Bible against such criticism, arguing the Bible is completely pro-green. The Earth Bible Project has developed a more critical attitude.[26] This latter project, which has been the most dominant in the field, has developed six ecojustice principles to biblical hermeneutics:

1. Intrinsic worth of the universe and its components
2. Interconnectedness (and interdependence) of all living things
3. Voice of Earth as a subject, rejoicing or speaking against injustice
4. Purpose of the universe and all its components in a dynamic cosmic design
5. Mutual custodianship in acting as partners with Earth, rather than rulers
6. Active resistance of Earth and its components in the struggle for justice

The primary "sin" of a biblical passage – if it falls short of these principles – is anthropocentrism. The method of approach is, therefore, not naively thinking the Bible will be pro-ecology or "green," but to read it with suspicion as well as retrieval strategies, modelled on existing feminist reading strategies. The Exeter project headed by David Horrell and his colleagues sought a middle path, bringing ecological ethics into greater dialogue with theological ethics in interpreting biblical texts.[27] These are only some of the major trends, but many other scholars have contributed to an increasing wave of ecological readings of the Bible and ancient Christianity.[28]

Few scholars, however, have explored such ecological issues in relation to animals in the gospels. Most have turned to other parts of the Bible. Much of the blame and defensiveness has been addressed at the "Old Testament," usually Genesis, but other places as well. Some may say that it is not a major part of the gospels; others like Richard Bauckham suggest instead, "the eyes of modern urban readers still need to be opened to that dimension of human life, our relationship to the non-human environment and its creatures, that to the biblical writers was self-evidently of huge importance."[29] Bauckham has been one of the few scholars who have turned to the gospels for ecological readings. In some ways, the objectives of this book are narrower. Ecology must consider all organisms – plants, animals, and humans – as well as other elements in an environment to promote sustainability. This project only focuses on a few of those organisms: animals and that peculiar representative, humans.

Adjacent to ecological ethics, a less trodden path would consider ancient literature in the wake of animal ethics, which has primarily followed three paths: animal liberation though utilitarian philosophy, particular Peter Singer's *Animal Liberation*; neo-Kantian animal rights ethics in conversation with and in critique of Tom Regan's *The Case for Animal Rights Ethics*; and ecofeminist engagements with animals within human communities.[30] For Singer, the great "sin" is "speciesism," the attitude that one's species is more important than any other or does not give other species equal consideration when making ethical decisions that impact their suffering or ability to experience pleasure. Singer, who is cited more frequently among biblical studies scholars than Regan, directly relates speciesism to sexism and racism, ultimately following up on some side comments that Jeremy Bentham made in a footnote towards the end of his *Principles of Morals and Legislation*. There, Bentham had noted the parallels between the treatment of animals and of human slaves and redirected moral consideration away from the ability to reason or speak to whether or not one can suffer.[31]

Regan is critical of consequentialist ethics, such as utilitarianism, and shifts the language to rights. While he is indebted to the utilitarian shift of ethical consideration of all beings who can suffer rather than all beings who can reason or speak a language, his model is Kantian, shifting Kant's second articulation of the categorical imperative under the formulation of the "end unto itself" to include more than humans.[32] Both Singer and Regan, however, are critical of the biblical influence of dominionist readings drawn from Genesis 1–3 for current attitudes towards animals. The mode in ecological and animal rights scholarship is not classificatory as studies directly relying on the natural sciences were but ethical and, when taken up by biblical studies scholars, regularly apologetic.

Ecofeminists have varied approaches to the problem of animal suffering and rights; most ecofeminists emphasize the complex ways human lives are enmeshed with other animal lives in communities of care.[33] Ecofeminists argue that anthropocentric attitudes that centre and privilege humans are inextricable from androcentric attitudes that centre and privilege men: that is, dominion of nature is rooted in patriarchal social norms.[34] Speciesism and sexism go hand in hand, such as treating women like "pieces of meat."[35] As Carol Adams writes, "Feminism challenges the gender binary. But it is also an analytic tool that helps expose the social construction of relationships between humans and the other animals."[36] In contrast to utilitarian and deontological efforts, ecofeminists tend to emphasize community and interconnectedness.[37] Some of these themes of interconnectivity – or entanglement – re-emerge in posthumanist discourse, especially in the posthumanist feminist writings of Donna Haraway.

The most recent way most scholars approach biblical animals and animality has been through the categories of posthumanism, nonhumanism,[38] and new materialisms. These interrelated streams of study have challenged the category of "human" as self-contained or undermined humanity's singularity compared to other forms of existence, particularly animals but also AI and biotechnologies. Gilles Deleuze and Félix Guattari, Jacques Derrida, and Donna Haraway among others have rethought animals, animality, humans, humanity, and the physical and symbolic interactions among them.[39] Much of the posthumanist impetus has arisen through engagement with the posthumously published works of Jacques Derrida, particularly *The Animal That Therefore I Am* and the two-volume *The Beast and the Sovereign*.[40] Also partly inspired by Bentham's musings,[41] the first part of *The Animal That Therefore I Am* includes a series of interactions between a naked Derrida coming out of his shower, his cat gazing at him, and Genesis 1–3. While the title and the content of this essay are a reference to and a critique of Descartes's "cogito ergo sum," they are also a reference to the "I am" of Exodus 3:14; therefore, Derrida seeks to entwine his reflections on contemporary philosophical thought with biblical themes.

A substantial number of scholars have entangled the posthumanities with Deleuze and Guattari's two-volume set on "capitalism and schizophrenia": *Anti-Oedipus* and *A Thousand Plateaus*, with their assemblage of "becoming-animal" that spills across their work.[42] Unlike Derrida and his pet cat, Deleuze and Guattari prefer the wild pack of wolves, though they sometimes may think of the collective wolf.[43] In their analysis, there are three kinds of animals: (1) "individuated animals, family pets, sentimental, Oedipal animals each with its own petty history, 'my' cat, 'my' dog" – these are "regressive" animals, victims of and contributors to bourgeoise human narcissism; (2) "animals with characteristics or attributes" – paradigmatic or mythic animals; and (3) "more demonic animals, pack or affect animals that form a multiplicity, a becoming, a population, a tale."[44] One does not become part of the pack, what they call "becoming-animal," by filiation or heredity, but by contagion. As a pack, animals are rhizomatic in their evolving assemblages.[45]

Donna Haraway, whose work has explored the various posthumans from cyborgs to animals, has provided a pointed critique of Derrida and Deleuze and Guattari.[46] While she acknowledges her debt to Derrida's animalistic readings of the Western canon, she finds that eating-and-excreting animals get lost in his philosophical and literary wanderings.[47] It was a failure of curiosity: "as a philosopher he knew nothing more from, about, and with the cat at the end of the morning than he knew at the beginning, no matter how much better he understood the root scandal as well as the enduring achievements of his textual legacy."[48] This failure of curiosity in an otherwise curious person she finds surprising. His shame about his nakedness before his cat short-circuited his curiosity. Ultimately, we never know much about Derrida's cat. Even after he goes on and on about naming, he does not mention his cat's name. But we do know Donna Haraway's dog, its breed, the history of its breed, the various entanglements and ethical issues raised by the history of the breed, and, of course, that her name is Cayenne.[49] We get a situated specificity that we do not get from Derrida.

I would add to Haraway's critique: Derrida becomes fixated on the gaze of his cat, the mutual look that gets theorized repeatedly from different directions. His privileging of seeing – and to some degree hearing and speaking – goes back to Plato and Aristotle.[50] As Cary Wolfe notes, speaking more about animal rights, "the philosophy of animal rights ... remains tied to the theoretical topos of the mirror and the look, and as such it reorients the question of the alterity of the nonhuman other once again toward the figure of the human. What seems to be needed, then, is a framework for thinking about the problem of subjectivity and species difference in terms of embodiment and multiplicity rather than identity."[51] Wolfe uses this as a launching point to discuss Deleuze and Guattari's work, which I will reinvoke in chapter 5; nonetheless, I think if one seeks to consider the situatedness of animals and animality in contact zones, other senses should come into play that would likewise redirect us in terms of multiplicity and embodiment: smell, taste, touch, and balance.

Speaking more programmatically, Haraway says, "I think we learn to be worldly from grappling with, rather than generalizing from, the ordinary."[52] And the ordinary can be differentiated here from just any kind of specificity. Deleuze and Guattari are fascinated more by the anomalous rather than the specific ordinary, even as they try to consider the tension between the multiplicity (pack) and the anomaly.[53] Haraway's critique of Deleuze and Guattari is much stronger than her reading of Derrida: they, more so than Derrida, lose the actual animals, even as they refer to many animals throughout their collaborative work, and lack curiosity about (or are even openly despising of) the mundane and the ordinary in their deterritorializing "lines of flight."[54] Another theorist, Baudrillard, notes the paradox in their thinking here: "to take the animal as a model of deterritorialization when he [*sic*] is the territorial being par excellence."[55] Deleuze and Guattari are too sublime; Haraway, by contrast, prefers to stick to the mud and slime of mundane critters, even as she acquires their preferred terminology of "becoming" and "assemblages" and their shared emphasis on symbiosis.[56]

Her critique would also stand against Georges Bataille, who begins his *Theory of Religion* with animality, defining the animal and animality as "immediacy or immanence."[57] While he cuts off transcendence for the animal, he dismisses animals as "water within water."[58] They are indistinguishable from their immediate surroundings, as animals eat other animals. Nonetheless, Haraway – and Derrida – would critique Bataille's use of "the" animal rather than simply animal or animals or a particular species of animals. A discontinuity opens between the animal and the human in the latter's use of positing an object; that is, a tool.[59] This creates the subject-object distinction, and the object spreads to other things and ascribe to objects transcendence.[60] Yet this overlooks animals who use tools. Nonetheless, it is this act in thought of the creation of the subject-object split that allows humans to view animals as things: "The animal has lost its status as man's fellow creature, and man, perceiving animality in himself, regards it as a defect. There is undoubtedly a measure of falsity in the fact of regarding the animal as a thing."[61] On the other hand, religious activities seek a lost intimacy that was part and parcel of our animality.

As this analysis will look at long-dead literal and still-living metaphorical animals in the gospels, I am sensitive to Haraway's critique. Gospel animals generate a different order of entanglements than Derrida has with his anonymous cat or Haraway has with her Australian shepherd, Cayenne. Can we have it both ways: to have animals and animality?[62]

These streams are not mutually contradictory categories; they engage one another, criss-cross and overlap. Posthumanist studies are interested in ethics, while they seek to undermine the taxonomic thinking of previous generations, more interested in undermining, blurring, or complicating boundaries. A posthumanist thinker, such as Cary Wolfe, for example, can also speak against the speciesism of much of the humanities and social sciences.[63] Moreover, White, Singer, and Derrida all alternately fixate on as well as blame Genesis 1–3 for Western culture's anthropocentrism and speciesism.[64] The appropriations of ecological, animal rights, and posthumanism among scholars of the biblical materials, Judaism, and Christianity attempt to show this equation is reductive, even if not entirely false.[65]

These streams have had an impact on biblical studies and related fields.[66] I have found many of these studies interesting, thoughtful, provoking, and strange. Nonetheless, my starting point has come from a different source: my students. I used to teach "Religion and the Environment" and would get the minimum number of students to hold a class. When I renamed the course "Religion, Agriculture, and Ecology," the course enrollment hit capacity! Why? Many of my students were or are farmers; they came from farming families, and they will farm after they leave college. A few of them have already begun investing in their own farms. Many of my students raise animals for the purpose of selling them for food, dairy products, or eggs. They raise several animals, particularly chickens and hogs but also goats as they expand their markets into the increasing Muslim demographic of central Illinois. For them, the starting point is not Derridean deconstruction; it is more direct and economical: while Derrida developed his provocations by watching his pet cat watch him, my students interact with domesticated working animals on a regular basis. Their interactions with animals intersect the intimate and personal with the instrumental and economical; that is, they are raising animals to make a living or supplement a living. Some of them are doing it to help pay their tuition. In short, they are part of the intermediation that transforms cows, pigs, and chickens – among other animals – from animals or fellow creatures into dead meat.[67]

Most of us live in an age of what the historian Richard Bulliet calls "post-domesticity."[68] Since the domestication of certain animals thousands of years ago, humans have lived in close, intimate relations with animals used for work, clothing, food, and sacrifice.[69] Historically, most people were familiar with domesticated animals mating, giving birth, being raised, and being slaughtered. The first acts of sex and violence that most people witnessed in their lives would have been part of this process. Today, after the rise of industrialization, urbanization, and the "green" revolution that gave rise to corporate farming, fewer people in North America, Europe, and Australia have these experiences. Our dominant intimate animal relationships are with pets, as was the case with Derrida and his cat or Haraway and her dog. As Baudrillard notes, "The violence of sacrifice, which is one of 'intimacy' (Bataille), has been succeeded by the sentimental or experimental violence that is one of distance."[70] Queer theorist Jack Halberstam refers to this primacy of pets as their zombification.[71]

Bulliet argues that the displacement of animal sex and violence that humans have been privy to for thousands of years has had wide-ranging social consequences, including the rise of animal rights ethics and posthumanism. He, however, suggests that posthumanism is thrusting humans back into the "pre-domesticity" stage; humans are thinking thoughts that have not been thought in a sustained way since before this domestication, thoughts about the relationship between humans and other animals and how slippery those categories can become. These pre-domesticity considerations survived in Bulliet's imaginative historical reconstruction in mythic and legendary fragments, in transformations and blurrings that give rise to the "monstrous" and feelings of the uncanny.[72]

Nonetheless, my students both contribute to and buck this trend, since they remain privy to animal sex and animal violence that has become hidden for most of us and on which the rest of us depend for food, clothing, and other animal products. So what can taxonomies, ecological and animal ethics, or posthumanism mean for them? Given the excesses in factory farming,[73] I hope a lot, but I think as we analyze how various gospel writers represent animals, their relations to humans, and their non-relations to humans, with an eye on the starting point (but not the ending point) of an animal on a farm – born, fed, raised, cared for, sold, and slaughtered – we may see something differently, allowing my students to bring their perspectives to bear on and allow their views to intersect with these broader currents of thinking about animals and our varied relationships to them.

So can we have our fish and eat it too? Again, Haraway provides a way out of the morass of blame and defensiveness found in the literature on animals – and their broader ecological relations – in biblical and related literatures, looking both beyond and to the side of posthumanism and nonhumanism.[74] She looks at animals – both like and unlike my students – not only as categories to think with but as micro-relationships – sympoiesis she would say – of being- and becoming-with;[75] all animals and living things for that matter are "companion species" of some sort. She writes: "Companion species are relentlessly becoming-with. The category companion species helps me refuse human exceptionalism without invoking posthumanism … In human-animal worlds, companion species are ordinary beings-in-encounter in the house, lab, field, zoo, park, truck, office, prison, ranch, arena, village, human hospital, forest, slaughterhouse, estuary, vet clinic, lake, stadium, barn, wildlife preserve, farm, ocean canyon, city streets, factory, and more."[76] Hers is a world of "com- / cum-" or "sym-": it is always "with" and not "post." She describes her work as not "posthumanist" but "compost" – that is "making" and "unmaking" "with": composing and decomposing at once with companion (cum panis) animals from microbes to dogs to feral pigeons to spiders coming together at the table.[77] "Humans" are "humus" rather than "Homo" or "Anthropos," much like Adam ("human") is Adamah ("dirt" or "ground") in Genesis.[78] It is not (only) "thinking with" animals as categories, but "becoming with" them; living with specific animals and finding the spidery webs of relationships that we spin together with our own and other species.[79]

Unlike in Haraway's works, one will find it difficult to locate specific animals in the gospels. The gospels mostly handle "types" of animals rather than a specific animal that has a situated history. We will try to unravel, however, as much as we can in the specific locations that the animals appear in narratives, parables, aphorisms, and miracle stories. By recapitulating well-known, forgotten, and missing animals from the starting point of the gospels, we can trace several entangled threads and make something that has been "absent present."[80]

I too have discomfort with the sign of "posthumanism" and, to some degree, "nonhumanism," though not for the same reasons as Haraway. I hope it is a productive discomfort rather than a dismissive or reactionary discomfort. So the starting point here is not whether the gospels, ancient Judaism, or ancient Christianity are to blame for the attitudes that undergird anthropomorphism or speciesism or whether we need to defend the Bible from such charges, though I will point out such issues as they arise. The interplay of accusation and apology is not particularly productive. Instead, it is about an opening up, an exploration, so that we can see gospel animals in their entanglements with one another, with human animals, and with divine and demonic animals anew. We will see the ways in which these entanglements relate, compare, and contrast current animal and human and other intra-actions. I want to follow the criss-crossing trails of animals in the (mostly) canonical gospels and see where it leads. While I am not going to dismiss potential ways the gospels "think with" animals,[81] I will also look at other intra-active becomings as they emerge.

MISSING ANIMALS AND ANIMALITIES IN THE GOSPELS

Before we proceed, however, I would like to introduce a gospel passage as both an example and a warning. I refer to canonized gospels as "domesticated" since we have become so familiar with them that we have lost sight of some of their more feral and wild elements in their original contexts. Extracanonical works were once familiar to some groups long ago but are not anymore; they seem "feral" to us. But there is sometimes something uncannily familiar about them even as they simultaneously seem strange to modern readers who are used to the more domesticated gospels. One of my favourite passages in all of the gospels – canonized (domesticated) and extracanonical (feral) – comes in the historically popular Proto-Gospel of James. At the very moment of Jesus's birth, Joseph stops and takes in his surroundings. From his first-person perspective, Joseph recounts:

> I looked up to the vault of the sky, and I saw it standing still, and into the air, and I saw that it was greatly disturbed, and the birds of the sky were at rest … I saw a flock of sheep being herded, but they were standing still. The shepherd raised his hand to strike them, but his hand remained in the air. I looked down at the torrential stream, and I saw some goats whose mouths were over the water, but they were not drinking. Then suddenly everything returned to its normal course. (18)[82]

When Jesus breaks forth into the world, time stands still, but Joseph retains the consciousness to observe it. The world around him is like a three-dimensional still photograph; someone has hit the pause button on reality. He takes time to soak in his surroundings. When everything stops, he notices everything that we would otherwise take for granted: the birds of the sky, the sheep, the goats; that is, the essential yet unnoticed elements of Joseph's daily life. The extraordinary moment of Jesus's birth makes the ordinary visible again.[83]

By contrast, what's arresting when one reads the domesticated gospels with a multi-focal lens from posthumanism to agriculture is the lack of animals where we would expect to find them; we imaginatively fill them in as the feral gospels and modern media do, from paintings to film.[84] One can see the absence and our imaginative reconstructions by looking at birth stories from Matthew and Luke. Following Luke's narrative from the beginning, bolstered by centuries of paintings, photographs, and retellings through plays and film, we imagine Joseph leading Mary on a donkey from Nazareth to Bethlehem. After Jesus is born, he's placed in a food trough for animals. He emerges into a world teeming with domesticated animal life. Looking at Matthew's narrative thread, we imagine three Magi traversing the desert on camels as they come into Jerusalem and then, finally, Bethlehem to find baby Jesus. While there is no feed trough, we then imagine Joseph, Mary, and young Jesus escaping to Egypt on a donkey.

But read the stories again: not a single animal is mentioned except for the shepherd's flocks in Luke. There is no indication that Mary at the end of her pregnancy rode a donkey. Maybe she did; maybe she was pulled behind in a cart; maybe she varied modes of transportation throughout the journey. All these options are historically plausible, but Luke has not bothered mentioning them. They are taken for granted. While Jesus is placed in a feeding trough, there is no mention of animals. While the Magi – and we don't know how many there were – likely did not walk on foot from Persia (if that was their starting point), and the use of camels is a very good guess, it is just that: a guess. Likewise, in Matthew, when Joseph, Mary, and Jesus flee Bethlehem to Egypt and then return from Egypt and go up to Nazareth, no one in their travelling party explicitly rides an animal in Matthew's narration.

Moving along in the gospel narratives, did the centurion in Capernaum (Matt. 8:5–13; Luke 7:1–10; cf. Acts 10:1–48) come to Jesus on a horse?[85] Did Jesus and the disciples actually walk everywhere, save for on Palm Sunday, when Jesus rides on a donkey – and, in Matthew, straddles two animals at once (Matt. 21:1–7; Mark 11:1–11; Luke 19:28–38; John 11:12–19)?

These gaps and absences spread throughout all of the biblical accounts – we know animals were there, just as we know women were there, though they are rarely noted or named.[86] If we apply the insights of the androcentric sexism of biblical writers pointed out by feminist biblical criticism to other phenomena, we – alongside ecofeminists – note the accompanying anthropocentrism of the biblical writers and figures, ignoring the obvious, everyday presence of animals.[87]

Not only are animals missing where we might expect to find them in the narrative texture itself, but those coming from other fields may be surprised at what *types* of animals and animality are missing in the gospels. Some types of animal tales found in the Hebrew Bible, second-temple Judaism, Rabbinic texts, contemporary Greek and Roman texts, and even other works now in the New Testament are absent in the gospels. The gospels do not have anyone transforming from human to animal or vice versa as in Ovid's *Metamorphoses*, Lucius Apuleis's *Golden Ass*, the "Dream Visions" in 1 Enoch, or the "Myth of Er" in Plato's *Republic*. There is no discussion of human-animal sex as found in the Hebrew Bible (Lev. 18:23; 20:15–16), Rabbinic texts (e.g., *m. Sanh.* 7:4; *t. Sanh.* 10:2; *b. Sanh.* 55a–b),[88] as well as Greco-Roman texts (*Golden Ass*).[89] There are no animals endowed with human speech, such as the serpent in the Garden of Eden, Balaam's donkey, or Aesop's fables.[90] There are no human-animal-angelic hybrids, such as in Ezekiel 1, Revelation 4, or Jerome's *Life of Paul* 7–8. There are no mentions of the Roman *venationes*, or "wild beast hunts," which occurred throughout stadiums, arenas, and amphitheaters throughout the Roman world, and, according to Josephus, occurred in Jerusalem at least during Herod's reign (Josephus, *War* 1.21; *Ant.* 15.8).[91]

Despite these absences, animal traces and tracks faintly appear in the literary and archaeological record. Richard Bauckham has listed twenty-one animals in the gospels: "bird, camel, chicken (cock and hen), dog, donkey, dove, fish, fox, gnat, goat, moth, ox, pig, raven, scorpion, sheep, snake, sparrow, viper, vulture, wolf."[92] He notes eight are domesticated animals and all would be at home in ancient rural Palestine. Animals do sometimes appear in these stories, and since they seem to be a taken-for-granted daily reality,[93] we need to think carefully about why they appear when they do appear.

My readings in historical reconstructions, archaeological survivals, ecological and animal ethics, posthumanism and nonhumanism, and queer theory, as well as where my students are and where they are going, have led me to the read the Bible, especially the gospels, with a heightened sensitivity to the physical intra-actions between humans and other animals, how humans represent animals, and how the representation of animals often reflects ancient ways of viewing other humans. I have begun to think about the various animalizations of humans that occur in the gospels: negative "out-group animalizations" by calling human beings by names of animals (vipers, fox, dog) and positive "in-group animalizations" – "be wise as serpents and innocent as doves" (Matt. 10:16).[94] The gospels contain the consumption of animals; the use of animals for clothing and other elements; working animals that one rides; and the phenomenon of divine animality.[95] These categories express many of the relationships Deleuze and Guattari mention in the third epigraph to this chapter:[96] animals and animality become entangled in a wide range of relationships between and among humans and other animals and, by extension, divine and demonic entities. In short, as Beth Berkowitz notes in her study of animals and animality in the Babylonian Talmud, "The texts are anthropocentric, yet animal perspectives percolate up."[97]

JOHN THE BAPTIST AMONG THE ANIMALS: UNFOLDING THIS BOOK

The following chapters begin to unfold with material and physical entanglements between humans and other animals, engaging eating-and-excreting animals and how humans relate to them through various forms of consumption: eating, wearing animal products, using animal labour, and sacrificing animals. Then this book takes a more symbolic direction, turning to how humans animalize other humans through name-calling and how the divine and demonic become entangled in animality. The last chapter recapitulates these overlapping entanglements in the visual-sonic experience of the film *Son of Man*. Throughout, gospel animals compose, decompose, and recompose social relationships among humans and between humans and animals and other nonhuman actors, including demonic and divine figures. The conclusion takes us in new directions with a queer and trans reflection on gospel beasts.

Most of these categories appear in a single pericope in the synoptic gospels: the story of John the Baptist at the beginning of Jesus's ministry.

CONSUMING ANIMAL PRODUCTS "Now John was clothed with camel's hair (*trichas kamelou*), with a leather belt (*zonen dermatinen*) around his waist, and he ate locusts and wild honey (*akridas kai meli agrion*)" (Mark 1:6; Matt. 3:4). The most conspicuous elements of John the Baptist's story in the gospel accounts to modern readers are what he eats and what he wears. Food and clothing, discussed in chapters 1 and 2 respectively, are the areas of life in which humans rely on animals the most. The use of eccentric clothing, even of a domesticated animal, and the consumption of wild animals (locusts) and animal products (honey) indicate someone on the edge of civilization, neither fully in nor fully out. John's entanglement with animals expresses his feralness, even perhaps wildness, which threatens the society of his day.

SACRIFICING ANIMALS As discussed in chapter 3, the sacrificial system hums in the background of the gospel accounts, vaguely alluded to in oblique ways. One oblique way could be that John's baptism was for the "repentance for the forgiveness of sins" (Mark 1:4; Luke 3:3) or, in Matthew's version, repentance and confession of sins (Matt. 3:1–12); that is, John's baptism encroached on a function of the temple, where one would give a sin offering. If John the Baptist was offering an alternative to or critique of sacrificing in the temple,[98] then a critique of sacrifice may stem from the beginning of Jesus's ministry, but, then again, Jesus didn't always follow John the Baptist's example – for example, the fasting of John the Baptist versus the feasting of Jesus (Mark 2:18–20; Luke 7:33–5).

ANIMALIZING HUMANS "Brood of Vipers" (*gennemata exidnon*) (Matt. 3:7–10; Luke 3:7–9): John the Baptist uses animals in name calling, or what I call "out-group animalizations," when he calls groups who have come to be baptized by him a "brood of vipers." Discussed in chapter 4, "Affective Animals and Social Identity in the Gospels," out-group animalizations use animals to characterize someone of a different group, to delineate the difference between "them" and "us" at the other group's or person's expense. The use of animals in name-calling is meant to dehumanize, usually with an animal that connotes negative traits in that culture.[99] Racialized out-group animalizations occur all the time, but such animalizations can be class-based, gender-driven, or ideologically driven. In this case, John the Baptist calls the "out-group" a "brood of vipers." John's name-calling does not rely on a difference of gender and race, but an affective othering due to ideology and, depending on which gospel one focuses on, class.

ANIMALIZING THE DIVINE AND DEMONIC "And just as he was coming up out of the water, he saw the skies torn apart and the Spirit descending like a dove (*hos peristeran*) into (*eis*) him" (Mark 1:10 adapted; Matt. 3:16; Luke 3:21–2; John 1:32). Jacques Derrida coined "divinanimality" to discuss the relational similarity of animals and the divine to humans as Other. All four gospels include this account, except that in the Gospel of John, John the Baptist relates it as a past occurrence rather than happening in the literary present. Was this a simile? The spirit alighted upon Jesus *as* a dove would? Did the spirit appear literally in dove form? Did the spirit come embodied as a dove? There is a connotation with Genesis 1, in which the Spirit hovers over the primordial waters in avian language. The hovering, alighting Spirit connects, therefore, the primordial waters of the creation account with this new creation of Jesus's baptism. Afterward, this spirit leads him to the wilderness (a place of undomesticated, wild, and feral animals). As further explored in chapter 5, "Into Gospel Wilds: Divine, Demonic, and Animal," the spirit is wild and the wildness is both creative and dangerous.

In short, the story of John the Baptist, at the very beginning of the domesticated gospel accounts, anticipates most of the ways in which the gospels represent animals and, through them, other humans and even the divine. The question remains: Why would John the Baptist / Jesus's baptism pericope have such a high density of animal associations, including locusts, camel hair, vipers, potential sacrifice, and the dove? Could it be that John the Baptist, more than anyone else in the gospel narrative, operates in a liminal space between this world and the next (however one chooses to define that), but, more importantly, between civilized (domesticated) and wild? Does his feral liminality attract an animality that can alternately illuminate, reinforce, and threaten to undo the basic binaries of human/nonhuman, civilized/wild, us/them, and, by extension, other overlapping binaries, such as man/woman?

Beyond John, this book continues with filmic adaptations of the gospels, which, like the extracanonical gospels before them, fill in gaps as the filmmakers must choose whether or not to include animals visually or aurally in their presentation, but also use animals as socially and spiritually significant symbols of unjust violence and God's justice.

We are now ready to begin. As Derrida writes, "The animal looks at us, and we are naked before it. Thinking perhaps begins there."[100]

I

Eating Animals in the Gospels

> To repeat myself, outside Eden, eating means also killing, directly or indirectly, and killing well is an obligation akin to eating well. This applies to a vegan as much as to a human carnivore. The devil is, as usual, in the details.
>
> Donna Haraway, *When Species Meet*[1]

The first entanglement of humans and other animals occurs through eating. Eating is an intimate, multi-sensory experience. You see, touch, smell, taste, and may even hear (if there is a crunch) as you incorporate food into you. We categorize animals based on what they eat: carnivore, herbivore, omnivore, insectivore, frugivore, detritivore.[1] *What* humans eat and *with whom* we eat have long been understood to have social, even cosmic, significance and not just caloric importance. As Mary Douglas states, "Like sex, the taking of food has a social component, as well as a biological one."[2] This sociobiological fusion resembles what Donna Haraway calls "naturecultures." Social theorists, such as Mary Douglas or Emile Durkheim before her, regularly turn to food to map social relations and broader symbols of the world views of various groups from the high school lunchroom to the Eucharist.[3]

Yet eating involves killing. We must absorb living and nonliving matter to survive, to live, to thrive. As Carol Adams writes, "Behind every meal of meat is an absence: the death of the animal whose place the meat takes."[4] Humans are omnivores; we can eat animals but do not have to eat animals to survive. Eating involves choosing, even if those choices are constrained. When, if ever, should one eat an animal? If one follows the utilitarian tradition from Jeremy Bentham through Peter Singer, then it is what causes the least suffering for all involved, including the nonhuman animals. The philosopher Georges Bataille notes that when one kills, cuts up, and cooks an animal, this act posits the animal as a thing or an object; the animal is no longer considered a fellow creature, since one only posits the same operations for a human with abhorrence and revulsion.[5]

Even though many people keep animal suffering within the realm of ethical consideration, Bataille's observation reflects a pervasive attitude. Especially in the twenty-first century, many of us are further removed than ever from the process that turns fellow creatures into meat. Our hands or our clothes are rarely covered with hot sticky blood, but we are still entangled in this process even as it has become increasingly invisible. Recounting a hunt that took place when he was younger, biblical studies scholar Robert Seesengood brings the process of animal slaughter into dialogue with biblical materials. He writes, "the biblical injunctions describing which animals are food and which are not … recognize the necessity of animal murder even as they attempt to contain its scope."[6] To put it into Haraway's terms, the biblical food restrictions assist one to kill well and to eat well.

In this chapter I ask a simple ethical question that will guide us through the material: would Jesus eat an animal? But behind this question are more difficult issues: not just what would Jesus do, as so many Christians across the theological spectrum would ask, but how do the domesticated gospels portray the eating of animals? And, returning to the opening inspiration from Mary Douglas: what social and symbolic relationships does this particular human entanglement with other animals unveil?

The archaeological record reveals evidence of varied meat-eating in first-century Palestine. The bone deposits from Qumran demonstrate that communal meals included sheep, goats, lambs or kids, calves, and cows or oxen, with a predominance of sheep or goat bones. Large numbers of poultry bones were found at Ein Boqeq from the late second temple period, and small amounts of gazelle and deer bones were found from same period in Jerusalem.[7] Put simply, ancient Judeans and Galileans ate animals.

The gospels present several food scenes. Many studies in the "third quest" for the historical Jesus made a lot of hay about Jesus's dining patterns.[8] Moreover, the gospels are – like modern scholars – more concerned about with whom Jesus dines than what is served.[9] Dining is not just the consumption of calories, but a social activity that determines both in-group and out-group categorizations and often the hierarchy within a group. It can also be a site of social experimentation and challenge to these cultural norms.[10] In contrast to the typical ancient Roman dining experience that expressed the hierarchy of the group through where one sits, John Dominic Crossan has argued that Jesus practiced "open commensality" in his dining practices, creating a radical egalitarianism.[11]

Scholars have studied Jesus's experimental dining experiences, including eating at Levi's house with sinners (Mark 2:15–17; Matt. 9:9–13; Luke 5:29–32),[12] dining with Simon the Pharisee/Leper and the woman who anoints Jesus's head/feet (Mark 14:3–9; Matt. 26:6–13; Luke 7:36–50),[13] and dining with "a leader of the Pharisees" in the entirety of Luke 14. Jesus is regularly invited into the homes of various people of different social locations – though all with enough means to throw a banquet of some sort – and not once does it indicate what he ate. This does, however, shed light on social configurations and how meals can reveal and challenge such configurations. But what did Jesus and his fellow diners eat? Did he eat an animal? Being a good guest, would he eat whatever was offered to him? We need to look elsewhere for answers. The debate about whether or not Jesus ate animals stems from the ancient world and continues into the modern world. The stakes are high for those who tie their own behavioural norms in Jesus's actions as they are portrayed in ancient documents.

Paul's letters and the Acts of the Apostles also display meal scenes in which what was eaten was of concern for the creation and maintenance of local Jesus-following communities. Paul, for example, in Romans 14–15 and 1 Corinthians 8 and 10 brings up the issue of meat-eating versus those who only eat vegetables, trying to heal rifts in these churches based on who eats with whom, which in turn is based on who eats what.[14] Acts 15:19–20 also assumes that meat is being eaten at early Christian meals and states that it should not come from animals who have been strangled and must not be consumed with blood.[15] If other early Christian documents discuss it openly, why are the gospels so elusive on this point?[16]

The gospels present Jesus and animal-eating in several ways. Most of the time, the gospel writers evade the issue or simply do not see it as worth bringing up. Nonetheless, the explicit consumption of animals appears in Jesus's parables and his miracles. Even if the gospels rarely clearly depict Jesus eating an animal, Jesus enables others to eat animals, particularly fish. Though, really, he ate fish, right?

Most studies of Jesus and meals focus on with whom Jesus ate rather than what he ate. As these studies have shown, there are important social arrangements and hierarchies – and critiques of these arrangements and hierarchies – that can be enacted through meals.[17] Nonetheless, I want to explore in my studies on animals in the gospels the portrayal of the consumption of animals as food.[18] *What* one eats has social significance just as *with whom* one eats. In what follows we will discover how through class status, religious remembrance, group differentiation, or simply good parenting, the eating of animals in the gospels provides a social map, or, as Mary Douglas might say, what one ingests in the body provides a microcosm of ordering of society. We will see this through John the Baptist's wild diet, Jesus's fishy miracles, the Passover lamb, Jesus's fatty parables that reflect patterns of eating, and finally Jesus's meaty aphorisms, which create and maintain in-group and out-group status.

THE VEGETARIAN JESUS: ANCIENT AND MODERN QUESTIONS OF WHAT JESUS WOULD EAT

What's at stake with eating? Why might Jesus's meat-eating be controversial? As ethicists discuss the problems with eating animals and people increasingly turn to vegetarian or vegan diets for ethical and health reasons, the question must arise for vegetarians and vegans within Christian social networks of whether Jesus would encourage animal consumption.[19] If it is unethical to eat animals and you think Jesus is an important ethical exemplar, then Jesus must have been vegetarian, right?

This is not just a modern question, but an ancient one as well. The Gospel of Ebionites – as reported by Epiphanius – presents a vegetarian version of the gospels. It begins with John the Baptist: "And so John was baptizing, and Pharisees came out to him and were baptized, as was all of Jerusalem. John wore a garment of camel hair and a leather belt around his waist; and his food was wild honey that tasted like manna, like a cake cooked in olive oil" (Epiphanius, *Panarion* 30.13.4–5).[20] In it, John the Baptist does not eat locusts, but eats pancakes instead. Pancakes recall the manna of the Israelites wandering in the wilderness. "Locusts" (*akrides*) and "pancake" (*egkris*) have only a couple letters of difference in Greek, so a bit of wordplay is going on as well.[21] John the Baptist, however, still wears camel hair and leather, so this gospel does not seem to be opposed to using animal products, but just eating them. Some non-vegetarian modern scholars who simply have a difficult time understanding that a person would voluntarily eat insects also cling to this possibility.[22] In a stronger vegetarian vein, the strongest readings of the later text *Life and Martyrdom of John the Baptist* portray John the Baptist "eating tips of plants and the sap in the plants" (1.2).[23]

Finally, Jesus's vegetarianism is also established when he refuses to eat the Passover lamb. Whereas the other gospels simply omit whether Jesus ate lamb, here Jesus directly opposes eating animals. Epiphanius writes: "For they [Ebionites] had the disciples say, 'Where do you want us to make preparations for you to eat the Passover lamb?' And they made him respond, 'I have no desire to eat the meat of this Passover lamb with you'" (Epiphanius, *Panarion* 30.22.4).[24] While this is close to Luke 22:16, where Jesus says he will not eat the Passover meal *until* the kingdom, there is a difference.[25] For Luke, Jesus will eventually eat of it. In the Gospel of the Ebionites, Jesus flatly rejects lamb-eating. It appears that the Ebionites were ancient Christian vegetarians who – like Christians everywhere – imputed their beliefs onto Jesus (and here John the Baptist). For John the Baptist, this involved changing a few letters to shift "locust" to "pancake." For Jesus, this involved disambiguating Jesus's unclear attitude toward sacrifice in the canonical gospels as well as the unclarity around whether or not Jesus ate the Passover lamb.

Modern vegetarian theologians, such as Andrew Linzey, also try to portray Jesus as a vegetarian who may have occasionally eaten fish either to not draw attention to his dietary choices or in circumstances of need.[26] That is, they argue that Jesus was vegetarian in principle, but to preserve human life, would allow occasional animal consumption to fight hunger. Yet, no matter how you slice it, a fish is still an animal, guts and all. Peter Singer partially sympathizes: "Certainly those who continue to eat fish while refusing to eat other animals have taken a major step away from speciesism; but those who eat neither have gone one step further."[27] As we will see, Linzey smartly covers his tracks by admitting Jesus would promote fish death in special circumstances, yet such arguments smell fishy with a strong whiff of apologetic posturing that explains away uncomfortable scenes in the gospels. The problem with these arguments is that Jesus never objects to eating animals in the domesticated gospels. Yet the Ebionites illustrate that this is not just a modern concern. In what follows, we will see that Jesus most likely did eat animals and definitely enabled others to do so. Not only did he tolerate and reflect the sociobiological systems of animal consumption, he contributed to them, unveiling, composing, and decomposing social boundaries that come with eating.

JOHN THE BAPTIST'S FASTING AND LOCUSTS

As mentioned, the most conspicuous elements of John the Baptist's story in the gospel accounts, to modern European and American readers at least, are what he eats and what he wears.[28] Food and clothing are the areas of life in which humans rely on animals the most. This only shows up in two domesticated gospel accounts: Matthew and Mark. Luke doesn't mention it. Neither does John. John the Baptist's diet locates him on a purposeful periphery, neither fully in nor fully out of society, providing a powerful platform to critique those at the centre: "Now John was clothed with camel's hair, with a leather belt around his waist, and he ate locusts and wild honey (*esthion akrides kai meli agrion*)" (Mark 1:6). Or, as Matthew put it, "Now John wore clothing of camel's hair with a leather belt around his waist, and his food was locusts and wild honey (*he de trophe en akrides kai meli agrion*)" (Matt. 3:4). This short passage raises some preliminary observations and questions. First, there is a difference in Mark and Matthew's versions here. Mark merely notes *that* he ate these things – locusts and wild honey – whereas Matthew implies that he *only* ate these things.[29] It is unlikely that locusts and wild honey alone would provide enough calories to survive, even for the smaller stature of a first-century person.[30] Second, it is also unclear why Luke and John exclude this information.[31] Even if Luke does not indicate what John ate, he does tell us what he avoids: that he ate no bread and drank no wine, wine and bread being basic first-century meal staples and, eventually, the elements of the Eucharist (Luke 7:33). Such abstentions would have removed John the Baptist from the daily life rhythms of Judean society.

Third, it is unclear if "locust" is the most accurate translation.[32] The Greek word could also mean "grasshopper," which might be preferable since it does not have the same connotations of plague that "locust" does. The term can cover both. Moreover, it may not be "bee honey" as most people assume today, since the word "honey" (*meli*) was also used to refer to "date honey" and other sweet fruit products.[33] So it is unclear whether or not the honey John the Baptist ate was an animal or fruit product. If the honey is bee honey, then the "locusts" and honey are both an animal and an animal product.[34] Neither is a domesticated animal, but they both are kosher. Leviticus 11:20–3 specifically states that eating a locust is fine: the locust, the bald locust, the cricket, and the grasshopper (according to their kinds). Though Deuteronomy 14:19 appears to exclude the eating of locusts and grasshoppers, most ancient Jewish interpreters, including the *Letter of Aristeas*, Philo, the Dead Sea Scrolls, and the Rabbis have sided with Leviticus.[35] Basically, one should only eat winged insects with four feet. The Qumran sect allowed the consumption of locusts so long as they were cooked alive beforehand (*11QT* 48:3–6; *CD* 12:14–15), while the Rabbis allowed live and dead locusts to be eaten (*m. Ter.* 10:9; *m. Ber.* 6:3; *m. 'Ed* 8:4; *m. Hul.* 3:7; *m. 'AZ* 2:7; *t. Ter.* 9:6).[36]

While the eating of locusts or grasshoppers would not be out of place in the ancient world, despite some modern Western hesitancy,[37] it was starting to become less commonplace by the first century CE,[38] and there has to be a reason for the gospels mentioning it. John the Baptist's diet and clothing place him in between the civilized and the wild; he is feral. While locusts and wild honey itself would have been unremarkable and plentiful not just in the wilderness, Kelhoffer argues that Mark has endowed with prophetic significance what would have been for John the Baptist fairly ordinary, making him the herald from Isaiah 40:3.[39] This would be confirmed by his location as well in the wilderness at the Jordan River – a place of liminality.[40] John's food choices may reflect his ascetic lifestyle and a concern with purity, since he consumed wild rather than processed food (cf. 2 Macc. 5:27).[41] Finally, it provides a contrast with Jesus and his disciples: John and his disciples fast, while Jesus and his disciples feast (Mark 2:18–20; Luke 7:33–5). John's food choices place him on the periphery of first-century Judean society; they place him between domestic and wild. He opts out of the regular rhythms of life with fasting, avoiding bread and wine. But his food choices are kosher; he is still "inside" the bounds of Jewish practice in terms of his foodways.

FISHY MIRACLES: ENABLING OTHERS TO EAT ANIMALS

Turning now from John back to Jesus, we look at how while Jesus often appears in dining scenes in the gospels, he is rarely portrayed as actually eating. The dinner scene, instead, sets up another issue or teaching from Jesus, although occasionally that teaching reflects ancient dining practices, such as their hierarchical arrangement and Jesus's potential challenging of that hierarchy. Nonetheless, even if it is rare to find a place where a gospel writer writes "Jesus ate," there are places where the domesticated gospels portray Jesus enabling other people to eat animals: his miracles.

While Linzey seeks to defend Jesus's lapse of allowing others to eat fish by saying that it was in response to an immediate need – and indeed it was – queer theory reminds us that things can always be otherwise.[42] A choice is involved here. Jesus could have just multiplied the bread and not multiplied the fish, but he multiplied the fish too.

In all of the domesticated gospels, Jesus performs miracles concerning fish.[43] This ichthyic focus makes sense since some of his disciples – e.g., Peter, James, and John – come from fishing backgrounds (Matt. 4:18–22; Mark 1:16–20; Luke 5:1–11). In the domesticated gospels, Jesus is teaching, and the people are hungry. There are only five loaves and two fish for everyone (Matt. 14:13–21; Mark 6:30–44; Luke 9:12–17). Jesus takes the loaves and the fish, looks up to heaven, blesses them, and then breaks them up. And not only is there enough bread and fish for everyone to have their fill, but there are twelve baskets of leftovers. This repeats again later with seven loaves and a few small fish with seven baskets left over (Matt. 15:32–8; Mark 8:1–9). In John's version (6:1–21), there are five barley loaves and two small fish, and they fill up twelve baskets of leftovers (it says from the fragments of loaves left over). Curiously, when Jesus reflects later on the miracle of the multiplication of food, he only mentions the bread, and not the fish (Mark 6:52, 8:14–21; Matt. 16:5–12). Fish are part of the original narration of the miracle, but in the later recounting they disappear; the secondary reflections show the erasure of gospel animals already in the gospels themselves.

Modern scholarship has articulated differing social meanings for these feeding miracles. For John Dominic Crossan, they broach the question of authority and leadership, since Jesus works through his disciples as intermediaries of his authority.[44] It creates a hierarchy in the community with Jesus at the centre, the people at the periphery, and the disciples in between them. For Hal Taussig, they are about social experimentation, since the crowds include many kinds of people of different backgrounds, and they all eat their fill, unlike many Hellenistic and Roman meal representations, in which the most important people in that particular context get more food than others.[45] For Taussig, they do not create distinction, but remove distinctions.

The creating and dissolving of social boundaries is an important theme in gospel accounts of eating, but I want to think about this in a different way. Thinking otherwise, why fish and not lamb or a fatted calf? Why fish and not pork? Or put another way, Jesus used what was at hand, but why was fish at hand and not something else? Rephrasing the question based on the food multiplied and eaten reveals a different set of social boundaries that are economic and ethnoreligious. Pork is not kosher of course; it would not be economically feasible for other animals to just be at hand. Fish – around the Sea of Galilee – would make economic and religious sense. Jesus's miracle makes what would be taken for granted visible: people have fish and bread as part of their daily meals; it is nothing special. It only becomes special in terms of the miracle.

But what about a non-anthropocentric reading? What kind of fish were they? Perhaps they were Galilee sprat or sardine – which in modern times accounts for about 60 per cent of all fishing in the Sea of Galilee, or perhaps tilapia, two subspecies of which are also indigenous.[46] How were the bread and fish multiplied? That is, let's look at this from the perspective of the (likely dead, but fresh?) fish. First, it is clear that the actual food multiplied, and Jesus didn't just increase the nutritiousness or filling-ness of the fish and bread – that is, it isn't the same number of grams of fish meat but just making you feel fuller than usual – otherwise there wouldn't be more leftovers than the original amount of bread and fish. Did Jesus expand their meat so that there were the same number of fish (two), but the fish got bigger? Or every time a piece of fish was taken, did it replenish itself – a sort of immediate regeneration of the fish? Or did Jesus make "more" than two fish? If so, were these synthetic fish? Were they sort of fish that have never actually lived (sort of like meat grown in a lab today) and never enjoyed a swim in the Sea of Galilee, but whose existence prevented living fish from being eaten?[47] Since such animals never experience pain or pleasure, would they be permissible to eat according to figures like Linzey? While from an anthropocentric perspective it doesn't matter (fish meat is fish meat no matter where it came from), from the fish perspective, it is significant: did more than two fish have to die? If there are more than two fish now, did the others ever live? Or did the two fish continually replicate or regenerate? This imaginative speculation has a point: how does one balance animal pain with human hunger? As queer thinkers remind us: you can always think otherwise. Jesus could have multiplied just bread – and the bread seems to be the point of the secondary reflection on the significance of the miracle. But fish were there.

Jesus also enables the eating of fish at the end of the Gospel of John. In John 21:4–8, Simon Peter is fishing along with the other disciple, and they haven't caught anything all day. The post-resurrection Jesus – unrecognized as of yet – tells them to try the other side of the boat, and the nets become so full they cannot haul them in. The beloved disciple recognizes it is Jesus, while the other disciples begin to haul in the huge catch. Next (vv. 9–11), the disciples find a fire along the shore with fish and bread on it, Jesus asks them for some of the newly caught fish, and Jesus cooks and serves the fish and bread to the disciples. The Gospel of John uses a different word than the typical *ichthus* here, using instead *opsarion*. It was probably just a synonym or could refer to fish you eat rather than living fish, much like the words "beef" or "pork" do for us. John uses the word *opsarion* five times, but it shows up nowhere else in the New Testament.[48]

In all the domesticated gospels, Jesus enables and encourages fish death. By contrast, in the feral gospels we see an exception to this pattern of enabling fish death, but it comes from a late manuscript variant of the Infancy Gospel of Thomas. In this case, Jesus takes fish that have already been caught and salted and throws them back into the sea. He commands them to shake off their salt and swim in the water (Infancy Gospel of Thomas C, 1).[49] In this case, Jesus restores life to the fish rather than enabling their death or enabling their consumption.[50]

Overall, through his miracles Jesus has enabled the consumption of an animal along with bread, even if it is unclear whether he ate it himself. While some modern critics give Jesus a pass since he was alleviating hunger, the Infancy Gospel of Thomas imagines things could have been otherwise. As an omnivore, eating means choosing, even if that choice is constrained; likewise, Jesus chose which food to multiply. He does not criticize the eating of animals at any point; instead, he facilitates this consumption.

DID JESUS EAT LAMB AT PASSOVER?

Jesus may have eaten meat at the Passover meal, where lamb would be served after being ritually slaughtered (Mark 14:12; Luke 22:7). Passover, as a temple festival in which an animal is slaughtered and handed over to a family, binds those family groupings to the rhythms of the temple. It was a religiously and politically charged event in the first century as ancient Jews remember in ritual and story gaining freedom from a foreign oppressive power. At the centre is a lamb, entangling humans and animals, priests and people, past and present, and God and people. Passover is an important part of all four gospels, because the Passover meal is enmeshed into the events leading up to Jesus's crucifixion. Moreover, the Gospel of John has three Passovers narrated, while Luke writes that Jesus's family – when he was younger – would go to Jerusalem annually for the Passover (a difficult thing to do while living in Galilee; Luke 2:41–52).

Mark refers to when exactly the Passover lamb is sacrificed (14:12), but the narration does not show Jesus and his disciples eating the meat, but eating bread (Mark 14:20, 22–5). Did Jesus or his disciples have a bit of lamb too? Luke is more forthcoming than Matthew on this issue, referring to the sacrifice of the Passover lamb (Luke 22:7) and preparing the Passover meal in the very next verse (Luke 22:8). This sequencing strongly implicates Jesus and his disciples in eating a Passover meal (Luke 22:15), though never directly depicts him eating the meat as it does the wine and bread. Jesus, in fact, claims that he will *not* eat this Passover meal now, but further affirms that he *will* in the kingdom (Luke 22:15–16).[51] This verse is tricky, however. In all manuscripts, Jesus claims he eagerly desired to eat of the Passover meal with his disciples before he suffered. In some manuscripts, Jesus claims he will not eat of the Passover meal until the kingdom is fulfilled, indicating he will not eat it now but will later; in other manuscripts, he says he will not eat of it *again* until the kingdom is fulfilled, suggesting he is eating it now as he eagerly anticipated but will not do it again until all is accomplished. In the first, it is not the eating of it as such that bothers Jesus; it is only the timing. In the second, he does eat it! In all versions, there is also no hint that Jesus dissuaded his disciples from consuming it. John is no help on this: for the second Passover, the only food is loaves and fishes, and only bread is discussed (John 6:4–21, 26).

It is likely that Jesus and his disciples would have partaken in eating lamb at Passover, and the narratives (excepting perhaps Luke) never explicitly say that Jesus refrained. Since refraining would have been the weirder course of action – and would, therefore, probably have been commented on – it seems more likely they would have eaten. But, due to the Passover meal / Last Supper becoming the blueprint for the Eucharist, the focus here is on bread and wine.

Jonathan Klawans forwards the counter-argument that – while generically held within the context of Passover – the Last Supper was a simple traditional Jewish meal, for which the basic elements are the bread and wine, and not a Passover seder.[52] There is a parallel in the *Community Rule* from Qumran, in which a meal must have a minimum of ten members present and a priest would bless the bread and then the wine (*1QS* 6.4–6), the same order as in the synoptic gospel stories and the reverse order of Jewish tradition today. Since bread and wine were not the only things eaten at this meal – or at Jewish meals today – the bread and wine are thought to be symbolic of the entirety of food and drink at the meal, since bread at least was a staple.[53]

The meal was not a Passover seder in the modern sense of it, since there has been so much development of the seder meal since the first century. Yet I am not concerned about whether Jesus's Last Supper was historically a Passover meal, as are Klawans and his interlocutors; I am concerned about the fact that the gospels portray it as one – something that is especially clear in Luke – something that even Klawans assents to and tries to account for. Nonetheless, just because the bread and wine are the only elements mentioned in the gospel accounts (though Luke's "Passover" in 22:15 refers to the entire meal, including lamb) does not necessarily mean that they were the only elements consumed. They are simply the only elements considered worth mentioning given their symbolic import for the storytellers. We, unfortunately, do not know with absolute certainty whether Jesus and his disciples ate lamb at the Last Supper or at any other Passover meal, but it would have been historically probable that they would have, and it would be strange if they abstained (as Jesus does in some manuscripts of Luke 22:15). In the texture of the gospel narratives, this lamb-centred freedom festival directly leads into Jesus's arrest, trial, and crucifixion. It shows Jesus felt compelled enough to travel to Jerusalem from Galilee to participate in this major festival, central to which are stories of freedom and the slaughter of lambs, one of which, according to John, was Jesus himself.

CHEWING THE FAT IN JESUS'S PARABLES

In addition to Jesus's miracles, which enable people to eat animals, Jesus's parables include animal consumption as verisimilitude of daily life, reflecting social, religious, and economic differentiations through animal consumption. I want to focus on two different parables. One, unique to Matthew, uses fishing as a metaphor for the judgment of the kingdom, in which consuming animals becomes symbolic of one's ultimate destiny; the other, unique to Luke, involves multiple economic reflections through eating animals and what animals eat: the story of the lost, or "prodigal," son.

Matthew – in a parable reminiscent of some of Jesus's "fishy miracles" – speaks of the kingdom of heaven as being like a net catching a lot of fish:

> Again, the skyward kingdom is like a net that was thrown into the sea and caught fish of every kind (*ek pantos genius sunagagousei*); when it was full, they drew it ashore, sat down, and put the good (*ta kala*) into baskets but threw out the rotten (*ta sapra*). So it will be at the end of the age. The angels will come out and separate the evil from the righteous (*aphoriousin tous ponerous ek mesou ton dikaion*) and throw them into the furnace of fire, where there will be weeping and gnashing of teeth. (Matt. 13:47–50 adapted)

In this parable, "good" and "rotten" fish parallel righteous and evil people at the end of the age. The terminology is important. There are good and bad, righteous and evil. The word for the good (*ta kala*) has a rich history in Greek philosophical reflection. Its base meaning is "beautiful," but Plato had long before then connected the "beautiful" with the "good" (see, e.g., Plato's *Symposium*). Its more direct antonym is *ta kaka*, which has associations with "ugly" and "bad." Instead, this parable has, more appropriate for its fishy context, *ta sapra*, which means the "rotten ones." It does not have the sense of moral badness but of a rancid stench. One, therefore, throws out the smelly ones! Yet the "good/beautiful" and the "bad/rotten" provide analogies for the "righteous" and the "evil" respectively. Like the parable of the sheep and the goats (Matt. 25:31–46), which is also unique to Matthew's gospel, animals provide a metaphor for God's selection of the righteous and unrighteous, between reward and punishment.

The emphasis on "every kind of fish" is also worth considering: it suggests both "clean" and "unclean" fish – that is, those fish with fins and scales (clean, accepted, kosher) and those missing one, the other, or both (e.g., shellfish). One may infer in Matthew's parable an association of "clean" with good and "unclean" with bad/rotten. For Matthew, moreover, the angelic sorting of the righteous and the evil parallels his explanation of the parable of the sower (13:36–43) as well as the sorting of the sheep and the goats (25:31–46).

There is one final parable that includes extensive animalistic imagery: the parable of the lost (or "prodigal") son in Luke 15:11–32, which, for Luke, comes in the chapter just after the parable of the great feast. The parable of the lost son is the third in a series of lost things, after a lost sheep and a lost coin. The story is well known, but here is a quick rundown of its contents: A man has two sons. The younger one asks for his inheritance, goes to a foreign country, and spends it all. He goes broke, there is a famine, and he gets a job feeding the pigs (*tous choirous*). He has gone so low that he finds the pig food appetizing. He decides to go home and become a hired hand of his father so he would not go hungry, because the hired hands have enough bread. His father runs to him when he sees him; the son says he's not worthy, but the father has his slaves bring the best robe out, a ring, and sandals for his son. He also throws a party, killing the fatted calf (*ton moschon ton siteuton*), with music and dancing. The older brother hears the party and finds out that his father killed the fatted calf for his younger brother. The older brother, angry with his father, notes he hasn't even gotten a young goat (*eriphon*) for a celebration, but his father has given his younger brother the fatted calf! The father notes that all he owns is the oldest brother's as well, but they should celebrate that what was lost is found, what was dead has come back to life.

Animals and animal consumption structure the narrative. It includes pigs, the fatted calf, and a young goat. The pigs represent the youngest brother's lowest point. He is in a foreign land (not Israel – pigs are not kosher) and is willing to feed and even fantasizes about eating the food of this unclean animal. While he does not eat a pig, the pigs would have been raised for their meat. He brings himself to the level of the pig by wanting to eat with the pig. Donna Haraway might see this as a potential "cum panis," "coming together at table" or mutual becoming of pigs and humans. Yet, if this a mutual becoming, an entangling of the pigs' and the son's lives, for Luke this represents the nadir of the lost son's life, marking him not only as animal, but an unclean animal; therefore, ultimately also realigning him as foreign.

Bread represents one's daily nourishment; it is freedom from hunger. It is something that even hired hands would get to eat, a step above eating with the pigs, but definitely below a fatted calf or even a young goat.

The fatted calf shows the father's compassion but also his relief and joy that his lost son has returned. The fatted calf represents the height of a party: slaughtering one is what you do when you go all out (also 1 Sam. 28:24; Amos 6:4). We can see this in other gospel passages as well. Matthew 22:1–14, Luke 14:15–24, and Thomas 64 provide another parable of the general banquet type. The three versions – Matthew, Luke, and Thomas – have quite a few variations.[54] In Matthew's version, the kingdom of heaven is like a king giving a wedding banquet for his son. He sent his slaves to invite the wedding guests, but the guests wouldn't come. He sent them again, saying: "Tell those who have been invited: Look, I have prepared my dinner, my bulls and my fat calves have been slaughtered (*hoi tauroi mou kai ta sitista tethumena*), and everything is ready; come to the wedding banquet" (22:4 adapted).[55] Some turned down the invite; others went so far as to mistreat and kill the king's slaves.[56] In Matthew, the King takes revenge on those who killed his slaves, and the slaves invited anyone they could find on the streets – the bad and the good (*ponerous te kai agathous*) – to the king's feast.[57] The idealized wedding feast Jesus imagines has bulls and fatted calves (literally "fattened ones") slaughtered for consumption. It makes one wonder if this would be the case at the banquets Jesus himself attended. And whether he ate some of this meat. Refusal to partake would have been noteworthy.[58]

The older brother's jealousy highlights the heightened role of the fatted calf. He cannot get over the fatted calf – he interestingly does not seem to care about the ring, the robe, and the sandals; he's not one of Joseph's brothers who cared more about fashion. He wants a party too, and he has not even been given a young goat to slaughter to celebrate with his friends. The young goat is not nearly as good as the fatted calf, but it would be something – and likely demonstrates what, for example, a less wealthy person might do when throwing a party.[59]

More so than the rest of the gospel narratives, Jesus's parables open up to eating more than the fish found everywhere else. Though fish are still present as metaphors of God's judgment, we see bulls, fatted calves, and a young goat. There is definitely a hierarchy of meat here as well: pigs are the lowest (unclean) and fatted calves are the highest. Since pork was considered the basic land-dwelling meat of choice in traditional Roman sources,[60] this parable is situated against broader Roman culture and aligns with traditional Judean foodways. A bull would not be as good for consumption, since it is more of a beast of burden, and, therefore, tough meat. The young goat seems to be a step down from the fatted calf, since the older brother has "not even" gotten a goat, while his younger brother gets the prized fatted calf. While these would be a special treat – thus, it appears in the celebrations of kings and the wealthy and, even there, on a special occasion – these parables open a window into religious and economic divisions implicated by different kinds of animal-eating while also imagining God's kingdom or reign analogous to a place of eating the best meats beyond just one's daily bread.

CAMEL SWALLOWERS AND SNAKE GIVERS: EATING ANIMALS IN JESUS'S APHORISMS

Jesus's parables provide short stories that imagine the kingdom, reign of God, and heaven as a banquet, with the recovery of lost children and so on, in which the best meats are served. Jesus's aphorisms, by contrast, tend to be biting and cynical. They are direct social critiques of Jesus's interlocutors. Animalistic aphorisms create or maintain in-group/out-group divisions that we will see re-emerge in chapter 4. These are not teachings about the kingdom to crowds or disciples as the parables were, though some of the parables contained social critiques that led to negative reactions from out-group people. Nonetheless, the aphorisms are more direct and have a venomous edge to them, directly addressed against out-group people instead of the indirection of the parables.

One animal-eating aphorism that is easy to miss is found in Matthew 23:24: "You strain out the gnat but gulp down the camel! (*hoi diulizontes ton kononta, ten de kamhelon katapinontes*)" (translation mine). Chapter 23 is Matthew's long diatribe against the scribes and Pharisees. It is full of hyperbole and this saying is no different. It comes just after Jesus noting that they tithe on little things – mint, dill, and cucumber – but miss the big things like justice, mercy, and faith (23:23). Jesus does not oppose such tithing, per se, but only the failure of the latter: "It is these [justice, mercy, and faith] you ought to have practiced without neglecting the others [tithing mint, dill, cucumber]." That is, do both.

How does this relate to straining gnats and camels? Both gnats and camels are unclean animals (Lev. 11:4, 20–3, 29–31). Anyone who has been outside when gnats are swarming – as is often the case in late May and early June where I live in central Illinois – knows it is difficult not to accidentally swallow one or even breathe one in, unless one is wearing a mask outside. Later rabbis recognized this and advised against straining gnats from liquids (especially wine and vinegar), indicating that some Jews (whom the rabbis here opposed) continued to be so scrupulous in a later period (*t. Ter.* 7:11; *b. Hul.* 67a).[61]

Clearly, Jesus is engaged in hyperbole, saying the scribes and Pharisees strain out (tiny) gnats but gulp down the (huge) camel. It is on par with taking the speck out of someone else's eye but having a log in one's own (Matt. 7:10). Of course, one cannot literally have a log in one's eye or accidentally swallow a camel. It is an exaggeration. It may also be a nice play on words. In Aramaic a gnat is *qalma* and a camel is *gamla*; when translated to Greek, it retains a bit of alliteration, with both words beginning with kappa.

But it is unclear whether or not Jesus approves of the practice of straining gnats. It could be on par with tithing mint, dill, and cucumber – do it so long as you also do the weightier things: be sure to strain gnats and not eat camels at the same time! Or it is so hyperbolic that it is "obvious" that such straining is a waste of time. Either way, Jesus – like most of us – probably accidentally ate or breathed in a gnat every now and then, but, like most of us, would not like to see a bunch of them in his wine.

A second saying is closer to the parable tradition, and, like the parables, is more directed to in-group people; it has an edge but is comparative as a parable is, yet it is not quite as developed. It is part of Matthew's Sermon on the Mount and paralleled in Luke (part of "Q"): "Is there anyone among you who, if your child asks for bread, will give a stone? Or if the child asks for a fish, will give a snake (*e kai ichthun aitesei, me ophin epidosei autoi*)? If you then, who are evil, know how to give good gifts to your children, how much more will your Father in the sky give good things to those who ask him!" (Matt. 7:9–10 adapted). Compare Luke's version: "Is there anyone among you who, if your child asks for a fish, will give a snake instead of a fish? Or if the child asks for an egg, will give a scorpion? (*tin ade ex humon ton patera ho huios icthun, kai anti ichthuos ophin autoi epidosei; e kai aitesei hoion, epidosei autoi skorpion*)?" (Luke 11:11–12). In both cases, this comes in the context of the famous paragraph, "Ask and it will be given to you." Jesus's rhetoric works from lesser to greater. If you – who are evil (what an extraordinary view of his immediate audience Jesus has) – know how to give good gifts (bread and fish) rather than evil gifts (stones and snakes), how much more will the heavenly Father give good things, and implied in Matthew is that the heavenly Father gives even better gifts than bread and fish. Luke is more explicit: the good heavenly gift the Father will give is the Holy Spirit (11:13).

While eating is not explicit here – no one is literally or parabolically sitting to eat a meal – and the context is gift-giving, the actual gifts here are food: the ubiquitous bread and fish (in Matthew). This likely reflects the food available to Jesus's audience in daily life, the food of regular folks who could not afford a fattened calf. Luke's version is an anomalous case, however, because this is the only place in the gospels (or the New Testament) that even alludes to humans eating eggs – and vegetarians and vegans can debate whether egg consumption counts as eating an animal or not.[62] At the very least, eggs are an animal product. The doubling of "bad" foods here to include scorpions also heightens the potential for danger, since snakes and scorpions can be venomous, though it shows how different a world we live in today where people do have scorpions and especially snakes, though not venomous snakes, as pets. Jesus, ultimately, reflects on eating bread, fish, and, in Luke, eggs as a matter of fact. He does not promote it, but he does not dismiss or dissuade from it either. It is just likely what his audience – and perhaps he – ate. Although snakes are edible for humans, it is assumed one would never give a child a snake. Jesus's animal aphorisms critique out-group practices and admonish and encourage in-group followers.

AND JESUS ATE ... TO PROVE HE'S NOT A GHOST

We have investigated a series of stories where different figures in the gospels eat animals, particularly John the Baptist and the crowds that surround Jesus. We have seen how Jesus reflects on or assumes the quotidian consumption of animals in his parables and sayings. We have further discovered how Jesus enables others to eat animals through his miracles. We have examined many instances where Jesus eats bread or drinks wine but, until now, none that clearly state that Jesus ate an animal, even though it is likely he did.

There is only one place in the domesticated gospels that unequivocally shows Jesus eating an animal: Luke 24:42–3. To really understand what is happening in this instance of animal consumption, let's look at the broader passage. It reads:

> While they were talking about this, Jesus himself stood among them and said to them, "Peace be with you." They were startled and terrified, and thought that they were seeing a ghost. He said to them, "Why are you frightened, and why do doubts arise in your hearts? Look at my hands and my feet; see that it is I myself. Touch me and see; for a ghost does not have flesh and bones as you see that I have. And when he had said this, he showed them his hands and his feet. While in their joy they were still disbelieving and still wondering, he said to them, "Have you anything here to eat?" They gave him a piece of broiled fish, and he took it and ate

> in their presence (*hoi de epedoken autoi ichthuos optou meros· kai labon enopion auton ephagen*). (Luke 24:36–42)

And so, here it is. The only place in the domesticated gospels that unambiguously states that Jesus ate an animal. What's peculiar is that it only occurs in the post-resurrection appearances of Luke's gospel. Nowhere in the domesticated gospels does the reader find Jesus eating animals in his pre-crucifixion life. The most likely reason for not portraying Jesus eating animals before his death was that there was nothing special in him doing so; it would have been unremarkable. What would be the point of bringing it up? Here there is a clear reason in bringing it up: it is making a theological point.

The story risks something, however, in placing fish in Jesus's mouth after he has been resurrected. Jesus is not long for this world – he is about to ascend to the heavenly realm (Acts 1:9). Yet, there is a shared understanding throughout the Mediterranean world that eating food of a particular realm binds you to that realm. This can be positive: eating food of the heavenly realm or divine realm is transformative, making you a part of that realm, a process Meredith Warren calls "hierophagy." This has a negative side, however: a being of the higher realm should not eat of the lower realms, such as when Persephone/Proserpina ate pomegranate seeds and became partly bound to the realm of Hades/Pluto/Dis.[63] In the Jewish tradition, this emerges in angels refusing to eat human food.[64] So, if Jesus – post-resurrection – is ready for the divine realm, why would he eat earthly food, re-binding himself to the earthly realm and, by extension, animal and human intra-active social and natural networks?

On the one hand, this, along with the multiplication of bread and fish earlier, may recall a primitive Eucharist meal and express Jesus's continued presence through the shared meal, here mediated by Jesus's disciples and expressed by Simon Peter (24:33–5).[65] Jesus appears to people after they know he has died. They have a very natural reaction to it: they think he is a ghost or spirit (*pneuma*). Like Thomas in the Gospel of John, he invites them to touch him to prove he is not merely a ghost. That is not good enough, so he asks for food and eats:

something a phantom cannot do. The broiled fish also reminds one of the end of John, when Jesus cooks fish for his disciples, enabling them to eat it – again after his resurrection (John 21:9–13). Of course, even the post-resurrection Jesus is an omnivore, so he could have just proven his embodiment through eating bread. Yet, here, as a guest, he took and ate what was given to him, just like he probably did as a guest in his pre-resurrection life. By doing so, he re-binds himself to the community and its continued entanglements with animals.

DECLARING ALL FOODS CLEAN?

One final issue needs addressing before wrapping up the discussion of eating animals in the gospels: the passage in the triple tradition in which Jesus declares all foods clean. This would, of course, have wide-ranging social implications for the earliest Jesus-followers as they moved out from strictly Jewish social networks to fold in more Gentiles, as Acts and Paul's letters amply illustrate.

Mark 7:1–23 is a long, complex, and difficult passage. The catalyst is that some Pharisees and scribes complain that Jesus's disciples do not wash their hands before they eat. While today this would be considered basic hygiene – especially if you are eating with your hands! – here it is framed in terms of ritual purity and impurity rules. Mark claims that it is a "tradition of the elders" and that all Jews – not just Pharisees – observe this custom. The passage also notes that they actually clean their pots, pans, and kettles too! Jesus, in turn, calls them hypocrites, has some weird retort that they have abandoned God's commandment and followed mere human tradition. It is notoriously difficult to parse out the meaning of Mark 7:9–13, but, luckily, we don't have to.[66]

After this, Jesus gathers a crowd and says that "there is nothing outside a person that by going in can defile, but the things that come out are what defile" (Mark 7:15). It sounds like Jesus just made a poop joke. The disciples ask for further explanation and Jesus says, "Do you not see that whatever goes into a person from outside cannot defile, since it enters, not the heart but the stomach, and goes out into the sewer?" (7:18–19a). Now while Jesus tried out some scatological humor, what concerns us here is the following verse. In what the NRSV puts in parentheses, the narrator says, "Thus he declared all foods clean" (7:19b). After this, there is a spiritual interpretation that deflates Jesus's joke, turning the saying of what comes out goes into the sewer into general sinfulness.

The point is Mark 7:19b. Jesus himself never says in the gospels: "I hereby declare all foods clean." It is a third-person parenthetical remark by the narrator: how the person who wrote Mark understood Jesus's words. Or it is an editorial intrusion. Matthew 15:1–20 and Luke 11:37–41 omit this remark. It only shows up in Mark. Nonetheless, it is now there. The broader point is that in declaring all foods clean, the editor of Mark was not talking about vegetables; since Jewish food laws focus on clean and unclean animals to eat (as well as how they are slaughtered and who slaughters them), it is focused on eating animals. In short, Jesus – according to the Markan editor – has declared all animals "fair game." If Mary Douglas is correct that the differentiation of what is clean and unclean among animals allows one to imitate God's holiness – separateness and wholeness – which also would demarcate oneself from non-holy people, then this remark would have wide-ranging social, in addition to the more discussed theological, implications.[67] It realigns holy and profane not just in terms of animals eaten, but, by extension, those who eat those animals. Mark's Jesus, therefore, while never directly eating an animal (this only happens in Luke), enables others to eat animals (through miracles) and makes all animals "fair game," to re-literalize the metaphor.

CONCLUDING OUR GOSPEL MEAL

While Jesus is only directly portrayed eating an animal once – a fish after he was resurrected – the domesticated gospels portray meat-eating in several contexts, usually in a positive or at least neutral fashion. There is no direct criticism of meat-eating in the domesticated gospels. Despite ancient and modern attempts to portray Jesus (and John the

Baptist) as vegetarian, it is not a question, therefore, of whether Jesus or his disciples ate meat, but which animals and why? Through animal consumption, Jesus becomes entangled in a series of sociobiological networks through his miracles, parables, aphorisms, and life narrative. He is implicated in the acquisition, slaughter, cooking, and eating of other animals. Social class distinctions arise based on what is eaten, as well as religious distinctions observed and undermined.

Before getting into this, we should acknowledge that most people in the ancient world did not eat as much meat as modern industrialized people do.[68] Most people maintained a largely grain- and vegetable-based diet due to necessity rather than ethical considerations.[69] Moreover, animals were often needed for something else: cows and oxen, for example, were work animals; sheep provided wool.[70] Only at special occasions would people eat a large animal.

Much of our lack of information on eating animals in the gospels may reflect the social settings of the recounting/reading of the stories of Jesus. We know in certain locales that the question of whether or not to eat meat – especially meat potentially sacrificed to Greek and Roman deities – was a live issue (1 Corinthians). By downplaying Jesus's consumption of potentially sacrificial meat (fish is non-sacrificial meat in both Jewish and Greek traditions), the gospel writers sidestep this potentially divisive issue. But, of course, there are fish.

Schools of fish swarm throughout the domesticated gospels: they appear as part of Jesus's miracles and what Jesus finally eats after his resurrection. On the one hand, there are times and places in the ancient world where fish would be considered delicacies or luxury items, from classical Athens to imperial Rome, especially if they were imported – and, in the Roman period, many sauces made from fish, such as garum, were popular products of trade. Even for most Israelites and Judeans, fish would have been largely rare. There was little direct access to the Mediterranean Sea; the primary sources were the Jordan and the Sea of Galilee. Most of the catches there would likely have been so small that they could only satisfy local markets and consumption; nonetheless, there is evidence that salted fish was exported from Judea to Egypt, likely beginning during Ptolemaic rule.[71] Thus, the ubiquity of fish in the gospel accounts is a mark of its specific situatedness. It is markedly Galilean. Local fish from the Sea of Galilee and bread would have been the staples only for those who hemmed closely to the Sea of Galilee, and likely very few others; that is, those who composed most of Jesus's most immediate audience.[72] Fish would have been the most accessible meat, other than insects, for non-elite classes of lakeside Galilee. These stories simply would not have resonated as well outside of this immediate setting. Moreover, many of his disciples – Simon (Peter), Andrew, James and John (sons of Zebedee) – were fishermen (Matt. 4:18–22; Mark 1:16–20; Luke 5:1–11). All of them were either fishing or mending their nets when Jesus found them. He calls them out of their jobs to fish for people – a "lesser to greater" statement? Moreover, fish – while subject to kashrut in terms of needing fins and scales – were not subject to the consumption of blood prohibition that land and aerial animals were subject to according to biblical and rabbinic rulings (Lev. 7:26–7; 17:10–14; *t. Ter.* 9:6; *Num. Rab.* 19:3), though the Qumran community believed that it extended to fish (CD 12:11–15).[73] They were, therefore, not subject to sacrificial rules either.[74] That is, they were fair game.

On the other end of the spectrum is the fattened calf, which only appears in elite contexts in Jesus's parables as kings or the clearly well-to-do father of the lost son. It is something only the wealthy can afford – or, if the case of Qumran is a guide, of a group, and even then it is for special occasions and not everyday consumption. It is part of how Jesus imagines the kingdom: a meal for people of all backgrounds, but including the best of meats. Bulls and a young goat – less costly and tougher meat than the fattened calf but more costly than a fish for a Galilean – also appear in these elite contexts, but, in the case of the young goat, as clearly second place to the fattened calf.[75]

Locusts, lambs, and pigs do not have the same class inflection as fattened calf versus fish, but they also have social significance. John the Baptist's consumption of locusts and wild honey locates him at the edge of civilization, between the wild and the domestic, in a continual liminality between the desert and the city and between the world and God's coming judgment. The lamb is of religious significance, since it is consumed as part of Passover, celebrating liberation from Egypt, a volatile time as Jews remember their former slavery to Egypt in light of their situation as subjected to Rome. It is unclear whether Jesus ate the lamb, but Mark and Luke seem especially interested in tying the Last Supper into the timing of the sacrifice of lambs.

There are also pigs, gnats, snakes, scorpions, and camels brought up for consumption. All of these are considered unclean by biblical food laws. For the lost son, seeking to eat with the pigs represents the nadir of his life, even though pigs were a staple of the Roman diet, while snakes and scorpions are obvious things one would not give a child instead of what they asked for: a fish or an egg. If one is so punctilious as to strain out a gnat – a difficult thing due to their ubiquity at certain times of year – then one should also consider weightier things. These are either eaten by out-group people (pigs or camels) or are considered "obviously" things you shouldn't eat or give a child to eat (scorpions and snakes). Nonetheless, at least according to Mark, Jesus declared all foods clean, erasing the in-group/out-group distinction, as well as part of the basis for "holiness" in Leviticus, based on food.

Jesus may disappoint modern animal ethicists as he remained fully entangled in the processes that enabled the consumption of other animals, and, for Jesus, these processes would not have been nearly as hidden from view as they are for us in the twenty-first century. Yet his literal and metaphorical gustatory habits also compose and decompose a variety of ideological, economic, and ethno-religious distinctions.

2

Prosthetic Animals: Wearing and Working Animals in the Gospels

The goat is for milking, the sheep for shearing, the hen for laying eggs, and the ox for plowing.

Babylonian Talmud, Shabbat 19b[1]

Humans do not only consume other animals through eating them; humans also become entangled with other animals through wearing animal products and using animals for labour, including involuntary labour. For example, Donna Haraway discusses the tangled histories humans and pigeons have had with one another: "The capabilities of pigeons surprise and impress human beings, who often forget how they themselves are rendered capable by and with both things and living beings."[2] In various ways, animals enable humans, whether it is through consumption of animals or through working animals. Non-vegetarian humans ingest animals, incorporating nutrients that become part of our bodies. Working animals, however, enable humans to do things that neither the human nor the animal could do alone: an example of what Haraway calls "becoming with."[3] It is an intra-active entanglement, and an unequal one.

While working animals of the past have been replaced by mechanization, today there are still working animals, especially dogs. As discussed by Laura Hobgood-Oster, dogs were the first animal to be domesticated, predating other domesticated species by millennia. Dogs likely aided humans in domesticating other species, including sheep and pigs, that humans use for food, clothing, and work. Modern humans became what they are through dogs; it is a co-evolution, an intra-active becoming.[4] Discussing border collies in Britain and the US, Donna Haraway notes "the dogs fall somewhere between livestock and coworkers for the human shepherds ... Working dogs are tools that are part of the farm's capital stock, and they are labourers who produce surplus value by giving more than they get in a market-driven economic system."[5] The idea of an animal as a "tool" pops up throughout animal studies literature. Hobgood-Oster similarly says, "Dogs were tools, but they were also companions."[6] The working animal has an ambiguous status, therefore: is it a co-worker, livestock, or a tool?

This concept of a "living tool" has ancient resonance, though not a positive one, relating to Aristotle's characterization of slave labour.[7] Aristotle notes that humans (or more precisely, free humans) have no friendship with inanimate objects, animals, or slaves; slaves are animate tools and tools are inanimate slaves. While slaves rank higher than animals insofar as they are human, insofar as they are slaves, like animals, they are living tools. Slaves and animals are objectified in the same breath, removed from any subjectivity, will, or desire of their own.

As sensitive as Haraway and Hobgood-Oster are as readers of human-animal entanglements, one must be sensitive to their characterization of animals as tools.[8] Animal rights theorists Sue Donaldson and Will Kymlicka note how easily using animal products and labour quickly turns into exploitation.[9] Haraway and Hobgood-Oster may be correct that this is how animals are treated: alternately as companions and tools, and all that implies for Haraway and Hobgood-Oster's respective projects, livestock, and objects.[10] While Haraway largely positively values this relationship between humans and companion species, such animal slavery and slave animality suggests we need a more critical reflection of such entanglements between humans and animals. The queer theorist Jack Halberstam offers such a critique in his book *Wild Things*.[11]

Halberstam aims his critique of what he calls "zombie humanism" – the turning of wild animals into commodities – at the pet industry. Pets do work too. They provide emotional support and attachment for humans. This type of support has been found to have much benefit, including health benefits, for humans, while puppy mills and the excesses of pure breeds have created problems for the animals themselves.[12] Halberstam uses the same language for modern-day pets as Haraway does for working animals. They are emotional prostheses for their human owners and similarly objectified.[13] He writes, "Accordingly, what I refer to as *zombie humanism* is a way of defining the human as alive only by positioning our humanity against other creatures that exist only as our prosthetic extensions."[14] Some animal rights ethicists also see the development and training of emotional support animals as exploitative.[15] Haraway and Hobgood-Oster see this relation as largely co-beneficial, though they are not blind to the negative impacts of, for example, modern breeding on animal, particularly canine, genetic diseases;[16] humans and animals, such as dogs, can only exist in intra-active relation to one another, and to understand what it means to be human means to examine other animals. As Hobgood-Oster writes, "humans can only really understand themselves when looking in a mirror that is smudged by a dog's tongue."[17] For Halberstam, this means a sacrificing of subjectivity of the other animals that humans define themselves against; it is an entanglement that unequally benefits humans more than other animals.

While Halberstam critiques the pet industry, this critique would stand for any animal life that exists as a prosthetic extension of humans: that is, most domesticated animals. Such animals, deprived of subjectivity and becoming objects, live half-lives, neither fully living (which Halberstam equates with being wild or feral) and neither fully dead.[18] This is codified in law, where animals are "things" and not "persons."[19] Thus, Halberstam calls them zombified. Both Haraway and Halberstam refer to working animals and pets as prostheses that allow humans to do things they could not do otherwise, but they evaluate this very differently. Haraway's slip, calling such animals "tools," unveils the persistence of a relation between humans and working animals as that of a form of animal slavery for human benefit.

In the ancient world, animals were living tools, livestock, and co-workers.[20] They allowed humans to do things they could not do otherwise; thus, they were prosthetic. Domesticated animals were part of what any basic settlement would need, making human civilization possible. Plato, when developing his ideal city in the *Republic*, has Socrates introduce the need for those who raise working animals: "Yet it [the city] still would not be a very large settlement, even if we added cowherds, shepherds, and other herdsmen, so that the farmers would have cows to do their plowing, the builders oxen to share with the farmers in hauling their materials, and the weavers and shoemakers hides and fleeces to use."[21] Plato puts together working animals and non-edible animal products. Both are "tools" or "materials" for various ancient jobs. They are prosthetic extensions.[22] While the use of animals as tools and materials was ubiquitous, it is in these categories that we find most of the "missing animals" of the gospels. The domesticated gospels do not portray Mary riding a donkey, the Magi riding camels, and the centurion riding a horse, for example, like we would expect. More to the point, Jesus is literally born in a feeding trough. Animals are assumed to be there, but they are not explicitly mentioned in Luke's narrative – at least not at Jesus's place of birth. Riding animals and animals pulling carts (which is just as likely an understanding of how Mary reached Bethlehem in Luke as riding on the back of a donkey) must have been present, but they are generally excluded from the account. But animals that work and the animals one wears do show up in the account at key points. They were taken for granted, as women, slaves, and children also were. In these accounts, animals and animal products become extensions of self, a living or once-living prosthetic.

As Plato's settlement illustrates, these prosthetics give rise to social categories. As was the case with eating animals, human entanglements with working animals and animal products, particularly used in clothing and accessories, intersect with social distinctions in the gospels. The animals one wears and the animals one uses in the gospels vary by occupation, economic status, ethnoreligious prescriptions, and gender.

WOOL, LEATHER, AND PEARLS: WEARING ANIMALS AND OTHER ANIMAL PRODUCTS

While clothing has a practical function to protect someone from weather or environmental conditions, it also has a social significance. What one wears and how one wears it signified in antiquity – as it does today – intersecting social distinctions, including gender, national and ethnic identities, status, stage of life, class, and occupation. Dress does not just reflect these social categories, but through its repetition it creates and maintains them; clothing can also cross, challenge, and modify them.[23] When one learns these codes of dress, one can create a "public self."[24] When one transitions in status, employment, life stage, or gender, one of the most obvious symbols of that change is changing clothes.[25] Clothing can disguise; clothing can express.

The Hebrew Bible and its ancient translations, for example, emphasize that Israelites and Jews are not to wear garments that mix different threads or *sha'atnez* (Lev. 19:19; Deut. 22:11), male Israelites should have tassels on their garments with a blue thread or *tzitzit* (Num. 15:38–9; Deut. 22:12), warriors should not wear women's clothing nor women wear warriors' clothing (Deut. 22:5),[26] and the priests have different – linen – garments than the rest of society and different garments they wear on special occasions.[27] Or, in the case of the Joseph novella, clothing – Joseph's princess dress – can propel the plot.[28] These rules create and recreate differences based on ethnicity and gender, as well as priestly versus non-priestly status. If how one dresses indicates status and group affiliation, then changes of dress regularly accompany and symbolize initiation, conversion, rites of passage, or other status transformations. These distinctions in dress, moreover, include materials used (such as linen or wool), dyes, cuts, and folds, as well as other adornments woven into or added onto the clothing. In antiquity as well as today, many of these materials derived from animal products.[29]

In the gospels clothing has a group-identity function. It differentiates Jesus's followers from the Pharisees and other authorities. It has ethnoreligious significance, separating Israelites from others and priests from regular Israelites. John the Baptist's clothing, like his diet, places him on the edges of society, while Jesus's own clothing draws attention due to its extraordinary properties. Finally, animal accessory products such as pearls signify luxury. Just as the kingdom will have the best meats, it will have or be symbolized by the most luxurious accessories.

When not using shepherds metaphorically to refer to Jesus and domesticated sheep (*Ovis aries*) to refer to his disciples (see chapter 4), the Gospel of Luke also depicts actual shepherds. Luke's narrative famously includes shepherds watching their flocks by night and an angel of the Lord appearing to them to instruct them to go visit the newborn Jesus (Luke 2:8–20). Shepherding reaches increased significance in the later feral gospel tradition; for example, Mary's father, Joachim, is a fairly wealthy shepherd according to tradition (Proto-James 4.2–4; Pseudo-Matthew 1.1). Shepherds tend flocks of sheep, to be sure! It is something that is obvious, but it is important to think about the economy here. They are watching their sheep to make a living. Some will likely be eaten or milked for milk or cheese,[30] while they will also be used for wool and therefore cloth, most likely dyed.[31] This is not remarked on because it would have been common for people to be wearing woolen clothing in ancient Palestine and the rest of the Mediterranean more generally. The indigenous species of sheep in Israel was the fat-tailed Awassi, which was usually white with brown or black head and feet; its light-coloured wool would have made the dyeing process easier.[32] Moreover, domesticated sheep must be shorn to protect from disease and overheating. If done by an expert shearer, it is in the sheep's interest to be shorn annually.[33] Plato has Socrates describe the process of preparing and dyeing wool:

> SOCRATES: You know, then, that when dyers want to dye wool purple, they first select from wools of many different colors the

> ones that are naturally white. Then they give them an elaborate preparatory treatment, so that they will accept the color as well as possible. And only at that point do they dip them in the purple dye. When something is dyed in this way, it holds the dye fast, and no amount of washing, whether with or without detergent, can remove the color. (*Republic* 429d–e, trans. Reeve)

Socrates discusses wool dyeing as common knowledge to draw on in his philosophical argument. Pliny, furthermore, remarks on various kinds of wool produced in different regions by different breeds of sheep, as well as embroidering and dyeing wool (*Natural History* 8.189–214). Embroidered and dyed wool would have been ubiquitous, even though the particular dye of purple (murex) Pliny refers to would have been a luxury.[34] In fact, with the exception of some sectarians who preferred linen, most Jews in the Roman period wore mostly or entirely wool.[35] Such an animal product would be omnipresent, but, due to its ubiquity, unmentioned unless it stood out in some way.

Wool and linen clothing show up throughout the gospels.[36] Wearing wool was far more common;[37] the rarity of linen, therefore, makes it more likely to catch attention and be remarked on. It was only used on special occasions or by special people. We see the "marked" attention to linen in a few places. Linen, and therefore not an animal product, shows up in an enigmatic verse in Mark 14:51–2, that "a certain young man was following him [Jesus], wearing nothing but a linen cloth. They caught hold of him, but he left the linen cloth and ran off naked." Burial also occurs using linen rather than wool. Jesus's own burial is in linen cloth (Mark 15:46; Matt. 27:59; Luke 23:53; John 19:40; 20:7; cf. John 11:44). The priesthood wore linen in the temple, and the Qumran sectarians also preferred linen in their community. Priestly clothing, which had to be linen while officiating, is briefly glimpsed in the gospels: the high priest tears his clothes (Mark 14:63). Priests also wore linen loincloths (Exod. 28:42–3; cf. Exod. 20:20; Lev. 16:4; Ezek. 44:18; cf. Josephus, *Ant.* 3.7.1–4 [151–8]), as did the Qumran sectarians in imitation of the priesthood.[38] Finally, there is a young man (angel) wearing a white robe at the empty tomb (Mark 16:5). If this angel is modelled off the priesthood, then he would have been wearing white linen, like a martyr (cf. Dan. 11:35; Rev. 7:9, 13).

Even if everyone else largely wore wool, how different groups wore it and how much of it they wore varied. Jesus's and John the Baptist's followers are marked by their simplicity of dress and their lack. John the Baptist tells those who have two coats ("tunics") to give away one (Luke 3:11). One set of clothes is enough. Jesus extends this minimalism to accessories: his commissioned disciples are to carry no extra tunic or a bag/knapsack with them (Luke 9:3). Mark also says to have "no money in their belts" and "to wear sandals and not to put on two tunics" (Mark 6:6b–9). It is unclear what material the belt would be: leather or perhaps a strip of wool. Sandals would most likely be made of leather. Matthew, however, has them avoid carrying "two tunics or sandals" (Matt. 10:10). In Luke 10:4, the commissioned seventy are also not to carry sandals as well as no bag and no purse.[39] All of the negations signify that following Jesus involved a transient lifestyle with no frills; Jesus's followers are marked by their lack of extra outfits.

By contrast, other figures exhibit excess dress. Whether or not the centurion had a horse, he most likely wore standard Roman soldier leather boots.[40] In Mark 12:38, Jesus tells his disciples to beware of the scribes who "like to walk around in long robes" (cf. Matt. 23:1, 6; Luke 20:45–7; 21:1–4; 11:43; 14:7–11). Similarly, while *tzitzit* or fringes and *tefillin* or "phylacteries" would have been ubiquitous for Jewish men in antiquity, Jesus speaks of their excessive use in Matthew 23, saying that the Pharisees "make their phylacteries broad and their fringes (*ta kraspeda*) long" (23:5). Fringes or *tzitzit* were attached to the outer garment and contained a blue (or bluish-purple) cord (see Num. 15:38–41; cf. Deut. 22:12). Like any garment mentioned, it is difficult to know whether the tassels were actually wool or linen, but we know they were regularly made from wool, since unspun wool intended for *tzitzit* was found in the Cave of Letters. Yet scholars have noted that *tzitzit* are the one exception for the average

Israelite/Jewish man for *sha'atnez* with the blue cord being wool and the white cords being linen.[41] The gospels also record that Jesus wore fringes, since they play a role in his healings: the hemorrhaging woman touches Jesus's fringe in Luke 8:44. Mark and Matthew also have people healed by touching the fringes on Jesus's garment (Mark 6:56; Matt. 14:35–6). While the term *ta kraspeda* could mean hem or edges, it is the same term used in the Septuagint and for Matthew's long-fringed Pharisees (see, e.g., Num. 15:37 LXX). *Tefillin* or phylacteries, commanded in Deuteronomy 6.4–9, were usually made of leather and, therefore, were also an animal product, some of which were found in Caves 1, 4, 5, and 8 at Qumran.[42] While Jesus and his male followers would also likely wear tzitzit and tefillin, the excess of the Pharisees contrasts the plainness of Jesus's disciples.

Jesus's own clothing draws attention as a conduit to his power but also reflects his life's journey: his birth, his power, and his true self, and even when he dies, his clothing is torn apart and he is buried in linen. When Jesus was a newborn, Mary swaddled (*esparganosen*) him, likely with bands of cloth (Luke 2:7, 12). As noted, the hemorrhaging woman touches the fringes on Jesus's clothes (Mark 5:28; cf. Matt. 9 and Luke 8). At the transfiguration his clothes become dazzlingly white; while cultural studies of changed clothing indicate a changed status, in this case Jesus's garments change to reveal who he already was, a previously hidden status revealed to a select trusted few (Mark 9:3; Matt. 17; Luke 9). Soldiers mock Jesus by giving him a purple cloak (linen or wool – but likely dyed with murex, which is also an animal product)[43] and then put his own cloak back on him (Mark 15:15–20). Finally, at the death of his body, the soldiers divided up Jesus's clothes (Mark 15:24); as his body is torn apart, so is his clothing. His clothing is a reflection of self, changing along with his own life and death.

The most famous clothing made from animals – because it does stand out – occurs in the John the Baptist story. Like his food choices, his clothing places him on the social periphery but also reflects his prophetic role. Matthew and Mark report – and Luke and John do not take notice – that John the Baptist wore a shirt made out of camel hair and a leather belt (Matt. 3:4; Mark 1:6). Even the *Life and Martyrdom of John the Baptist* – which makes him a vegetarian – retains the camel hair and leather belt (3.3). Supposedly it is to strengthen the connection to Elijah, though Elijah is simply hairy – he does not necessarily wear a hair shirt (2 Kgs. 1:8). Unlike with the case of wool coming from the kosher sheep, one is not allowed to eat camels according to biblical food laws. Thus, there is not a perfect correlation between eating and wearing, though both John and Elijah wear a leather belt, so they both wear animal products.[44]

Yet in the gospel tradition, John the Baptist's garments set up a contrast between those of the palace and the prophet in the wilderness (Thomas 78; Matt. 11:7–9; Luke 17:24–6). John the Baptist is not a "reed shaking in the wind" or one who wears soft clothes, unlike those who live in palaces; he is a prophet as his place (wilderness) and his dress (camel's hair) attest. Crossan even suggests that the implied contrast in clothing is between John and Antipas, John's eventual beheader.[45]

Pearls – an animal product used as an accessory – are a symbol of wealth and, in the gospels, the worth of the kingdom. Matthew – paralleled by Thomas – brings up pearls twice. Both instances indicate the value of pearls. The second is more metaphorical: "the kingdom of heaven is like a merchant in search of fine pearls (*margaritas*); on finding one pearl of great value, he went and sold all that he had and bought it" (Matt. 13:45–6; cf. Thomas 76). Pearls were a form of luxurious adornment deriving from oysters and therefore also an animal product. The most important pearl fisheries were off the coast of India and in the Persian Gulf. Pearls were mostly exported from India into Persia and ultimately into the Near East and into the Roman Empire. While trade had occurred beforehand, there was a large upsurge in pearl imports into the Roman Empire in the first century CE. Secondarily, pearls were fished from the Red Sea, which, although cheaper to produce due to a shorter trade route, still could fetch a high price in the Roman marketplace.

On the one hand, pearls could be prized in the ancient Near East and Middle East, leading to a lot of Christian reflection on a great pearl as a symbol for salvation,[46] and as the gates to heaven (Rev. 21:21). On the other hand, they could be thought of as a foreign luxury incompatible with Roman – and eventually Christian – values, becoming equated with effeminacy (1 Tim. 2:9; Rev. 17:4; 18:11; cf. 1 Pet. 3:3–4; Pliny, *Natural History* 9.96–124).[47] They were, however, without a doubt, valuable. Pliny calls them the "most prized of all jewels" (*Natural History* 9.106); Jesus advises that one should not throw them before swine, the quintessentially unclean animal in Roman-era Jewish practice (Matt. 7:6; Thomas 93).[48] The kingdom has the most luxurious imports.

Speaking of Roman garb, Carly Daniel-Hughes writes, "Romans variously constructed and employed modest garb and grooming to bolster their political ambitions and social position, or to undermine those of others."[49] In an intersecting manner, the gospel writers employ animal-sourced clothing to bolster minimalist clothing as proper while critiquing others' excessive clothing as emblematic of hypocrisy. Wearing animals and other animal products differentiated overlapping social groupings (Jesus's followers, scribes and Pharisees, or priests), located John the Baptist on the fringes of society, and had religious significance and metaphorical value.

ANIMALS AS TRANSPORTATION AND TRACTORS

The most conspicuous way animals become prosthetic extensions in the gospels, however, is as a working animal engaged in forced labour on behalf of humans, usually as transportation, but also as tractors. What one rode and whether one rode an animal at all could also indicate social status. In the domesticated gospels, as mentioned, Mary didn't ride a donkey, the Magi did not have camels, and the centurion didn't have a horse. Of course, they all might have, but we just don't know. Much like we do in modern retellings such as films, ancient writers began to fill in these gaps. The Proto-Gospel of James is the first to depict Mary riding a donkey with Joseph walking alongside (17.2–3).[50] The Gospel of Pseudo-Matthew follows suit with Mary riding a donkey (13).[51] Yet it also includes an ox and an ass bending knees in worship at Jesus's birth (14).[52] This same feral gospel even includes baby Jesus taming leopards, lions, and dragons, with the leopards and lions joining the pack animals (oxen and donkeys) in carrying the family's stuff to Egypt (18–19).[53] The feral tales of the Magi, however, rarely attempt to fill in these gaps, leaving us to wonder at their mode of transportation.[54] In fact, in the *Revelation of the Magi* 16, they explicitly walk their entire journey! Before all these gaps were filled in late-antique feral gospels, Jesus conspicuously rides a donkey (*Equus asinus*) in the domesticated gospels. Since the canonized gospels typically omit such references, one must attend to why they show up where they do. Jesus's donkey, in other words, is special.

Mark 11:2–6 and Luke 19:29–40 both state that Jesus rode a colt (*ho polos*) on his entry into Jerusalem; that is, he rode a young uncastrated male animal – a horse, pony, donkey, or mule.[55] In this case, it was likely a donkey.[56] In both cases, the colt had never been ridden on by anyone else. Jesus was its first passenger. John's version is more abbreviated, simply noting that Jesus rode on a young donkey (*onarion*) (John 12:14) with a quotation that is a fulfillment of not only Zechariah 9:9 (as the synoptics allude to or cite) but also Zephaniah 3:16. Matthew's version (21:1–10) is a bit different; in it, Jesus sits astride two animals at once: a donkey (*onos*) and a colt (*polos*). It is tempting to try to imagine how Jesus rides two animals at once, and this is sometimes thought to be either a careless or overly literal reading on Matthew's part of Zechariah 9:9–10 (cf. Isa. 62:11):

> Rejoice greatly, O daughter Zion!
> Shout aloud, O daughter Jerusalem!
> Lo, your king comes to you;
> Triumphant and victorious is he,
> Humble and riding on a donkey
> On a colt, the foal of a donkey. (Zech. 9:9)[57]

According to this view, Matthew misreads the biblical parallelism – which the author of Matthew cites as a composite citation of both Zechariah 9:9 and Isaiah 62:11 – as two animals rather than one. That is, Zion and Jerusalem parallel each other and stand in for each other, whereas donkey is paralleled and extended by colt, foal of a donkey. This overly literalized reading is a possibility. Also possible, and not mutually exclusive with this explanation, is that Matthew regularly doubles material taken from Mark; so, this may simply be another example of that.[58]

What's the upshot? Usually the Zechariah allusion and, in Matthew, direct citation is thought to represent humility and peace (Zech. 9:9–10). It is a humble donkey and not a warhorse (cf. Ps. Sol. 17).[59] Also, beyond a symbol of peace, Bauckham writes, "Jesus rides the animal that was every peasant farmer's beast of burden."[60] The extent and regular treatment of such a beast of burden rarely shines out in ancient literature; nonetheless, perhaps it emerges most conspicuously in Apuleius's *Golden Ass*, where the protagonist, Lucius, accidentally transforms himself into a donkey and one sees from his perspective the usual treatment of beasts of burden. Kimberly Stratton notes, "Lucius's experiences as a donkey, in fact, reveal the cruel, barbaric, and inhumane behavior that human beings regularly exhibit toward animals."[61]

The donkey occupies a similar space in ancient Jewish frameworks as the camel: it cannot be eaten or sacrificed, but it can be ridden and used.[62] Nonetheless, as the story of Balaam attests (Num. 22:21–39), the donkey can be appropriated by supernal beings, and maybe that connection is also important for the gospels.[63] Augustine called the donkey "the Lord's beast" (*iumentum domini*).[64] Ultimately, everyone agrees that the donkey has a social importance of locating Jesus amidst peasant culture.

Even though the gospels do not depict the Magi riding camels, the gospels have camels in their imagined menagerie, in addition to straining the gnat and swallowing the camel. It was forbidden to eat camels if following Jewish dietary rules; nonetheless, one could still ride them and wear them.[65] Pliny lists them as a beast of burden (*Natural History* 8.67–9). While we have discussed Jesus's biting aphorisms elsewhere, in Mark 10:23–5 he has another zinger. After dismissing the rich man, Jesus gives three parallel sayings:

> How hard it will be for those who have wealth to enter the Kingdom of God! (10:23)

> Children, how hard it is [for those who trust in riches] to enter the kingdom of God. (10:24)

> It is easier for a camel to go through the eye of a needle than for someone who is rich to enter the kingdom of God. (10:25)

For 10:24, there are some manuscripts that include what I have placed in the square brackets. The benefit of this reading is that we have three variations of the same aphorism. Some manuscripts, however, exclude what is in square brackets. Without it, it would not make much sense, making it then a mere lead-up to the camel saying.[66] Matthew's and Luke's versions reduce the first two statements to one before getting to the camel comparison (Matt. 19:23–4; Luke 18:23–5). After the first and the third statements in Mark, the disciples are perplexed and astounded. In Matthew's version, after the camel statement, they are greatly astounded (Matt. 19:25). In Luke's, there is no affective response, only a verbal one.

The example of the camel going through the eye of a needle seems absurd – and perhaps that is part of the point as it was when Jesus said the Pharisees strain the gnat and swallow the camel. It is a complete impossibility, one which later Christians who had wealth would wrangle.[67] It is a strange comparison. Horsley simply calls it "a piece of peasant humor."[68] Perhaps troubled by the absurdity, many people have tried to explain it away as a mistranslation: that in Aramaic camel and rope are similar – both with the root of *g-m-l* – and, when shifting to Greek, which also has similar words for camel (*kamelos*) and rope (*kamilos*), the terminology shifted from the original rope to camel. This term for rope, however, is not attested until a later period by a scholiast trying to make sense of this verse; that is, the reference to a camel may have driven the search for or even creation of a similar word for rope rather than rope being the source of the camel in this verse.[69] It seems to make some sense of the problem: instead of spun thread going through the eye of a needle – difficult, yet possible – it is rope, analogous to thread, but impossible. Yet, whether a letter got misplaced or not, the comparison still expresses utter impossibility. And that impossibility has become embodied in an animal.

Why a camel? Though there are periodic reflections on elephants used for military, entertainment, or luxury purposes (for ivory),[70] the camel may have been the largest animal anyone in this region would have seen.[71] It would, therefore, connote the concept of impossibility by having the largest animal (in the region) trying to squeeze through the smallest space in one's experience: the eye of a needle. In this way, it mirrors Jesus's gnat/camel aphorism: the largest and the smallest are juxtaposed.[72]

In addition to transportation, animals were tractors, allowing farmers to complete tasks they could not on their own. In the middle of a parable of a great dinner, one of the excuses for why people cannot attend is they just got some new oxen and want to try them out (Luke 14:19). This is a work animal – though there are references to eating oxen – and its primary purpose was plowing; the oxen were the ancient tractors. Pliny does not talk about oxen at all when discussing land animals; he tellingly only discusses them in terms of agriculture (*Natural History* 18.9–11, 296). The historian Moses Finley says, when speaking of the wider Roman economy, "The ox was the chief traction animal of antiquity, the mule and donkey his near rivals, the horse hardly at all."[73] For short distances of travel and farming, an ox or a team of oxen was preferred; for longer distances, due to how much oxen eat, travel by sea would be less costly than overland by oxen. In the gospel account, it is a flourish of daily colour that provides some verisimilitude, but one that would have been ubiquitous in the ancient economy for plowing and transporting cargo over short distances.[74]

Finally, there is a strange passage, the ultimate meaning of which I am unsure, that includes some working animals, again from Luke's gospel account: "Who among you would say to your slave who has just come in from plowing or tending sheep in the field, 'Come here at once and take your place at the table'? Would you not rather say to him, 'Prepare supper for me, put on your apron and serve me while I eat and drink; later you may eat and drink'?" (Luke 17:7–10). It is a dining scene that illustrates hierarchy: master and slave do not normally eat together. In fact, one may have been tempted to think of Aristotle's discussion of slaves as "living tools" just as working animals were "living tools" – Aristotle largely equates a slave and an animal, grouping them together as similar in terms of their usefulness for their master.[75] Slaves and animals are also grouped together as something between a person and a thing, as between a who and a what, as Haraway and Hobgood-Oster both strikingly seem to agree with at least in terms of animals. Jesus's parable reflects this persistent association of animals as tools, as objects, and as prosthetics that were entangled with slavery. Jesus speaks of a situation in the midst of slaves doing work: they are plowing the fields (again, this would involve oxen) or tending sheep for food or wool for cloth. They, in this sense, are a stand-in for their master; they are working with animals rather than working as animals. Nonetheless, they, like working animals, are prosthetic extensions of their master, doing human labour but as a living tool that is in charge of other living tools. Similarly, Aristotle did situate human slaves slightly higher than animal slaves in the labour hierarchy. Unlike other parables, such as the dining parables, where Jesus brings up a hierarchy to subvert it, Jesus in this case does not challenge the hierarchy between a master and the master's living tools (slaves and animals) or between those living tools (slaves above animals) but builds on it. In the broader context, Jesus is telling his disciples that they are in the position of slaves vis-à-vis God and do what they do out of obligation rather than for reward, ultimately reinforcing the zoo-anthropological hierarchy. That is, all humans are God's living tools as the human-animal entanglement reflects the divine-human entanglement.

USING ANIMALS AND ANIMAL PRODUCTS

Before tractors, there were oxen; before cars, donkeys and horses; and before synthetic fibers, wool. Riding animals, plowing with animals, and using animals for clothes or otherwise would have been the most ubiquitous presence of animals in the ancient world. Using animals was so prevalent that this activity went for the most part unnoticed. Yet these prosthetic extensions occasionally graze in and out of the gospel narrative, drawing attention to themselves. Animals, overlapping with human slave labour, were living tools and co-workers. They were extensions of free humans; they clothed humans and allowed humans to do things they could not do without them. Haraway and Hobgood-Oster have made similar observations about working animals today, but I find it difficult to avoid Halberstam's critique of this positioning of domesticated animals between tool and co-worker/companion. Betwixt and between a dead thing and a living being, this is what Halberstam calls "zombified life." Domesticated animals were (and are) considered objects without their own will rather than subjects. Aristotle explicitly had this view; the gospels do nothing to challenge it, but mostly reflect it.

These prostheses that cover the human body and allow human bodies to accomplish more work than they could do otherwise intersect with social patterns. When one wore an animal product (wool, special dyes, leather, pearls), how one wore it reflected one's social location in terms of gender, ethnoreligious group, point in the life cycle (birth through burial), social standing (priest versus non-priest), on the margins of society (John the Baptist), or whether one followed Jesus and was marked by a lack of extra clothes or was a scribe or Pharisee marked by excessive clothing. Accessories – such as pearls – also signified the luxury and worth of the kingdom.

The gospels were not as clear about how working animals reflected social delineation, yet there are some clues. Riding a donkey, as Jesus did, is considered more humble as a peasant's beast of burden than riding a horse, which one would expect a soldier or higher-ranking figure to ride. We find slaves entangled with working with plowing fields (with oxen) or keeping sheep (for wool), while also providing a metaphor of God's relationship to humans, making humans the tools of God as humans use other humans and other animals in forced labour. This creates a chain of unequal entanglements between humans, other animals, and the divine that will persist in other ways through sacrifice (chapter 3) and ultimately through the portrayal of the divine (and demonic) through animals and animality (chapter 5).

3

Jesus and the Ancient Abattoir: Sacrificing Animals in the Gospels

As a social animal, man is a ritual animal.

Mary Douglas, *Purity and Danger*

Sacrifice entangles human and other animals at the expense of other animals while organizing social relations among humans. In addition, sacrifice brings into relation other nonhuman entities, specifically the figure who is the recipient of the sacrifice. While sacrifice encompasses more than animal sacrifice since other things, such as grains and fruit, can be offered to a deity, sacrifice regularly includes the slaughter of animals.

Why do humans sacrifice nonhuman animals and sometimes other humans? Why did the ancient Israelites and Jews do it? And, while we are at it, the ancient Greeks and Romans? Because animal sacrifice has been so widespread in human behaviour, theorists obsess over its origins, functions, and symbolic significations. It could be simply a gift, tribute, or homage to the divine mirroring relations between subjects and royalty. Others see it as a shared meal between humans and the divine, making it a direct corollary to eating animals.[1] It could be a reflection or imputation of complex social forms onto the body of an animal, or, in some cases, a human.[2] Or it could be an outlet or release valve for social violence.[3] The sacrificial animal is a substitute for the entire community, as the community seeks to protect itself from itself by releasing its violence on an animal.[4] Or, since humans developed the subject-object relationship that does not exist among animals, humans became alienated from those animal objects. The destruction of an animal through sacrifice destroys not just the animal, but its utility as food or labour;[5] that is, it removes its "thingness" and restores a lost immediacy, immanence, or intimacy.[6] Or, the very opposite, it could be to create and reify distinctions between human, animal, and gods.[7] Or sacrifice is a patriarchal "remedy for being born of woman," establishing a social paternity that seeks a social transcendence of women's reproductive powers.[8] Because male descent cannot be a natural given, blood sacrifice enacts patrilineal descent, while standing in opposition to the blood of women's childbirth and menstruation. For readers coming from an ecological perspective, animal sacrifice is a "holy waste" of animals.[9] This is even more true of those coming from an animal ethics perspective, for whom it is a form of unnecessary cruelty.[10] Clearly scholars have a lot to say about animal sacrifice.

The slaughter of animals for the purposes of sacrifice hums in the background of the domesticated gospels, but I will mostly focus on the synoptics: did Jesus, according to the synoptic gospels, promote the slaughter of animals for sacrifice? One's immediate response would be negative, that Jesus would not: especially from a Christian perspective, Jesus does not promote animal sacrifice, because according to Christian theology he is the ultimate sacrifice, such as articulated in Hebrews or 1 John 1:7–2:2.[11] John treats Jesus as the sacrificial lamb, reflecting this developing trajectory (cf. Rev. 5:6). In addition to the theological argument, the Christian ecological apologetic argument claims that Jesus – as a good animal rights activist – would have been against the slaughter of animals for sacrifice.[12]

Upon further reflection, since Jesus was Jewish, he plausibly would have participated in traditional Jewish festivals, especially Passover, which included animal slaughter as a central element.[13] One may, of course, further reconsider that he was a Galilean, and Galilee was a region far away from the temple cult, which, moreover, had only come under Judean control about a hundred years before Jesus's birth.[14] Yet the archaeological record also reminds us that, on a material culture level, there were several entanglements between the Judean temple system and Galilean society.[15]

With all of these scholarly theories of sacrifice as well as theological, apologetic, and historical debates crowding the field of gospel studies, we need to return to the stories afresh to see what entanglements of humans, other animals, and the divine we find in the gospel narratives through sacrifice. While different domesticated gospels vary in their emphases, with some relatively more accepting of animal sacrifice than others, they consistently relativize the importance of sacrifice and decentralize the institution of sacrifice without rejecting it outright in the way that later feral gospels do. Instead of using the slaughter of animals as a primary way to organize human-divine relations, the synoptic gospels have Jesus suggest that human social interactions come first before attending to the human-divine relationship as expressed through animal sacrifice, which is secondary but never fully excluded.

BIBLICAL SACRIFICE AND ANTI-SACRIFICE

Bible scholars – often in conversation with theories of sacrifice – have developed many overarching frameworks of biblical sacrifice that would hum in the background of the gospels. Overlapping with sacrifice as tribute, meals, patriarchal lineage, recovering lost intimacy, holy waste, and animal cruelty, there are several theories of why the ancient Israelites and Judeans in particular sacrificed animals as well as other foodstuffs. Usually stemming from insights from the anthropologist Mary Douglas's work,[16] these theorists, including Mary Douglas herself, entwine sacrificial rules with purity rules, seeing the priestly legislation as a symbolic system. Douglas's own theory, picked up by others, is that sacrifice allows one to imitate God's holiness.[17]

Of those in Douglas's wake, I will highlight two: Jacob Milgrom and Jonathan Klawans. Jacob Milgrom argues, using the "sin offering" as his primary example, that the blood rituals surrounding sin offerings did not purge the one who offered it, but the sanctuary itself. Using Oscar Wilde's *Picture of Dorian Gray* as an analogy, Milgrom describes how various sins are attracted to various parts of the sanctuary depending on their degree of severity. The various sin offerings, and the ultimate sin offering on the Day of Purgation or Day of Atonement, cleanse the sanctuary of the mark of sin. Why is it important to purge the sanctuary rather than the sinner? Because the presence of God can only tolerate so much moral impurity; otherwise it will depart. Therefore, the ultimate purpose of the sacrificial system – using the piacular rites as the most important ones – is to maintain the divine presence.[18]

While parts of Milgrom's analysis have been effectively critiqued – the purgation rituals do, in fact, purge the offerer of sacrifice – his overall synthesis has been found perceptive.[19] Milgrom has also argued that the common denominator of the purity system is death avoidance. Every substance that one must avoid to enter the divine presence in the temple – a corpse, menstrual blood, shed human blood, semen, etc. – represents reproductive life and, ultimately, death.[20]

Jonathan Klawans has built on Milgrom and Douglas among others to formulate a dual purpose for the sacrificial system. Drawing on his previous work on the differentiation of ritual purity and moral purity, he argues that any systemic focus on the temple system must integrate both purity and sacrifice. He notes that three major forms of "moral impurity" (bloodshed, idolatry, and sexual immorality) defile the sanctuary and the land. Such impurity, distinct from "ritual impurity," is resolved by purgation (atonement), punishment, and exile. He finds the "organizing principles" of this overarching view of the temple system of purity and sacrifice to be (1) the imitation of God and (2) attracting and maintaining the divine presence.[21]

Now that we have some frameworks on sacrifice, what about the animals who are dying for this system to work? One line of discussion is the relationship between the animals humans eat and the animals humans sacrifice, aligning with the "shared meal" view of sacrifice. In biblical sources, there is an overlap between what animals one is permitted to eat and what animals one is permitted to sacrifice, but it is inexact. In the biblical system, one can eat all the kinds of animals one sacrifices, but one cannot sacrifice all the animals one eats (for example, fish or wild animals). One only sacrifices domesticated animals that one exerts a great deal of control over in a herd (cattle, sheep, and goats) as well as some domesticated birds.[22] But there are wild land animals one eats, but does not sacrifice, such as the ibex or deer.[23] In fact, one is required to sacrifice the first-born male of one's flocks of domesticated animals – just as one must offer (and redeem) one's first-born human male. The role of sacrifice with redeeming first-born male children brings the lineage of sacrifice into view. Moreover, sacrifice draws attention to the commonality of fleshly humans and animal flesh: for both the "blood is life."[24] The sacrificial "table" is stricter than the Israelite home table.[25]

The sacrificial system, human reproduction, and lineage intersect in ancient Israelite and Jewish thought. How one thinks about animals in sacrifice relates to social organization among humans. If sacrifice is a shared communion between humans and the divine, it also orders relationships among humans, between priests and non-priests, and between men and women. It can reconstitute one's Israelite bonds as in the Passover sacrifice. Moreover, sacrifice relates to the fertility of the land, one's flocks, and one's families. One offers sacrifices of first fruits, first born of flocks, and offers a substitute for a first-born male child, integrating family, animal, and vegetable lineages.

Yet if animal sacrifice orders relationships among humans and between humans, the divine, and other animals, what happens when one challenges animal sacrifice? Does a critique of sacrifice also mean a critique of the social order? Or does a critique of the social order necessarily include a critique of sacrifice? We find such sacrificial-social critiques not just among modern readers, but in the ancient sources themselves.

CRITICAL ATTITUDES TO SACRIFICE IN BIBLICAL SOURCES

If the sacrificial system, the food laws, and human reproduction (and family arrangement) are interrelated, what happens when one factor changes? What happens when the temple is destroyed and sacrifice suspended, Jesus (or Paul) declares all foods clean, or if one creates family bonds not based on genealogy but something else (Matt. 10:34–9; 12:46–50; 19:29; Mark 3:31–3; 10:29–30; Luke 8:19–21; 12:49–53; 14:26–7; 18:29)? Pull one thread out and the others may follow.

Alongside injunctions and obligations to sacrifice in biblical materials, one can find what appears to be anti-sacrificial sentiment in biblical literature; this, however, is usually couched in broader anti-worship sentiments, of which sacrifice is the central, but not only, element. Always in the prophetic literature, it is people's practice of sacrifice to and worship of the deity while neglecting the social values of justice, mercy, and compassion that rouses the prophetic rage of Amos, Isaiah, and Hosea.[26]

The doom-and-gloom prophet Amos (eighth century BCE) was one of the more socially responsible prophets. Amos predicted that God would destroy Israel for their bad behavior. He does not single out problems of worship, like idolatry, so much as problems of justice: failure to help the poor and needy (3:6–7; 4:1; 5:10–17) while indulging in luxury (3:13–15; 6:1–7). In this context, Amos makes a startling point: God does not want your worship. It is just noise. In fact, God will hate your worship if you worship God – even properly worship God – but are not just. One should not seek out God's traditional sanctuary, but seek the LORD (YHWH) (5:4–7).[27] Amos writes:

> I hate, I despise your festivals,
> and I take no delight in your solemn assemblies.
> Even though you offer me your burnt offering and grain
> offerings,
> I will not accept them;
> and the offerings of well-being of your fatted animals
> I will not look upon.
> Take away from me the noise of your songs;
> I will not listen to the melody of your harps.
> But let justice roll down like waters,
> and righteousness like an ever-flowing stream. (Amos 5:21–4)

While some of this is directed toward temple offerings – burnt (animal), fatted animals, and grain offerings – not all of it is. It includes all worship of God: festivals, temple service, and singing songs. This is all proper worship. But it is just noise to God without justice, without concern for the condition of the poor and the needy.

Hosea expresses a similar concern: "For I desire steadfast love and not sacrifice, the knowledge of God rather than burnt offerings" (Hos. 6:6). This is the passage Matthew's Jesus paraphrases in a couple places. In this case, the focus of piety is on inner disposition (love and knowledge of God) rather than one's exterior actions (sacrifice and burnt offerings). These dispositions, moreover, are the connective tissue of the covenant relationship – the primary theme of Hosea. Hosea, moreover, condemns Israel's festivals; drink offerings and sacrifices will not please the LORD (Hos. 9:1–7).

Isaiah likewise notes that people have failed to do good, that, to do good, one should seek justice, rescue the oppressed, defend the orphan, and plead for the widow (Isa. 1:17). Isaiah also notes that without justice, worshiping God is pointless:

> What to me is the multitude of your sacrifices? says the LORD;
> I have had enough of burnt offerings of rams
> and the fat of fed beasts;
> I do not delight in the blood of bulls,
> or of lambs, or of goats.
> When you come to appear before me,
> who asked this from your hand?
> Trample my courts no more;
> bringing offerings is futile;
> incense is an abomination to me.
> New moon and sabbath and calling of convocation –
> I cannot endure solemn assemblies with iniquity.
> Your new moons and your appointed festivals
> my soul hates;
> they have become a burden to me,
> I am weary of bearing them.

When you stretch out your hands,
I will hide my eyes from you;
even though you make many prayers,
I will not listen;
your hands are full of blood. (Isa. 1:10–15)

While there is a greater emphasis on the temple here, it is again inclusive of all worship activities, including festivals, and prayer.

In sum, God hates people's worship, including temple sacrifices, incense, festivals, songs of worship, and prayer, if those people are unjust, indulge in luxury while failing to help or even actively oppressing the poor and needy: the oppressed, the orphan, or the widow. That is, social ethics precedes all divine worship.

The "if" is important. What makes these critiques striking is how close these "prophets" were to the system. While many people think of "prophets" and "priests" as socially distinct figures, most prophets were priests themselves. Isaiah's own call vision was in the temple (Isa. 6:1). Jeremiah descended from priests (Jer. 1:1); Ezekiel was in exile, but was also from the priesthood (Ezek. 1:1–3). The critique is an internal one – not just internal to Israelites or Judeans, but to the priesthood itself, which relied on such "gifts" to the temple to sustain it. Acts of worship – of which they were specialists or related to such specialists – were meaningless without proper ethical and moral comportment. Yet these insider critiques did not seek to dismantle the temple system but to reorder the relationships between God, animals, and humans by elevating the social ethics of intra-human relationships above all forms of divine worship. Proper moral comportment – acting justly – makes worship, including animal sacrifice, meaningful again.

These prototypes of sacrificial critique were not the only ones. For those in the Qumran community, for example, the temple system in its ideal form was good, but it had become corrupted by the current occupiers of the high priesthood, the Hasmonean dynasty. At issue for them were the actions of the Hasmonean high priest, the 364-day, 52-week calendar, proper temple governance, ritual purity, and

Torah observance. They, therefore, separated themselves from the temple sacrifices and established their own community as a temple, developed their own idealized temple in the *Temple Scroll* and *New Jerusalem* texts, and engaged in heavenly worship (*Songs of the Sabbath Sacrifice*) with the angels in the heavenly sanctuary.[28] Therefore, critique of the temple did not mean rejection of some idea of the temple or temple service; it was typically a criticism of those in charge at the time.

JESUS AND THE CRITIQUE OF SACRIFICE

The domesticated gospels could likewise be critical of sacrifice. The clearest anti-sacrifice statement comes from Matthew, which, in its penchant for doubling things, has Jesus twice quoting Hosea 6:6, saying, "I desire mercy, not sacrifice (*thusian*)" (Matt. 9:13; 12:7). In the first quotation, Jesus is dining with tax collectors and sinners, while the Pharisees disapprove. He tells the Pharisees to go and learn what this means: "I desire mercy, not sacrifice." He then proceeds to say that he has not come for the righteous but for sinners. The second occurrence appears in the "lord of the Sabbath" pericope, in which he notes that the priests in the temple break the sabbath but are "guiltless." Matthew adds something not found in Mark's or Luke's versions: "I tell you, something greater than the temple is here" (12:6). Thus, the critique of sacrifice also appears to relegate the temple to a secondary status. In the first "controversy dialogue," Jesus sides with someone typically excluded – the tax collectors and sinners – while in the second, he defends his disciples' practice of plucking grains on the Sabbath, suggesting with the example of David eating the bread of the presence in the temple that basic human needs (hunger) supersede Sabbath and temple regulations, even if those regulations have divine origins.[29]

These bold statements are direct quotations of Hosea and in the same spirit as Amos and Isaiah. Also consider that John the Baptist's baptism was for the "repentance for the forgiveness of sins" (*metanoias eis aphesin hamartion*) (Mark 1:4; Luke 3:3) or, in Matthew's version, repentance and confession of sins (Matt. 3:1–12); that is, it encroached on the function of the temple, where one would give a sin offering (Lev. 4:1–35; 16:1–34). Is John the Baptist offering an alternative to or perhaps critique of sacrificing in the temple?[30] If this is the case, then a critique of sacrifice would stem from the beginning of Jesus's ministry, but, then again, Jesus didn't always follow through on John the Baptist's abstentions – for example, the fasting of John the Baptist versus the feasting of Jesus (Matt. 9:14; Mark 2:18; Luke 5:33). What is clear is that the gospel writers portray John's baptism as having an atoning quality.

Another critique could be teased from Jesus overturning the money changers' tables and those who sold doves for sacrifice in the temple (Matt. 21:12; Mark 11:15).[31] Luke, though, does not mention the doves (see Luke 19:45–8). While Luke does not bring animals into view, John's version, by contrast, begins the historical process of filling in gaps for verisimilitude by including a lot more animals in the temple scene: "In the temple he found people selling cattle, sheep, and doves, and the money changers seated at their tables. Making a whip of cords, he drove all of them out of the temple, both the sheep and the cattle … He told those who were selling the doves, 'Take these things out of here! Stop making my Father's house a marketplace!'" (2:14–16). While Jesus's body becomes the temple throughout John (2:21),[32] in this ambivalent scene Jesus whips not only the money changers out of the temple, but the animals themselves. Animal rights readers may be slightly pleased here: Jesus is removing the animals from the temple – they are "saved" from their immediate slaughter – but they are also being whipped. And, of course, the temple would have contained several kinds of animals ready to be sacrificed, unless it was an incredibly slow day.

In this symbolic action, then, did Jesus demonstrate an anti-sacrifice, pro-animal attitude? Jesus's motivation emerges through the quotation, which is a mash-up of Isa. 56:7 and Jer. 7:11: "Stop making my Father's house a marketplace!" It is the trade in the temple rather than the temple itself that foments Jesus's agitation. Klawans, who works through several different reasons behind Jesus's motivation, argues most clearly: "Jesus opposed those aspects of the temple system – the temple tax and the pigeon sellers – that required exacting money or goods from the poor."[33] Unlike John's account, most versions single out those who sold the doves, the sacrificial animal a poorer person would be most likely to offer. In fact, there was a dove breeding complex in Mareshah since the third century BCE that likely served as the basis of this trade as well as other dove consumption.[34] The elements that were economically unjust to the poor rather than the slaughter of animals anger Jesus here.

Finally, Mark includes a comment on sacrifice within the greatest commandment pericope – which is the most positive encounter between Jesus and a scribe in all of the gospels.[35] The scribe says to Jesus that loving God and loving one's neighbour "is much more important than all whole burnt offerings and sacrifices" (Mark 12:33b; cf. Matt. 22:34–40; Luke 10:25–8). Jesus agrees. Here the focus is on relative rather than absolute importance. Saying that loving God and neighbour are more important than the entire sacrificial apparatus does not negate the sacrificial system, especially since they both appear in the Torah (Deut. 65; Lev. 19:18); it just puts it in a subordinate position.

In all of the places where Jesus appears to critique sacrifice directly in the domesticated gospels, he does not criticize the slaughtering of animals, but the poor treatment of people. He does not seem to be angered by unjust treatment of animals, but he is worked up about unjust actions towards humans or the care of basic human needs. Jesus is, therefore, anthropocentric.

JESUS AS PROMOTING SACRIFICE

Otherwise, animal sacrifice is often assumed yet regularly hidden from direct view. We find it in hints, glimpses, and indirections here and there. It is assumed, yet not named directly, in a few places, present in the background. One obvious situation would be the eating lamb at a Passover meal (Mark 14:12; Luke 22:7).[36] Mark refers to when exactly the Passover lamb is sacrificed (14:12). Luke is more forthcoming than Matthew, referring to the sacrifice of the Passover lamb (Luke 22:7) and Jesus commanding his disciples to prepare the Passover meal in the very next verse (Luke 22:8). This more strongly implicates Jesus or at least his disciples in participating in a regular Passover meal (Luke 22:15). More to the point: he asks his disciples to prepare the "pascha," the same word the Septuagint uses for the lamb itself (Exod. 12:21 LXX). Whether or not Jesus ate, he enabled the eating of a sacrificed animal in this context, and, thereby, participated in the temple establishment. Moreover, earlier in the narrative, Luke writes that Jesus's family would go to Jerusalem annually for Passover, a pretty rare and difficult thing to do when so far away (Luke 2:41–52).

A clearer occasion occurs when Jesus himself commands the healed leper to show himself to the priest to be pronounced clean and to "offer (*prosenegke*) for your cleansing what Moses commanded as a testimony to them" (Mark 1:44; Matt 8:2–4; Luke 5:14; cf. Papyrus Egerton 2 frag 1 verso 2). This painfully awkwardly worded line keeps the Levitical system in the background of the scene. It has occasioned much commentary among the historical Jesus scholars. Crossan, for example, sees Jesus's healing of the leper as putting him on a collision course with the Jerusalem priesthood. Since Jesus has just broken purity rules by touching the leper, how can he turn around and have the leper observe the same rules Jesus just broke? While Jesus does not ultimately get along with the Jerusalemite priesthood, Crossan creates a much larger cultural divide between Judeans and Galileans vis-à-vis the temple than I think can be maintained, as archaeological evidence continues to show how priestly and temple-oriented Galilee actually was. Crossan sees the portion of the leper showing himself to the priesthood as a secondary alteration ("transmissional level") to show that Jesus was legally observant, but that Mark himself at the third ("redactional level") reworks the tradition to make it a standoff or confrontation between Jesus the healer and the priests – it is a "witness against them."[37]

Luke 5:14 is similar, and Luke 17:11–18 even repeats a different version, though, in this case, after ten lepers are healed and told by Jesus to show themselves to the priest, only one (the "foreigner") returns to thank Jesus. Matthew smooths over the leper scene by saying to offer the "gift," which is Matthew's preferred terminology for sacrifices and offerings made at the temple.[38] Crossan notes that Luke, unlike Mark, has Jesus act like a good, observant Jew, since he never physically touches the leper.[39]

However phrased, this "gift," according to Leviticus 14, is an animal sacrifice of two living birds and two male lambs (Lev. 14:1–32) in a ritual that has several resonances with the Day of Atonement ritual. There are, of course, substitutions for those who cannot afford it, mostly consisting of small animals. Whether Jesus is being ironic (as some of the third questers seem to think) or not, he still told the leper to kill some animals at the temple. Ironically killing an animal does not help the animal; it is still dead no matter how ironic one intends to be. The sacrificial system is now humming louder in the background of the gospels.[40]

Sacrifice also intersects with the various gospels' attitudes toward the Jerusalem temple, which itself is a complex issue, with Luke being the most eager to show Jesus and his disciples regularly hanging out and teaching in the temple, and using the temple to frame the entire gospel itself from Zechariah in chapter 1 to the disciples gathering there every day after Jesus's death and resurrection in 21:37–8. In between, Jesus and his disciples pray in the temple (Luke 18:9–14; story of Pharisee and the tax collector), teach in the temple (Luke 20:1–47), and watch a poor woman giving to the temple treasury, whom Jesus praises for doing so (Luke 21:1–4).

Luke, in fact, has several other instances of sacrifices being assumed and sometimes even depicted in the narrative. Zechariah tends to the incense altar in the inner shrine of the temple – of course, this is different from the outer altar, but still part of the general complex of offerings and gifts to Yahweh (1:9–11). Jesus's parents offer a sacrifice of either a pair of turtledoves or two young pigeons in the temple after Jesus is born (Luke 2:22–4; cf. Exod. 13:2, 12, 15; Lev. 5:11, 12:8). This is perhaps the most direct reference to a sacrifice in all of the canonical gospels, even using the proper word: *thusian*. Luke also contains the story of Pilate mingling the blood of Galileans with their sacrifices, suggesting that Galileans were offering sacrifices and undermining the idea that Galileans had a lukewarm attitude toward the temple and sacrifice (Luke 13:1; Josephus, *Ant.* 8.3.1–2; *War* 2.9.2–4).[41]

Despite attempts by different modern scholars to divorce Jesus from the Jerusalem temple, the gospel writers present various scenes in which they assume Jesus participated in the sacrificial establishment without criticism; in fact, he even encouraged other people to do so.

RESOLUTION: RESTATING THE PROPHETIC CRITIQUE

While tensions exist in all three synoptic gospels, they take on a different shape and intensity in each. Mark is the blandest on the issue – the strongest critique Mark contains is the scribe telling Jesus that loving God and neighbor is better than sacrifice – and perhaps John the Baptist baptizing for the forgiveness of sins. Luke is the most pro-temple and the least likely to criticize sacrifice – in fact, Luke multiplies scenes of implied sacrifice throughout and adds a direct scene of sacrifice, and seemingly approves of Jesus's parents fulfilling the rules of sacrifice. Except maybe for John the Baptist, there is not even much implied critique. Matthew is the most critical, yet balances clear preferences of mercy over sacrifice (twice) while including Jesus's command to sacrifice, surviving from Mark.

While we can create a spectrum in which Matthew is most likely to criticize sacrifice and Luke most likely to positively portray it, there remain some additional tensions. One possible way forward can be found in the contents of the Sermon on the Mount: looking at chapter 5 in the so-called "antitheses," couched in Jesus's prohibition against getting angry, we find the following: "So when you are offering your gift (*to doron*) at the altar, if you remember that your brother or sister has something against you, leave your gift there before the altar and go; first be reconciled to your brother or sister, and then come and offer your gift" (Matt. 5:23–4). While Matthew's doubled preference for mercy and not sacrifice may provide a starting point for modern Christian animal rights, Jesus never says that he thinks killing animals is wrong. It is the critique of using the sacrificial system for the forgiveness of sins without reforming one's behavior and attitude that seems to be at stake, as it was for Isaiah. Jesus's statement to leave the gift at the altar to make amends with someone whom you have wronged also includes returning to the altar once amends have been made. Social wrongs are more important than sacrifice in Jesus's system, but sacrifice is not negated, simply relativized.

Jesus makes a similar structural arrangement in the Lord's prayer: "And forgive us our debts, as we also have forgiven our debtors" (Matt. 6:12). Again, the horizontal social relationship comes before the vertical divine-human relationship. Divine worship through sacrifice and prayer is relegated to a secondary level. It is about relative value; that is, indeed, what the "greatest commandment" question was all about too: when the scribe in Mark agrees with Jesus that loving God and loving your neighbour are more important than all of the sacrifices put together, the scribe does not also conclude that one does not sacrifice at all. Neither does Jesus. Sacrifice again is not negated, but relegated to a lower rung. I find it difficult, therefore, to follow the argument that Jesus forbids animal slaughter or that Jesus was even a vegetarian, though like most ancient people, he probably would have eaten meat rarely.[42]

The tensions may be partly resolved, but there is another problem: Matthew and Mark attempt to hide the pro-sacrifice sentiments in plain sight or use hesitating language or euphemisms around sacrifice. Matthew includes Jesus telling someone to leave a "gift" at the altar and, eventually, to complete that "gift." "Gift" or "offering" is a regular term for sacrifice in ancient Israelite culture, reflecting the "tribute" theory of sacrifice, but it still avoids the clearer term, such as "sacrifice." "Gift" though was a widely used euphemism for anything one brings to the altar. There can be much slippage with this language; for example, regarding Cain and Abel's respective offerings to the LORD, Cain's vegetable offering can be called a *thusian* while Abel's animal offering can be called "gifts" (Gen. 4:3–5 LXX). Gifts can also refer to animal sacrifices in the Proto-Gospel of James (1.1–

2; 4.3–5). Thus gifts and even "sacrifice" can include grain or animals in available ancient evidence (cf. Pseudo-Matthew 1.1–2.1).[43]

While Matthew prefers the word "gift," Mark uses awkward terms to refer to a potential animal sacrifice. Luke most forthrightly uses the term "sacrifice." Why the variations from generic terms for any gifts given to God to specific designations of animal sacrifices? It is like animal sacrifice was there, but then erased, but not erased well enough that those with eyes to see could not reconstruct it. The tension, however, may not (only) be in the text; it may be in the reader. From our post-domestic ethical perspective we may merely be disgusted at the "holy waste," and, therefore, from a domesticity perspective (and a fairly anthropocentric one at that), not much tension remains to be resolved.

The larger difference comes between gospels: why do Matthew and Luke diverge so much on the issue of slaughtering animals? To put a finer point on it: though Matthew can use "gift" in a positive or neutral manner, whenever Matthew uses "sacrifice" (*thusian*), he criticizes it; when Luke does, he presents it positively. Part of this is shifts in social positioning from gospel to gospel. Both Matthew and Luke regularly speak of sacrifice in "controversy dialogues," where Jesus engages a potentially opposing interlocutor. In Matthew, this leads to vituperative competition with other figures of authority, especially Pharisees. In Luke, however, more common ground remains between Jesus and other groups' authority figures.

In these tensions and occasional hesitations we see the seeds of later increasingly anti-sacrificial developments. After Jesus's followers began to believe that Jesus not only died but had arisen from the dead and took the following step of his death as a sacrifice, and not only that, the sacrifice to end all sacrifices, memories of Jesus's encouragement of sacrifice likely began to become troubling, at least to Matthew and maybe Mark. But they could not be removed completely since they were embedded in some of the most memorable parts of Jesus's speeches and actions.

BEYOND THE SYNOPTIC GOSPELS: JESUS AS SACRIFICE AND AS ANTI-SACRIFICE

The early gospels of the first century had an ambivalent attitude towards temple sacrifice. This dissipates in the next century as gospels increasingly present Jesus as a sacrifice and as completely against animal sacrifice.

The latest of the canonized gospels – John – presents Jesus as animalistic, equating him with the Passover lamb. At the beginning of the gospel, John the Baptist proclaims: "Look, the Lamb of God (*ide ho amnos tou theou*) who takes away the sin of the world!" (John 1:29; translation mine). And again, "Look, the Lamb of God (*ide ho amnos tou theou*)!" (1:36; translation mine). John 19:36 – "None of his bones shall be broken" – refers to the Passover lamb (cf. Exod. 12:46). As the gospel reaches its climax, Jesus's death becomes entwined with the Passover lamb's death. Jesus is the ultimate, final lamb. As the Passion narrative comes into view, Jesus – uniquely to John – dies on the Day of Preparation, when all the lambs would be slaughtered (19:14; see Josephus, *War* 6.423; Philo, *Spec. Laws* 2.145).

Like the Passover lamb, Jesus is eaten. The Gospel of John serves up this critter Christ as the "bread of life" (6:35, 48) consumed like the manna of the wilderness. In John one eats Jesus's meat. In a complex passage that begins with the miracle of bread and fish and proceeds to bread from heaven to the proclamation that Jesus himself is the bread of life, Jesus brings the reader to the edge of literary cannibalism:

> I am the living bread that came down from heaven. Whoever eats of this bread will live forever; and the bread that I will give for the life of the world is my flesh … Very truly, I tell you, unless you eat the flesh of the Son of Man and drink his blood, you have no life in you. Those who eat my flesh and drink my blood have eternal life, and I will raise them up on the last day; for my flesh is true food and my blood is true drink. Those who eat my flesh and drink my blood abide in me, and I in them. Just

> as the living Father sent me, and I live because of the Father, so whoever eats me will live because of me. (John 6:51, 53–7)

Jesus basically says: "Eat me! Drink me!" Jesus is bread, but he is more: he is the Passover lamb and one is called to drink his blood – something that one is not even supposed to do with the Passover lamb, since, to be kosher, meat must be drained of blood (Gen. 9:2–7; Lev. 3:17; 17:10–14; Deut. 12:23–5). The consumption of the blood of an animal is a divine prerogative, because the blood is its life and life belongs to God (Gen. 9:4-6; Deut. 12:23). By consuming Jesus's blood – and flesh – one gains his life, the divine life, recycled back to the human meat-bags. The divine animal (Jesus) transfers the divine prerogative to anyone who consumes Jesus's blood. If this passage does not make you feel uncomfortable – that you are eating the meat of Jesus and drinking his blood – then you are not reading it correctly. Indeed, as the commentator to the Oxford Annotated Bible for the NRSV – Jerome Neyrey – notes, "Ordinarily, taking Jesus literally is folly, but here Jesus intends to be both literal and outrageous."[44] This is not anthropophagy – in what would be a misunderstanding of the passage – it is theophagy, the consumption of the enfleshed deity, the divine animal (see chapter 5).

In addition to a shift to Jesus as a sacrificial lamb whom one eats (and drinks), Jesus becomes increasingly anti-sacrifice in feral gospels. On the one hand, some feral gospels retain sacrificial overtones, especially, ironically enough, those that claim to be from the Matthean tradition: Proto-Gospel of James, Pseudo-Matthew, and to some degree Gospel of Nicodemus A (16). On the other hand, most take an anti-sacrifice stance. Whereas Jesus relativized the role of sacrifice but did not discount sacrifice completely in Matthew, Mark, and Luke, Jesus is virulently anti-sacrifice in the Gospel of the Ebionites: "I have come to destroy the sacrifices. And if you do not stop making sacrifice, God's wrath will not stop afflicting you" (Epiphanius, *Panarion* 30.16.4–5).[45] As noted in chapter 1, the Gospel of the Ebionites, which has a vegetarian bent, also claims Jesus did not eat the Passover lamb (Epiphanius, *Pa-*

narion 30.22.4). Consistent with this concern with animals, the gospel wipes out sacrifices completely.

While the Gospel of John presents the eucharist in sacrificial (and cannibalistic) overtones, the Gospel of Judas criticizes the eucharist as well as sacrifice (33.22–34.10). In the Gospel of Judas the disciples collectively dream that they see people offering sacrifices of their own children and wives to priests and committing many sins at a great altar, at which Jesus tells the disciples that they are the priests in their dream (37.20–40.26).[46] Elaine Pagels and Karen King write that this is a meditation on a contradiction in sacrificial logic that was emerging in second-century Christian thought "that while Christians refuse *to practice sacrifice, many of them bring sacrifice right back into the center of Christian worship – by claiming that Jesus' death is a sacrifice for human sin, and then by insisting that Christians who die as martyrs are sacrifices pleasing to God*."[47] The Gospel of Judas lampoons this contradiction. Judas, though, will also "sacrifice" the "man" that "clothes" Jesus to the lesser God of this world.[48]

Why the shift from canonized to extracanonical literature? Firstly, the synoptics were written at a time of trauma and turmoil during and largely after the Jewish War. The temple was destroyed, but there would have been some living hope for rebuilding just as had happened after the Babylonian Exile. As time passed, such hopes would have dimmed. Moreover, given most of these gospels are later than at least the synoptic gospels, it likely reflects a time when early Jesus followers were increasingly defining themselves against other forms of Judaism, especially as more Christians came from non-Jewish backgrounds. The Gospel of Judas, in addition, is seeking to distance itself from those who claim to follow Jesus's initial disciples, who represented the emergent dominant Christian group of the Roman empire that was pushing other forms of Christianity to the side. As April DeConick writes, "the barbs in the *Gospel of Judas* are many, all directed at the theology and practices of apostolic Christianity."[49] The fallout from the Jewish War and the destruction of the temple led to many different trauma responses, including – at least temporarily – hope for rebuilding and hope for another heavenly temple (e.g., Hebrews), while others relegated sacrifice to a secondary status and still others renounced temple sacrifice altogether. The temple's destruction could represent other forms of traumas related to diaspora.[50] All of these responses jostled with one another in the first couple of centuries after the temple's destruction.

CLOSING DOWN THE ABATTOIR

The animal rights philosopher Tom Regan edited a volume on animal sacrifice, bringing together perspectives from different religious traditions. *Animal Sacrifices*, however, is not about the animal slaughter we have been discussing. Regan and his co-contributors repurposed the word "sacrifice" to refer to the use of animals in science. That is, animals continue to be "sacrificed" for some perceived greater good, an ideal or idea rather than a deity. These metaphorical sacrifices have no theory of tribute, meals, lineage, immanence, or the social body, though one could perhaps develop one; they suffer or die for knowledge. Such animals are not sacrificed on the altar of a deity; they are studied in a laboratory. Many animals die for the improvement of science and medical insights that benefit humans and other animals.

The sacrificial language surrounding the use of animals in science does not crystallize around the same set of concerns as ancient sacrifice. In general, I cannot find the same concerns for animal suffering and death in the earliest strata of the Jesus traditions about sacrifice that one can find among modern ethicists. Jesus was not a utilitarian or Kantian philosopher; he did not have a framework of rights, whether human or other animal. On the other hand, one can see some increasing discomfort with sacrifice in later layers of tradition, though not for the reasons modern ethicists would have. These ancient reflections have different, more theological, concerns; yet, ultimately, the evidence is messy.

In the domesticated gospels, Jesus never speaks directly against the slaughter of animals in the temple. Jesus thought that other things were more important than sacrifice, such as loving God, loving one's neighbour, mercy, and justice. He relegated sacrifice to a secondary level of importance, but did not reject it. At no time does Jesus ever critique the slaughter of animals in the temple; he critiques injustice against other humans, but not against nonhuman animals. At other times, he directly participated in the ancient temple sacrificial system and encouraged others to do the same. In this he was less critical than Amos, who said that God hates your worship, and more moderate than the Dead Sea sectarians who opted out of the Jerusalem cult completely and set up their own alternative in the wilderness. Instead, human interpersonal ethics – mercy and justice – precedes sacrifice, but once one attends to justice and mercy, one ought to also return to the altar and offer one's "gift," a term that covers all sorts of tribute one might bring to the temple, including animal sacrifices.

Later gospel writers were less positive about temple sacrifice than what we see in first-century documents. While the temple's destruction would have been a recent memory for the synoptic writers, who may have also held out the possibility of its eventual rebuilding, by the second century, a full generation without a temple to the God of Israel had been born and grown old; at the same time, some Christians began trying to differentiate themselves from other forms of Jewishness and other Christ-followers, though this process remained messy and incomplete.[51] Certain Christians increasingly postulated Jesus's death as a substitute for an end of temple sacrifice: not just for Judean sacrifice, but also for all sacrifice. The modern appropriation of "sacrifice" to speak of how nonhuman animals suffer and die for the sake of others appears to participate in this later critique that now assumes that killing animals for one's deity is problematic.

4

Affective Animals and Social Identity in the Gospels

Has anyone ever called you a derogatory name? What made it derogatory? Was it the content of what was said? Was it a particular context? Was it how it was said? Have you ever called another human or has another human called you the name of a nonhuman animal? What was the social situation like? What power relations were on display? How did it make you feel? How did you respond?

Earlier chapters have focused on living, breathing, eating, and excreting animals. More accurately, these chapters have been on various forms of human consumption of other animals, whether for food, sacrifice, work, or clothing. But what if an animal isn't always just an animal? Or, when is a human not always a human? One of the more striking – and socially interesting – mentions or uses of animals in the domesticated gospels is for animalizing humans, or what Wendy Doniger and Patricia Cox Miller call "zoomorphism."[1] It is the flip side of anthropomorphizing animals. What does it mean to call a human or group of people the names of animals?[2] This is a different kind of entanglement as we leave behind living, breathing, eating, and excreting nonhuman animals. But just as eating, wearing, and sacrificing living animals did, animalizing humans has a direct social significance that manages social boundaries.

Clifford Geertz teases out various social patterns of Bali based on cock fighting and the gambling at the cock fights: "much of Bali surfaces in a cock ring." He continues,

> *Sabung*, the word for cock ... is used metaphorically to mean "hero," "warrior," "champion," "man of parts," "political candidate," "bachelor," "dandy," "lady-killer," or "tough guy." A pompous man whose behavior presumes above his station is compared to a tailless cock who struts about as though he had a large, spectacular one. A desperate man who makes a last, irrational effort to extricate himself from an impossible situation is likened to a dying cock who makes one final lunge at his tormentor to drag him along to a common destruction. A stingy man, who promises much, gives little, and begrudges that, is compared to a cock which, held by the tail, leaps at another without in fact engaging him. A marriageable young man still shy with the opposite sex or someone in a new job anxious to make a good impression is called "a fighting cock caged for the first time."[3]

The cock reveals both patterns and anomalies. Geertz is able to map social relations onto the cockfight, but he also notes that the Balinese have an aversion to anything animal-like, creating deep ambivalence toward their cocks.[4]

Though with the fragmentary evidence I am working with I cannot spin a web covering as thick a description of social relations through animality as Geertz does, in this section I will consider three kinds of animalizations: first, out-group animalizations (turning rival groups into animals), in what often amounts to a specific kind of socially fraught name-calling; second, in-group animalizations, in which Jesus seeks to cultivate a quality associated with an animal with a human being, usually his disciples (though it can also serve other purposes as well); and, finally, cases when Jesus compares humans in general to animals or a certain kind of animal, usually in lesser (animals) to greater (humans) comparisons. This last set of sayings displays Jesus's anthropocentrism most clearly. While many modern readers resist anthropocentrism and speciesism, they regularly give Jesus a pass. But Jesus was part and parcel of his society and regularly expresses broader ancient anthropocentric attitudes.

Animalizing metaphors create and manage insider/outsider statuses at an affective level by associating mostly negative predatory and feral qualities to outsiders, creating a sense of danger around them, and mostly positive domesticated attitudes toward insiders, creating a sense of communion and comfort in the herd.

This chapter, more than any other, will look at how animalization works through affect, the emergent impressions and sensations that flow between, around, and through bodies that sometimes evolve into feelings and more complex emotions.[5] Donovan Schaefer writes that "animality is compulsory affectivity, to be en cavale, horsey, butterflyesque. Bodies are desire in motion. Animals are moved by subtly rich and urgently necessary landscapes of emotion."[6] Though he subtly elides animality and animals, the movement, sliding by, and stickiness of affects and emotions entangle bodies, human and nonhuman, and animalities together.[7] Kathleen Stewart writes, "Ordinary affect is a surging, a rubbing, a connection of some kind that has an impact. It's transpersonal or prepersonal – not about one person's feelings becoming another's but about bodies literally affecting one another and generating intensities: human bodies, discursive bodies, bodies of thought, bodies of water."[8] Landscape may suggest a stable topography, but this is as much an impact of the networks of affects as it is something that pre-exists the affects. Instead, they are intra-active: as Schaefer writes concerning Sedgwick's reading of Proust, "a queer affectscape that emerges out of a topography of interactions between bodies and worlds."[9] While those labelled – by themselves or others – as participating in affect theory are diverse in their thinking, they agree that affects are public and not merely private sensations. These affects, sensations, feelings, and emotions don't just exist within oneself; they do something; they circulate; they have public impacts. So, alongside Sara Ahmed, I do not seek to (only) name them, I want to know what they do: in particular, how they bring certain bodies together while separating out other bodies.[10] Or as Ahmed writes, emotions are always directional toward or away from an object, sticking to some objects. We become attracted to those objects, while when emotions stick differently to other bodies, we become repulsed by those bodies.[11]

In the gospels, we only hear one side of the story. Only Jesus and John the Baptist – the "good guys" – actually throw animal names at their opponents; never does a Pharisee, Sadducee, or scribe do this. We only hear from those on "our side." Therefore, at the very level of reading or hearing the gospels, one is drawn to align with the positive insider animals (sheep, cattle, doves) and avoid the negative outsider, largely predatory animals (vipers, dogs).

Yet a warning about animal metaphors and social relationships is necessary. Those using these terms view language as less nominal and more substantive: they believe they are expressing something essential about the nature or character of those humans described as animals.[12] Even when metaphorical, they are never merely metaphors.[13]

VIPERS, WOLVES, FOXES, AND DOGS: OUT-GROUP ANIMALIZATIONS IN THE GOSPELS

Out-group animalizations are common in all societies. Calling others, whether rivals or people of a different race, ethnicity, class, sexuality, or gender, the name of an animal is often thought to degrade, to dehumanize. Donna Haraway writes, "The discursive tie between the colonized, the enslaved, the noncitizen, and the animal – all reduced to type, all Others to rational man, and all essential to his bright constitution – is at the heart of racism and flourishes, lethally, in the entrails of humanism."[14] As Cary Wolfe argues, this operates on an assumption of speciesism; that is, the "discourse of species" operates to differentiate humans from animals, which, then, can be used to justify or even just tolerate others' violence against such other species. This violence then slips via animalization into other kinds of differentiations of gender, race, and class.[15] As Carol Adams has argued, sexism and speciesism in particular have gone hand in hand, as women and animals are objectified through real or symbolic dismemberment, renaming bodies and body parts, and foregrounding edible and sexually charged body parts from the male gaze or stomach.[16] Animalization also contributes to anti-queer and anti-trans violence. If there is no institutionalization of speciesism in place, then the act of dehumanizing others through animalizations becomes incomprehensible. This act is only comprehensible with the assumption of speciesism or anthropocentrism.

Ancient Romans regularly animalized lower classes, particularly slaves, as well as subjected peoples.[17] There is a power play involved here: when someone calls someone else by the name of an animal, they seek to dehumanize them, putting them below themselves, who remain "human." Usually this precedes, justifies, or coincides with some sort of violence, particularly colonial violence.[18] There are four – on my reading – clear instances of "out-group" animalizations that occur in the domesticated gospels to refer to real or perceived outsiders. All four major instances refer to or create outsiders by affiliating them with the names of wild predators or feral animals. The gospel writers create objects of repulsion by attempting to stick negative affects to them. By doing so, the gospels largely create an aura of fear and danger around the predatory figures of serpents, wolves, and even foxes, while attaching feelings of contempt for the lowly foreign dogs. The former are largely affiliated with ideological and political opponents; the latter are affiliated with those who are ethnically different. Yet these affects cannot be fully contained; that which repels can also fascinate.[19]

Fear and Danger: Animalizing Ideological Opponents

Sara Ahmed asks, "Which bodies fear which bodies?"[20] The synoptic gospels tend to attach fearful animalizations to ideological opponents, designating them as dangerous. It is a simultaneous process of distancing and intimacy: one only creates fear for objects that are a threat; those must be things that can somehow reach you. Ahmed writes, "fear works to secure the relationship between those bodies; it brings them together and moves them apart through the shudders that are felt on the skin, on the surface that surfaces through the encounter."[21] The best-known out-group animalization in the domesticated gospels is when John the Baptist calls a group of people a "brood of vipers." This occurs in Matthew and Luke, being part of the "double tradition" or "Q," but there are some important variations of whom John the Baptist is referring to and how it fits within the texture of the rest of the gospel.

Let's start with Matthew's version:

> But when he [John] saw many Pharisees and Sadducees coming for baptism, he said to them, "You brood of vipers (*gennemata echidnon*)! Who warned you to flee from the wrath to come? Bear fruit worthy of repentance. Do not presume to say to yourselves, "We have Abraham as our ancestor"; for I tell you, God is able from these stones to raise up children to Abraham. Even now the ax is lying at the root of the trees; every tree therefore does not bear good fruit is cut down and thrown into the fire. (Matt. 3:7–10)

This scene drips with social tension. The Pharisees and Sadducees have come to be baptized – not to criticize or mock John and his followers. Yet, as Ahmed points out, "we fear an object that approaches us."[22] The approach creates an intense sensation that one seeks to repel. They have come to be incorporated into the "in-group," but John's comment recreates their "out-group" status: they are a brood of vipers. His language is full of eschatological judgment about how they cannot rely on their status as physical heirs of Abraham, since God can create new heirs of Abraham from stones.

This fits with Matthew's use of "vipers" as well as Matthew's negative – yet sometimes ambivalent – attitude towards Pharisees. In Matthew, Jesus takes up this venomous name-calling elsewhere. In 12:34, after responding to the Pharisees' accusation to cast out demons by Beelzebul, Jesus expounds on a long discourse against them. In it, he says, "Either make the tree good, and its fruit good; or make the tree bad, and its fruit bad; for the tree is known by its fruit. You brood of vipers (*gennemata echidnon*)! How can you speak good things, when you are evil? For out of the abundance of the heart the mouth speaks" (12:33–4). The passage continues in the language of judgment. Jesus's language resembles John the Baptist's. Both call Pharisees a "brood of vipers," both speak of trees and fruit, and both speak of judgment. In this case, Jesus is flipping the tables on the Pharisees. They have accused him of being in league with the prince of demons; he, in turn, has called them vipers and suggests that they bear bad fruit and speak evil from the abundance of evil that exists within them.

Finally, Jesus calls Pharisees (and scribes) "vipers" in 23:33 within a long screed against the hypocrisy of Pharisees that comprises the entirety of chapter 23. This snake-calling emerges while Jesus accuses the ancestors of the Pharisees of shedding the blood of the prophets. In the midst of it, Jesus says, "You snakes, you brood of vipers! (*opheis, gennemata echidnon*)." As with John the Baptist, the screed includes a question concerning the Pharisees' learning of or inability to escape the coming wrath, in this case, the "judgment of Gehenna." Matthew brings up the brood of vipers three times and each has additional linguistic ties with each other: all three include the Pharisees and the first two include issues of bearing good fruit. All three include judgment.[23]

Luke's version of John the Baptist also includes the name-calling of "brood of vipers (*gennemata echidnon*)!" (Luke 3:7–9), but it is not directed at the Pharisees, but at the "crowds." While the pericope continues the same way with judgment and bearing good fruit, the next segment changes the entire affect of the passage, as the crowd then asks what they need to do; that is, they earnestly seek to "bear good fruit." There we learn that among the crowd are tax collectors and soldiers. In this case, the accusation of "brood of vipers" creates distance as it does in Matthew, but, unlike in Matthew, that distance is overcome by the crowd seeking to close this gap. As Schaefer writes concerning this same process in calling others "savages," "The affective responsivity of bodies to other bodies is not limited to the hedonicity of hate: there are also compulsions pulling bodies across bounding lines, a recalcitrant compassion."[24] This might be because, as Ahmed argues, hatred has an intimacy to it that makes it ambivalent. The ambivalence of hate may open a space to overcome that hate. Inversely, love is often a precondition for hate as well.[25] This intimate relation to hate explains both its being overcome in Luke and its vehemence in Matthew.

This name-calling does not as easily fit within the texture of Luke's gospel. Luke does not bring up the "brood of serpents" again, so it does not accumulate the repeated ties as it does with Matthew to create in-group and out-group through the themes of vipers, fruit, and judgment. There are some variations, since Luke does not have the same level of antipathy towards Pharisees. Moreover, the passage introduces some of Luke's themes of economic justice (3:10–14) as well as setting up redemption of tax collectors (and other sinners) as well as soldiers (e.g., the Centurion), though both of these elements can be found in Matthew as well.

So why the serpent and, not just a serpent, but a "brood of vipers"? Brood (*gennemata*) indicates a grouping – a group of people rather than individuals. But more than that, it is literally "begettings" or "those born of" vipers. The term suggests not just a grouping but something about in-born nature. In the ancient world, vipers were popularly thought to kill their mothers, who, in turn, had killed their fathers.[26] Whether or not John, Jesus, or the audience of the gospels had this in view, "begettings of vipers" already suggests an alternative genealogy to those who, in especially Matthew's view, claim false descent from Abraham, Moses, and other past righteous figures (Matt. 3:9; 23:2; 23:29). Vipers are, moreover, venomous. So perhaps this refers to the "poison" of the Pharisees (for Matthew) or the crowd (for Luke) (cf. Rom. 3:13). For Matthew it becomes associated with hypocrisy, and so the forked tongue may resonate. Luke, however, does not develop these connotations.

While ancient views of serpents were both positive and negative, negative imagery of serpents regularly stuck to out-group peoples. The Dead Sea Scrolls, for example, provide several examples of using serpentine imagery to refer to out-group people, referring to the kings of Greece as the "head of asps" (CD VIII, 9–11; CD XIX, 22–3 on Deut. 32:33) and relating the evil of serpents to the begetting of evil, discussing serpent eggs (CD V, 14; *4Q266* 3 II; on Isa. 59:5).

Moreover, the speech of one's opponents is equated to the venom of serpents (*1QH^a* 12 X, 26–7; *4Q429* 9–10), like Jesus's references to the Pharisees' evil speech.[27] In ancient visual culture represented in the Great Altar of Pergamon the enemies of the Olympian gods – in this case, the giants – could be portrayed as chthonic figures with coiling serpentine legs.[28] Serpents are, symbolically, the other to proper order. Finally, serpent imagery is possibly an allusion to the other serpent in Genesis 2–3. If that is the case, deceit – as well as potential judgment – would be in the background for Luke and explicitly developed in Matthew.

The serpent – especially the viper – therefore carries with it a host of negative connotations that have carried over into the modern period. Derrida recalls how John Llewelyn recalls a question that he (Llewelyn) posed to Levinas: "Does an animal have a face?" Here a "face" means being given ethical consideration in the sixth commandment, "thou shalt not kill." In response, Levinas retorts, "I don't know if a snake has a face." He does not bring up a dog, cat, or a chimpanzee, but an animal that, seemingly, closed off further debate, and, ultimately, ethical consideration.[29] The snake, it seems, is an ultimate "other" among animals, whereas humans can find easier recognition of a "face" in more closely related animals, such as most mammals. One may kill one without a "face" without remorse. Oddly, Levinas leaves the question in the air; the snake's face is undetermined, underdetermined, or undeterminable. Returning to the ancient text, the slithering, scaly – potentially faceless – serpent can be the cipher for the most venomous dehumanization. It makes one shudder.

A less venomous case of dehumanizing name-calling occurs in the Sermon on the Mount: "Beware of false prophets, who come to you in sheep's clothing (*en endumasin probaton*) but inwardly are ravenous wolves (*esothen de eisin lukoi harpages*)" (Matt. 7:15). Like the "brood of vipers," this is a group animalization. Also like vipers, there is an emphasis on deceit. False prophets are people who claim to be "in-group" – thus the sheep – but are really "out-group": wolves. They claim to be domesticated, peaceful, docile or harmless, but they are really predatory, harmful, and wild. This combination has the potential to heighten paranoia. The serpentine Pharisees were recognizably out-group; but the sheep-clothed wolves are out-group people hidden among us.

Nonetheless, the "wolf in sheep's clothing" is odd, since wolves could attract positive associations in the ancient world. Notably, however, in Isaiah's eschatological vision, wolves and lambs dwell together peacefully (Isa. 11:6; 65:25).[30] Wolves famously hunt in packs. Their pack status could lead to admiration, applied to army standards, for example, and fear in the ancient world.[31] Here they display the duplicity usually associated with a "fox" or later tales, such as *Little Red Riding Hood*.

Speaking of foxes, a passing out-group reference occurs in Luke 13:32. Like the third viper reference in Matthew, this one occurs in the context of the killing of the prophets. In this case, however, the Pharisees come to warn Jesus that Herod is out to kill him. Jesus responds, "Go and tell that fox (*te alopeki taute*) [for me], 'Listen, I am casting out demons and performing cures today and tomorrow, and on the third day I finish my work. Yet today, tomorrow, and the next day I must be on my way, because it is impossible for a prophet to be killed outside of Jerusalem'" (Luke 13:32–3 adapted). The Pharisaic attitude towards Jesus here is noteworthy: they are more aligned with one another than either is with Herod Antipas. Thus, ideological opponents could work together in the face of a more powerful threat. Though Jesus's only other reference to a fox is fairly neutral (Matt. 8:20; Luke 9:58), in this case fox is clearly a slur. But it is unclear what kind of slur. Foxes are generally associated with slyness, but they are also a threat to one's small domesticated animals. Nonetheless, when Jesus says that "foxes have dens," he is referring to a fox as a fox, but when he calls Herod a fox, he is dehumanizing him. One may not fear a fox the way one fears a venomous snake, but they are interlopers who threaten. As Ahmed writes, "Through the generation of 'the threat,' fear works to align bodies with and against others."[32] One both creates and recreates social boundaries through the animalized threats.[33]

Contempt: Animalizing Foreigners

The final "out-group" animalization is more involved and is affectively different; it is the story of the Syrophoenician/Canaanite woman in Mark 7:24–30 and Matthew 15:22–8. Whereas the previous three animalizations were directed at out-group opponents who posed an ideological threat, this is not the case here. Instead, Jesus dehumanizes a foreign woman in terms of contempt.[34] She is not venomous; she is feral. She does not attack the herd; she begs for scraps.

In both gospels, by going to Tyre (Mark) or Tyre and Sidon (Matthew), it is the only place in the gospels where Jesus travels beyond the traditional boundaries of Israel in his ministry – even if he otherwise ends up in Gentile-dominated places.[35] In Mark's version, a Gentile Syrophoenician woman, whose daughter has an unclean spirit, comes to Jesus, bows at his feet, and asks him to cast out the demon.[36] Jesus retorts harshly, "Let the children be fed first, for it is not fair to take the children's food and throw it to the little dogs (*tois kunariois*)" (Mark 7:27 adapted). The woman does not accept this answer. She responds cleverly, "Sir, even the little dogs (*ta kunaria*) under the table eat the children's crumbs" (Mark 7:28 adapted). She accepts Jesus's terms but resists his conclusion. For her clever retort, Jesus says to her that the demon has left her daughter.

The woman in this tale is triply excluded in the narrative: as a woman, as a foreigner, and through Jesus's own speech, as a dog.[37] Though Jesus may, in fact, be calling the woman's daughter the dog, the triple exclusion would also apply, instead of male, Israelite, and human, as Jesus would be himself. The use of the plural "dogs" may include both of them. By contrast, Jesus never calls male non-Israelites by the name of animals (e.g., the Centurion). Therefore, even though the term here is grammatically neuter plural, it still likely has gendered associations.

Matthew's version has some minor changes that heighten the social distance between Jesus and the woman (and her daughter). While Syrophoenician already designated "foreign," Matthew calls her a Canaanite, a title redolent with violence and dispossession in the

Hebrew Bible. She refers to Jesus as "Son of David." Matthew's dialogue is more involved. The woman begs for help, but Jesus does not answer her. Jesus then says that he has only come for "the lost sheep of the house of Israel (*ta probata ta apololota oikou Israel*)." Finally, he calls her (and/or her daughter) a dog. The contrast is partly between dog and human, but it is also between dog and sheep. She is a foreign (feral?) dog who failed to be a domesticated sheep, a typical in-group animalization in the gospels (see below). Her retort is the same, but his final response is a little different, exclaiming on her great faith rather than her cleverness. Either way, hers is the first female voice we hear in the domesticated gospels as they now stand.[38]

Refusing the miracle, at least initially, and calling the woman and/or her daughter a dog is harsh. The word translated as "dogs" is really the diminutive neuter form: "little dogs." While some modern scholars have tried to mitigate the offensiveness of Jesus's remark, suggesting it implies something like "puppy,"[39] calling a man or a woman a "dog" is a term of reproach that goes back to Homer and continues to be a major negative slur today in the eastern Mediterranean and the Middle East.[40] To get the degree of insult across, one could perhaps translate this as "bitch," though "dog" – again here in the grammatical neuter – could refer to both men and women in a way that the modern "bitch" does not. Nonetheless, one should keep the animality of both gender and ethnicity in mind as one considers this passage.

Today dogs are primarily viewed as companion animals, who are both the subject and commodities of a vast animal market,[41] and there are ancient writings that positively reflect on dogs in this way, such as Odysseus's faithful dog, Argos, in the *Odyssey*. Socrates waxed rhapsodic about the philosophic nature of dogs in the *Republic*, regularly comparing the nature of a dog – friendly to those it knows and fierce to those it does not know – to the qualities necessary for the guardians of his imagined city (*Republic* 375a–b, 375e–376b). Pliny also reflects on the faithfulness, loyalty, memory, and hunting skill of dogs (*Natural History* 8.142–53).[42]

Unlike the earlier animalizations of fear, ancient biblical and related texts usually referred to dogs with contempt.[43] In the Hebrew

Bible, dogs were primarily viewed as unclean scavengers. In Exodus 22:31, one gives the meat of mangled animals in the field to the dogs, because they are unclean for human consumption. In the Elijah-Elisha story, dogs lick the blood off dead bodies and eat the dead bodies of Jezebel and those belonging to Ahab who die in the city (1 Kgs. 21:19, 23–4; 22:38; cf. 2 Kgs. 9:35–7). They, moreover, eat their own vomit (Prov. 26:11; cf. 2 Pet. 2:22). As Ken Stone remarks, dogs in the Hebrew Bible are anomalous – in Mary Douglas's sense – because they are neither domesticated nor wild.[44]

Another example of the broader prevalence of this association, the Homeric epics largely cohere with this view of dogs as scavengers and consumers of dead human bodies. Both the Hebrew Bible and Greek epics portray dogs eating dead human bodies as a curse for the body not having had a proper burial (*Iliad* 1.1–5; *Odyssey* 22.474–7; see *Iliad* 23.179–87, where Aphrodite protects Hector's corpse from being eaten by dogs). Some ancient Mesopotamian curses say just as much. A curse from Ashur states, "may all these [various gods listed] curse him with a curse which cannot be relieved, terrible and merciless, as long as he lives, may they let his name, his seed, be carried off from the land, may they put his flesh in a dog's mouth!"[45] Dogs are also associated with the demonic realm related to the ancient Mesopotamian demon Lamastu, a demonic association that re-emerges in the Greek Magical Papyri.[46] Something of this scavenging attitude is likely reflected in the dogs licking Lazarus's sores in the story of the rich man ("Dives") and Lazarus in Luke 16:21.[47] As Crossan, moreover, in a provocative chapter called "The Dogs Beneath the Cross," referring to the work of Martin Hengel, reminds us, dogs and birds of prey would have been waiting to scavenge on the meat of crucified victims.[48]

The Bible also has metaphorical dogs as a term of reproach. When David faces off with Goliath, the giant retorts: "Am I a dog, that you come to me with sticks?" (1 Sam. 17:43). When Saul seeks to kill David, but David, in a turn of events, spares Saul's life, David says ambiguously to Saul: "Against whom has the king of Israel come out? Whom do you pursue? A dead dog? A single flea?" (1

Sam. 24:14). It is unclear whether David is saying he is as insignificant as a dead dog or a flea or that Saul should not underestimate David by thinking he is merely a dead dog or a flea. The same phrase occurs later, when David seeks to help Jonathan's son, Mephibosheth, who is crippled. This is after David's rise to prominence and after the deaths of Saul and Jonathan. Mephibosheth says to David, "What is your servant, that you should look upon a dead dog such as I?" (2 Sam. 9:8). The same phrase, "dead dog," occurs again in 2 Samuel 16:9. In all cases, it expresses one's complete insignificance. Returning to the Elijah-Elisha cycle, Hazael refers to himself as a servant, a "mere dog," to Elisha in what is clearly a form of self-abasement (2 Kgs. 8:13; cf. 2 Sam. 3:8). This, again, has parallel with Homer, in which Helen self-deprecates by calling herself a "dog" or "dog-face."[49]

The books of the New Testament elsewhere associate the term "dog" with negative character traits or one's opponents. Paul uses the term "dogs" (*tous kunas*) to refer to those who prescribe circumcision – "those who mutilate the flesh" – to those who join the movement (Phil. 3:2).[50] Moreover, in Revelation 22:15, dogs are listed alongside sorcerers, fornicators, murderers, and idolators as those who will remain outside the gates of the new Jerusalem.[51] Dogs are associated with the greatest of sinners and the lowest of the low; they are even listed first in the list. While most commentators take the dogs to be metaphorical here, there may be a reason for this: literal dogs were profane, unclean animals, and not fit to be in the eschatological sacred space. Philippians and the Psalms also mention dogs hand in hand with evildoers (Ps. 22:16, 20; Phil. 3:2). Whether literal or not, according to Revelation, no dogs go to heaven. In the Gospel of Thomas, Jesus says the Pharisees are "like a dog sleeping in the cattle's feeding trough. For it neither eats nor lets the cattle eat" (102).

One might compare the Qumran sect, which states that "one should not let dogs enter the holy camp because they might eat some of the bones from the temple with the flesh on them" (*4QMMT* 58–9).[52] This coheres with the primary image of a dog as a scrounging scavenger. *Miqsat Ma'ase ha-Torah* (4QMMT) considered Jerusalem the "holy camp," and, therefore, thought all dogs ought to be banned from Jerusalem.[53]

More contemporary to the gospel writers, Josephus refers to his opponent, "Apion," as having the mind of an ass and the impudence of a dog (*impudentiam canis*), which, for men, is what the slur of "dog" often connoted: rashness or impudence (Josephus, *Against Apion* 2.85).

Finally, in the post-gospel period, rabbis regularly referred to or equated Gentiles with dogs, as Jesus does with the woman. One finds dog animalizations for the hateful (*b.* ʻAZ 54b on Deut. 4:24; *Tanh.* 100a on Mal. 1:3), the ignorant (*Lev. Rab.* 9.110d), the godless (*Exod. Rab.* 9.73c on Ps. 110:2; 59:7), and the pagan (*Mid. Ps.* 11:24a; *Gen. Rab.* 81.52a; *y. Shab.* 9.11d, 23, *b. Meg.* 7b; *PRE* 29; *Num. Rab.* 15.179b; *Mid. Ps.* 2.115a).[54] Though, notably, the Mishnah does not include the use of "dog" as a cipher for "gentile," so these are late associations compared to the gospel usage.[55] Nonetheless, *Mishnah, Berakot* 5:6 comes close, indicating that selling forbidden food to a Gentile is the same as "throwing it to the dogs."[56]

Yet, except for cases that post-date the gospels, there are no cases that use the term "dogs" as an *ethnic* term of reproach – they are mostly terms of individual self or other abasement – not group deprecations. Paul uses it as a term of group reproach, but it is ideological: those who claim that those who join the movement should be circumcised. Jesus's usage here, therefore, appears to be novel in using it in an *ethnic* means of differentiation of insider versus outsider.

Dogs were, however, long associated with *women* in the Greek tradition. Hesiod claimed Pandora had a *kuneos noos,* which Vernant translates as "the spirit of a bitch" (Hesiod, *Works and Days* 67).[57] Clytemnestra is called "dog-face" and Agamemnon says, "Is there anything more like a dog than a woman" (*Odyssey* 7.216; 11.427). Clement of Alexandria follows suit in this tradition, also saying there is nothing more like a dog than a woman.[58] In short, when Jesus called a woman (and/or her daughter) a "little dog," it was hardly a compliment, but a saying that – even in its neutered diminutive form – took on gendered and ethnic dimensions. The Syrophoenician woman, however, cleverly takes Jesus's terms and turns the tables on him, speaking back to power in a case Mitzi Smith calls "sass."[59]

In addition to the woman-as-dog, there is another "dog" saying in the gospels. In Matthew 7:6 Jesus says, "Do not give what is holy to dogs and do not throw your pearls before swine, or they will trample them under foot and turn and maul you." While not paralleled in the domesticated gospels, one can find parallel sayings in the Gospel of Thomas 93 and the Didache 9:5. Thomas 93 reads: "Do not give what is holy to dogs, lest they throw them on the dung-heap. Do not throw the pearls to swine, lest they grind it [to bits]." A further negative conjunction of swine and dogs occurs in Papyrus Oxyrynchus 840, where the Saviour, in the temple, says, "Woe to you blind who do not see. You have washed in these waters that have poured out, in which dogs and swine have wallowed night and day" (recto 30–4).[60] Here the swine and dogs are not literal – there would be no swine in the temple – and likely refer to the people who seek to cleanse themselves in the *mikvaot*. The element of giving what is holy to dogs likely refers to the leftovers of the sacrificial animals, relying on the aforementioned issue of dogs scavenging. Jesus controversially challenges those who claim to be ritually clean that they are not morally clean. Again, the cultural attitude towards dogs and swine is entirely negative. These biblical authors would ultimately agree – though for different reasons – with Deleuze and Guattari that "*anyone who likes cats or dogs is a fool.*"[61]

We have looked at the social attitude towards dogs in the discussion of the Syrophoenician woman; dogs were largely considered lowly scavengers. We will later discuss pigs with the Gerasene demoniac, and pigs were, of course, unclean animals. Are these literal animals? Or metaphorical animals? Or both? What is the "holy" thing one should not throw to dogs? The phrase may derive from the idea that dogs should not have access to sacrificial meat, something the Qumran sectarians seem to have been worried about.[62] Is this literal meaning operative here?

The *Didache* 9:5 interprets the saying as the "holy" food being the Eucharist and the "dogs" being anyone who has not been baptized into the name of the Lord: a social distinction. As with the Syrophoenician woman, dogs are outsiders. But for the Didache, they are anyone who has not been baptized, whereas for the story of the Syrophoenician woman, it was a non-Israelite. Nothing, however, in Matthew's or Thomas's contexts indicates that this has anything to do with the Eucharist. Could "dog" mean the same thing as it did for the Syrophoenician – or in Matthew, the Canaanite woman – story? A non-Israelite? Then it would be not to give what is "holy" to non-Israelites – or, as Jesus would say, keep it for the "lost sheep of Israel"?

Most interpreters read it in terms of Matthew 7:1–5 on not judging others too harshly, and it can, therefore, be a juxtaposition that balances the laxity of vv. 1–5 with the harshness in v. 6.[63] Yet Thomas allows for greater triangulation. Both Matthew and Thomas put the saying next to sayings about "seek and you shall find" and "knock." There may be a thematic connection in that the first is about (im)proper giving and the other about proper receiving.[64]

When turning to the Pseudo-Clementine *Recognitions* 2.3 and 3.1, however, the light of analysis shines a little differently. It highlights a similarity with Thomas 93: both are about giving truth to those who are worthy or, I would more accurately say, to those who seek it. April DeConick reads this as operative in Thomas and Pseudo-Clement and even later Islamic readings, but absent in Matthew itself.[65] I find myself in agreement with the spirit and disagreement with the letter. I agree this is what the pericope is about; I also think it is there in Matthew, however: the juxtaposition of seeking and finding, knocking and the door will open, is indeed about seekers seeking "good gifts." The reciprocity of gift-giving and receiving is in play here and how to receive and how (not) to give. Where all of these readings, no matter how discordant amongst themselves, intersect is the belief that dogs/pigs are outsiders and not worthy (or not ready for) certain teachings. It is an insider/outsider dynamic already present in Jesus only explaining parables to his disciples (Matt. 13:11; Mark 4:11; Luke 8:10).

Dog, whether little or not, in Jesus's mouth becomes a slur with ethnic and gendered dimensions to it, evoking broader cultural affects of contempt. Instead of outsiders to be feared, they are outsiders looked down upon. Yet due to the woman's clever response, she elicits a "recalcitrant compassion."[66] Not all "dogs" are so lucky.

Affective Outsiders

Out-group animalizations run a gamut between wild (serpents, wolves), feral (dogs), and domesticated (swine). In all cases, either Jesus or one of the "good guys," like John the Baptist, does the name calling. There is not a single instance of a Pharisee, scribe, Sadducee, Herodian, or Gentile calling Jesus or one of the disciples an animal as a slur. Of course, the story is told from that perspective, and it does not record any animal slurs against John the Baptist, Jesus, or his disciples, even though these authors are willing to record other slurs (such as being in league with Beelzebul). At the level of reading or listening to the gospels, one affectively associates ideological opponents with danger and foreigners with contempt, though there are cases where the initial feelings are overcome. Nonetheless, there are "in-group" animalizations that do occur, though for different reasons. Jesus – usually – calls his followers names of docile, domesticated animals.

SHEEP, CATTLE, SERPENTS, AND DOVES: IN-GROUP ANIMALIZATIONS IN THE GOSPELS

Unlike predatory or scavenging outsiders, Jesus repeatedly calls his own followers domesticated animals. He mostly calls them sheep, but also cattle, serpents, and doves. This does not seem very flattering; this listing makes Jesus's followers sound docile and stupid. In philosophical discourse, being like "cattle" means to be without reason and given to pleasures. Aristotle writes, for example, "Now most of the utterly slavish sort of people obviously decide in favour of a life that belongs to grazing cattle."[67] Kant speaks of people who fail to think for themselves and have others – "guardians" – who do their thinking for them as cattle.[68] But, as Donna Haraway notes in her discussion of Navajo-Churro sheep, sheep can be intelligent and actively discriminate among themselves, between themselves and humans, and between different humans: "the sheep themselves are active participants in the interlaced relational worlds. Like all sheep, they recognize hundreds of faces; they know their people and their land."[69] These animalizations do not trigger a threat; they do not put one into a fight-or-flight or freeze response. As an insider domesticated animal, one can find rest or comfort in exchange for absolute obedience. So let's take a closer look at the human sheep or sheep-like humans in the gospels.

In the "double tradition" or "Q" Jesus sends out his disciples as "sheep" (*probata*; Matthew) or "lambs" (*arnas*; Luke) "into the midst of wolves" (*en mesoi lukon*; Matt. 10:16; Luke 10:3). Matthew adds "so be wise as serpents and innocent as doves (*ginesthe oun phronimoi hos hoi opheis kai ekeraioi hos hai peristerai*)." The combination of serpents and doves along with sheep and wolves also appears in Papyrus Oxyrynchus 4009 recto. Luke does not include the serpents/doves. We have already seen the dual characterization of sheep versus wolves with the "wolves in sheep's clothing" saying. In that case, "sheep" denoted insiders and "wolves" outsiders posing as insiders. Here there is no pretense to the wolves. They are pure outsiders. The imagery is that the disciples (sheep/lambs) must be aware and on guard against hostile people (wolves).[70]

Matthew characterizes this awareness with the admonition to be like serpents and doves (cf. Thomas 39). On the face of it, Jesus's admonition juxtaposes two qualities associated with opposing animals. While wisdom and innocence are not necessarily opposed, the association with serpents and doves does create an underlying tension. While serpents – especially vipers – carry a negative valence elsewhere in Matthew, here they are uniquely used for an in-group quality of wisdom.

This ambivalent use of the snakes in Matthew becomes heightened since it also likely recalls that the serpent in the garden was, in fact, similarly "wise." The Septuagint says that "the serpent was wiser than all the animals that were upon the land" (*Ho de ophis en phronimotatos panton ton therion ton epi tes ges*; Gen. 3:1 LXX, translation mine). This is the same word for "wise" that Matthew uses: "*ginesthe oun phronimoi hos hoi opheis.*" The close proximity between the word "serpent/s" (*ophis/opheis*) and this root word for "wise" (*phronimotatos/phronimoi*) would strongly conjure Genesis 3, which makes it all the more fascinating that this is a quality that Jesus seeks to instill into his disciples.

Phronesis, however, had a positive valence in broader Greek culture. Plato used it and *sophia* interchangeably. Aristotle more specifically used *phronesis* as a virtue to cultivate in his *Nicomachean Ethics*, and one could translate it there as something like "practical wisdom."[71] For him, instead, *sophia* indicated intellectual accomplishment or theoretical wisdom. In Palestinian culture, the serpent could also have a dual nature and was also associated with the critical reflection of the sages (*m. Avot* 2:10).[72]

Doves, however, have clearer positive valence in the gospels at the outset when the (Holy) Spirit descends on Jesus as a dove (Mark 1:10–11; Matt. 3:16; Luke 3:21–2). Overall, this is a rare case when Jesus refers to animalistic qualities directly. Usually, an animal is simply named, and one has to guess at the implied connotation; here it is explicit.

Jesus likewise refers to his disciples as sheep throughout the domesticated gospels. While we may think of sheep as "sheepish" or blindly following, mostly Jesus means this in a positive sense: they follow their shepherd (Jesus) well and will be rewarded. There is one place, however, where Jesus calls his disciples sheep in a potentially negative key: "And Jesus said to them, 'You will all become deserters; for it is written, "I will strike the shepherd and the sheep will be scattered (*pataxo ton poimena, kai ta probata diakorpisthesontai*)"'" (Mark 14:27; cf. Matt. 26:31; cf. Zech. 13:7; cf. Papyrus Vienna G 2325 [Fayum Fragment]). Jesus predicts his disciples' desertion when he is arrested and crucified. When they become leaderless, they will scatter (cf. John 16:32). Domesticated sheep cannot take care of themselves.

Jesus uses a similar phrase in another pericope in Mark 6:34 and in Matthew 9:36. In it, however, Jesus does not refer to the disciples, but the crowds, as the sheep: "Then Jesus went about all the cities and villages, teaching in their synagogues, and proclaiming the good news of the kingdom, and curing every disease and every sickness. When he saw the crowds, he had compassion for them, because they were harassed and helpless, like sheep without a shepherd (*hosei probata me echonta poimena*)" (Matt. 9:35–6; cf. Mark 6:34). While Mark's and Matthew's versions occur in different places in the narrative, in both Jesus has compassion for the leaderless crowds. Such shepherdless sheep are not fully in-group like the disciples, but not fully out-group either like the Pharisees. They are something in the middle. They are the "lost sheep of Israel," as Jesus says to the Canaanite woman. He is seeking to "find" them to become their shepherd. Indeed, not long after this, Jesus commissions his disciples to avoid Gentiles and Samaritans, "but go rather to the lost sheep of the house of Israel (*ta probata ta apololota oikou Israel*)" (10:6). Sheep without a shepherd to refer to leaderless people, moreover, is a trope in the Hebrew Bible (Num. 27:17; 1 Kgs. 22:17; Ezek. 34:7–10; Zech. 10:2; Zech. 13:7).

This sheep-like imagery is not limited to the synoptics. Jesus is, in the Gospel of John, the "good shepherd." Jesus says:

> Very truly, I tell you, anyone who does not enter the sheepfold (*ten aulen ton probaton*) by the gate but climbs in by another way is a thief and a bandit. The one who enters by the gate is the shepherd of the sheep (*poimen estin ton probaton*). The gatekeeper opens the gate for him, and the sheep hear his voice (*ta probata tes phones autou akouei*). He calls his own sheep by name and leads them out (*ta idia probata phonei kat' obama kai exagei auta*). When he has brought out all his own, he goes ahead of them, and they sheep follow him because they know his voice. They will not follow a stranger, but they will run from him because they do not know the voice of strangers. (John 10:1–5)

This language continues all the way through verse 18. Jesus is, in this instance, both the "gate" (John 10:9) and the "good shepherd" (*ego eimi ho poimen ho kalos* in John 10:11). Further sheep imagery appears in vv. 26–30, where Jesus reiterates that his "sheep" know his voice and he knows them (cf. Ezek. 34:11–31), with a strong emphasis on hearing, knowing, voice, and name. There is an auditory connection between shepherd and sheep that establishes their "knowing" each other. The connection between hearing and knowing is an important theme in the Gospel of John.[73] This is a quality known in sheep; as Donna Haraway reminds us, sheep recognize and discriminate between different human faces.

The knowledge of animals, particularly domesticated animals – in contrast to human ignorance – shows up already in Isaiah 1:3: "The ox knows its owner, the donkey its master's crib; but Israel does not know, my people do not understand." While the people are not called by the sign of an animal here, the animal analogy demands that we see God as owner and God's people as in the place of animals, but as failing to be as knowledgeable as such animals! Wild animals also know better than people what they should do (Jer. 8:7).[74] The animals know what's expected of them, but humans do not. Indeed, one should "go to the ant, you lazybones; consider its ways, and be wise" (Prov. 6:6). Even Job laments that the animals, the birds, the plants, and fish all know what his human interlocutors seem to miss (Job 12:7–10).[75] Luckily, Jesus's human-shaped sheep know his voice in the Gospel of John.

Toward the end of John's gospel, after Jesus has been resurrected, Jesus passes the baton to Peter, asking him three times, if he loves him, to feed his lambs/sheep (*ta arnia/ta probata*) (John 21:15–17), which reminds and counteracts Peter's three denials of Jesus at his trial. This is generally reminiscent of Moses passing the baton to Joshua, using shepherding language in the process (Num. 27:17). In fact, the second time Jesus asks Peter whether he loves him or not, he responds to Peter's positive response by saying, "Shepherd my sheep" (*poimane ta probata mou*). The sheep, therefore, are no longer shepherdless. Or, put another way, Peter's status has been transformed from sheep to shepherd, from cattle to human.

Finally, returning to Matthew, Jesus reiterates the "insider" status of sheep in judgment: "When the Son of Man comes in his glory, and all the angels with him, then he will sit on the throne of glory. All the nations (*panta ta ethne*) will be gathered before him, and he will separate people one from another as a shepherd separates the sheep from the goats (*hosper ho poimen aphorizei ta probata apo ton eriphon*), and he will put the sheep at his right hand and the goats at the left" (Matt. 25:31–3). There is an ambiguity with the phrase "all the nations" (*panta ta ethne*). Are they all nations inclusive of Israel or, following general biblical parlance, including elsewhere in Matthew (e.g., 28:16–20), does this mean only "gentiles"?[76] The use of "all" suggests inclusion of Israel, especially since it is unclear who's who until the sorting happens. And, further down in the passage, who are the "least of these" (Matt. 25:40, 45): Jesus's disciples or all people in such a condition?[77] The rhetoric of the passage – and the surprise of both groups – indicates that the insider-outsider dynamic does not fall on the least-of-these versus everyone else, but on how one treats the least of these. I, therefore, find the idea of the "least of these" being the disciples unlikely. The disciples, and all others who do these things, would be the sheep.

Moreover, realizing that in the ancient world the right hand is the good side and the left hand the bad side, one should know where this is going. The right-hand sheep are "blessed" and "righteous" and will inherit the kingdom, because they fed the Son of Man when he was hungry, gave him drink when he was thirsty, welcomed him as a stranger, gave him clothing when he was naked, and visited him in prison, and because they did so to the least of these. The left-hand goats who are "accursed" will inherit "eternal fire prepared for the devil and his angels" because they failed to do all of these things. Clearly sheep represent the blessed and righteous and the goats represent the cursed.

The sheep among the nations are the insiders who go to the kingdom; the goats the outsiders who go to eternal punishment (25:34–46). This language develops Ezekiel 34:17: "As for you, my flock, says the Lord GOD: I shall judge between sheep and sheep, between rams and goats." Both Ezekiel and Matthew create a judgment scene from the metaphor of the shepherd/judge separating out animals that belong from animals that don't belong. But socially these animals mix; therefore, there could be "sheep" among the "goats" and "goats" among the "sheep." It seems, based on the judgment scene, that no one knows if she is a sheep or a goat until the moment of separation.

Such shepherd and sheep imagery flashes throughout the Hebrew Bible and the ancient Near East.[78] Literal shepherding is an activity that is associated with great leaders in Israelite history, including Moses and David (Exod. 3:1; 1 Sam. 16:11; 17:15; 17:34–7). David is figuratively called a "shepherd" in his role as king (2 Sam. 5:2). Kingship is so tied with shepherding that the language of "sheep without a shepherd" regularly indicates leaderless or potentially leaderless people (Num. 27:17; 1 Kgs. 22:17; Ezek. 34:8; Zech. 10:2; 3:7). When such people are leaderless – or if they have "bad" shepherds – then sometimes God seeks out his own sheep (Ezek. 34:11–31). Famously, in Psalm 23 (22 LXX), "The LORD is my shepherd," which in the ancient Near Eastern context could be understood as "The LORD is my king." The shepherd/king and sheep/people analogy seems to permeate many societies of the ancient world. The Pharoah's "crook" he holds is a stylized shepherd's staff. Agamemnon is the "shepherd of the people."[79] If one has the examples of Moses and David – as well as the numerous other places shepherding is equated with a king-like leader – then, when applied to Jesus in the gospels, such language will have a royal ring to it.

In Plato's *Republic*, Thrasymachus presents his difficult-to-overturn argument that laws are made for the stronger at the expense of everyone else; that is, the strong define what is justice, and others must follow this, using sheep and cattle analogies: "You [Socrates] think that shepherds and cowherds consider what is good for their sheep and cattle, and fatten them and take care of them with some aim in mind other than what is good for their master and themselves. Moreover, you believe that rulers in cities – true rulers, that is – think about their subjects in a different way than one does about sheep, and that what they consider night and day is something other than what is advantageous for themselves" (*Republic* 343b, trans. Reeve). Thrasymachus thinks

Socrates is wrong, and Socrates struggles to overcome this argument, which takes him the rest of the book to do. Nonetheless, it draws the common view of rulers as shepherds and cowherds and the ruled as sheep and cattle together in the same passage.

Similar to the extensive sheep in-group animalization, Jesus refers to his followers as cattle in one place: "Come to me, all you that are weary and carrying heavy burdens, and I will give you rest. Take my yoke upon you (*arate ton zugon mou eph' humas*), and learn from me; for I am gentle and humble in heart, and you will find rest for your souls. For my yoke is beneficial, and my burden is light (*ho gar zugos mou chrestos kai to phortion mou elephron estin*)" (Matt. 11:28–30 adapted).[80] The Gospel of Thomas has a similar saying: "Come unto me, for my yoke is beneficial, and my lordship is mild, and you will find rest for yourselves" (Thomas 90; translation mine). In this case, his followers are oxen – those who have a yoke for plowing – and Jesus's yoke (that is, Jesus's teachings or "Torah" and obligations he lays upon his disciples)[81] is lighter and more beneficial,[82] though it is still a yoke, and his followers are still cattle. Yet instead of burdens, Jesus offers rest.

In the context of Sabbath disputes that follow (12:1–21), of which one is about saving an animal versus healing a human on the Sabbath (12:9–14), one might recall that the Sabbath rest is for humans and domesticated work animals, such as an ox or a donkey (Exod. 20:8-11; Deut. 5:12–15). Mary Douglas notes that based on this, "Cattle were literally domesticated slaves. They had to be brought into the social order in order to enjoy the blessing. The difference between cattle and the wild beasts is that the wild beasts have no covenant to protect them."[83] While this is not Douglas's immediate point, the result of this is that insiders are compared to animals that are already socialized, even already part of the covenant, receiving the blessings of the Sabbath.

This domesticating in-group animalization of yoking is a common metaphor in ancient Jewish thought – the commandments that God places on his people are the "yoke." In Sirach 51:26, one submits to Wisdom's "yoke"; that is, her teaching, which is Torah (cf. Sir. 6.25–6).[84] Indeed, the word "burden" used here is also used in

Matthew to refer to Pharisaic legal interpretation (Matt. 23:4); thus, Jesus's "yoke" (Jesus's Torah) is lighter than the Pharisaic "burden" (Pharisaic Torah).[85] The text of 2 Enoch 34.1–2 refers to God's commandments as God's yoke; 2 Baruch 41.3–5 further refers to the "yoke" of God's law, equivalent to the covenant itself, which the people have cast off from themselves. A yoke is a sign of submission to someone's rulership; note the symbolic valence of Jeremiah wearing an ox's yoke to symbolize the submission to the yoke of Babylonian hegemony (Jer. 27–8) or that God broke the yoke of slavery (Lev. 26:13). Paul in Galatians 5:1 also refers to the "yoke of slavery" (cf. 1 Tim. 6:1).[86] In Acts 15:10, Peter argues that Gentile converts to the Jesus movement need not be circumcised and keep the law of Moses, asking why those who claim they should (Pharisaic members of the movement) are "placing on the neck of the disciples a yoke that neither our ancestors nor we have been able to bear."[87] Didache 6:2 also refers to bearing the "whole yoke of the Lord," referring now to Christian rules and obligations.[88]

The "animal apocalypse" (1 Enoch 85–90) operates similarly to the gospels by using different kinds of animals to differentiate in-group and out-group, but keeping cattle and sheep – that is, domesticated and kosher animals – for in-group associations. In this apocalypse, Enoch dreams of the history of humanity from Adam to the end of the world as a series of animals. The humans, including Adam to Noah, are all bulls and cows. The "good" lineage through Seth is designated as white, whereas "bad" lineages are black and others – for example, Abel – are red. But the "black bulls" that came from heaven (the fall of the watchers) produced other kinds of animals, such as elephants, camels, and donkeys (out-group). Surprisingly, Noah was born a bull, but becomes a "man" – that is, he rises above animality to humanity, as Peter does as he shifts from sheep to shepherd at the end of John. In this vision, this means that the human Noah became angelified or divinized. After Noah, the true lineage of Israel remains a white bull, but other nations are signified by lions, leopards, wolves, dogs, hyenas, wild boars, foxes, conies, pigs, falcons, vultures, kites, eagles, and ravens.[89] There are also boars and a white ram, which, in turn, begets twelve sheep – the twelve tribes of Israel. From this point on, the Israelites are sheep; the Egyptians are wolves. The "Lord of the sheep" appears to be god, and one of the sheep becomes a "man" (as Noah did); this likely refers to Moses becoming angelified or divinized. Upon entering Canaan, the sheep are surrounded by dogs, wild boars, and foxes (local Canaanite tribes) that seek to devour the sheep (Israelites), but God raises a series of "rams" (Joshua and then any major leader among the Israelites is a "ram") among them to butt heads with the other animal species. God also raises up a total of seventy shepherds for the sheep; most of these shepherds, however, were "bad shepherds." At the end of time, the Lord of the sheep comes back and turns all the sheep back into white cattle. Ultimately, cattle and sheep are God's people, the in-group. All other animals – wild, feral, predatory, or unclean – represent out-group peoples in this apocalyptic dream vision.[90] The gospels follow this same pattern of in-group and out-group animalistic designations that differentiate between domesticated and clean versus wild, feral, and unclean.

Predators and wild and feral animals tend to be out-group, and prey and domesticated animals tend to be in-group. There are exceptions, such as being wise as serpents, but this is the overwhelming tendency. Being sheep or cattle is the sign of true followers who follow their leader and, when leaderless, do not know what to do. They, however, will be rewarded for their sheep-like characteristics. Cattle share Sabbath blessings and, as Mary Douglas reminds us, they are "brought into the social order" already.[91] They are prepackaged "in-group" animals. Even Socrates can wax rhapsodic about how one "should graze freely in the pastures of philosophy" (*Rep.* 498c, trans. Reeve). When one blindly follows one's shepherd, one can be at peace.

WORTH MORE THAN BIRDS: JESUS'S ANTHROPOCENTRISM IN MATTHEW AND LUKE

Beyond using animals to create social identities between human groups, one finds sayings in the gospels that compare humans as a whole with other animals. A few sayings lay bare Jesus's anthropocentrism to a degree that should make many modern eco-apologists uncomfortable, though oddly these same sayings often form a part of their favorite "eco-texts." Most of these sayings work by similar forms of reasoning: from lesser (animals) to greater (humans), especially in Matthew's gospel.

The first operates within the controversial dialogues of the legality of Sabbath healings. Jesus healed a man with the withered hand (Matt. 12:9–14). When asked whether healing on the Sabbath is permitted, Jesus responds, "Suppose one of you has only one sheep and it falls into a pit on the sabbath; will you not lay hold of it and lift it out? How much more valuable is a human than a sheep (*posoi oun diapherei anthropos probatou*)" (12:11–12). Jesus is anthropocentric. Whereas Jesus regularly associates people – his followers or leaderless people – with sheep, here the association of sheep-like characteristics stops. He assumes – does not argue that – human life is much more valuable than a sheep's life. If we are willing to help out a sheep on the Sabbath, how much more should we be willing to help a human being? The same episode in Mark (3:1–6) omits the reference to sheep or any animals for that matter. The point – that one can do good deeds on the Sabbath – can be made without the anthropocentrism found in Matthew's version.

Luke has a different Sabbath healing episode in which a woman has a spirit that has crippled her for eighteen years (Luke 13:10–17). Jesus heals her on the Sabbath, and the leader of the synagogue opposes the healing on the Sabbath – any other day of the week would be just fine. Jesus responds: "You hypocrites! Does not each of you on the sabbath untie his ox or his donkey from the manger (*ou lieu ton boun autou e ton onon apo tes phates*), and lead it away to give it water? And ought not this woman, a daughter of Abraham whom Satan bound for eighteen long years be set free from this bondage on the sabbath day?" (Luke 13:15–16). The logic in this healing is not quite as anthropocentric as Matthew's version, where the question was, if you are willing to do this for an animal, *how much more so* should you be willing to do it for a human being? In Luke, if you are willing to do this for an animal (here give it water), *just so* should you do it for a human being – a daughter of Abraham for that matter.

Another Sabbath-healing controversy occurs in the next chapter (a rare doublet for Luke), in which a man with dropsy comes to Jesus for healing (Luke 14:1–6). Jesus says, "If one of you has a child or an ox (*huios e bous*) that has fallen into a well, will you not immediately pull it out on a sabbath day?" (Luke 14:5). There is a text-critical issue here: some manuscripts read "child" (*huios*); others read "donkey" (*onos*).[92] Scribes likely later substituted the original "child" with "donkey" to conform with the wording of Luke 13:15. No matter how one resolves the text-critical problem here, it is almost exactly the same counterexample given in Matthew: if a living being falls into a well on the Sabbath, you will try to get it out. In Matthew, it just happens to be a sheep; in Luke it is an ox and something else. Nonetheless, Luke still does not follow exactly the same reasoning as Matthew and does not clearly argue that animals are lesser and humans are greater as Matthew does. If, in fact, "child" is correct here, then what matters is not animal versus human, but giving life to those who need it, whether animal or human.

Another example of the animal-to-human argumentation occurs in Matthew's Sermon on the Mount and in Luke's parallels. In the portion about not worrying about basic necessities, Jesus says: "Look at the birds of the sky (*emblepsate eis ta peteina you ouranou*); they neither sow nor reap nor gather into barns, and yet your skyward Father (*ho pater humon ho ouranios*) feeds them. Are you not of more value than they (*ouch humeis mallon diapherete auton*)?" (Matthew 6:26–7). Luke 12:24–6 is very similar, except it refers specifically to ravens (*tous korakas*) and refers to "God" rather than "your skyward father." The switch to ravens recalls Psalm 147:9: "He gives to the animals their food / and to the young ravens when they cry.

This is a favourite text for ecological gospel readings, since it demonstrates God's providential care for all living beings (cf. Job 12:10; 38:39–39:30; Ps. 36:6; 104:19–30; 145:15–16; 147:9).[93] Yet, it is anthropocentric in its lesser-to-greater rhetoric.[94] It may heighten the lesser-to-greater argument, in this case, since ravens – as scavengers – were considered unclean (Lev. 11:15; Deut. 14:14). Nonetheless, "ravens" were one of the birds Noah used alongside doves to check for land when the flood waters were receding (Gen. 8:7). Matthew's version, on the other hand, may bring the birds and God closer together. Unlike the simple ravens of Luke, in Matthew they are the "birds of the sky *(ta peteina you ouranou)*," which could be alternatively translated as "the birds of air/heaven." And God is not simply God as in Luke, but "your heavenly/skyward father" (*ho pater humon ho ouranios*). The air/heaven and heavenly father place both birds and God in the sky/heaven. Overall, however, both Matthew and Luke maintain an anthropocentric assumption that humans are worth more than animals.[95]

Matthew has a similar saying later in the gospel: "Are not two sparrows sold for a penny (*ouchi duo strouthia assariou poleitai*)? Yet not one of them will fall to the ground apart from your Father. And even the hairs of your head are all counted. So do not be afraid; you are of more value than many sparrows (*pollon strouthion diapherete humeis*)" (Matt. 10:29–31). Luke says that five sparrows are worth two pennies, but otherwise has the same material as Matthew (Luke 12:6–7). So, while Luke did not have the same anthropocentric attitude as Matthew in terms of the Sabbath-healing controversy dialogues, here they both are clear: you, human, are far more valuable than animals. If God watches and takes care of even minor or unclean birds (or birds not highly valued by humans),[96] then how much more so will God take care of you?

One final place to consider is when Jesus says, "Foxes have holes and birds of the sky have nests, but the human one has nowhere to lay his head" (Matt. 8:20; cf. Luke 9:57–8; Thomas 86). This is Jesus's response to a scribe (Matthew) or just someone (Luke) willing to follow him. It reflects Jesus's radical itinerancy and also provides a contrast to animals, but in a different manner than the others. Here the human has nowhere to sleep, whereas wild animals do. Jesus's apparent inferiority to the birds of the air – or at least their living conditions – stand in tension with Jesus's statements of human superiority to birds before.

The elision of the "human one" and the animal come together in Jesus's death interpreted as sacrifice. If sacrifice was originally an animal, then Jesus becoming a sacrifice animalizes him. If Jesus's blood is the "blood of the covenant" (Matt. 26:27–8; cf. 20:28), evoking Exodus 24:5–8, then Jesus is being placed in the position of an ox. Of course, he is also the "lamb." At this point, his human/animality slippage blurs into the human/divine slippage in the gospels, as Jesus becomes both slain beast and divine sovereign (see chapter 5).

Jesus is the most anthropocentric in Matthew and Luke and less so in Mark. The most anthropocentric statements occur in Matthew and Luke's shared material (Q). A question remains unresolved: Why would Q be more anthropocentric than Mark?

BECOMING HUMAN THROUGH OTHER ANIMALS

Posthumanism has caused us to go back and rethink what it means to be human. In this sense, Jesus's attitude both relies on and challenges the dichotomy between humans and other animals. They are – as fellow creatures of God – something to compare and contrast with humans; they are used to illustrate qualities within individual and collective humans. Animals are – as Beth Berkowitz has shown in her book on animals in the Talmud – useful to think with, though without the extensive argumentation found in the Talmud.[97] While the gospel animals are off-the-cuff illustrative rather than extensively discussed as in the Talmud, they are still useful to think with to make comparisons between humans and animals and to draw social boundaries between otherwise proximate groups, whether marked by gender, ethnicity, ideology, or a combination of these.

If we read alongside those who work with domesticated animals on a daily basis, such as my students or Jesus's earliest hearers, then we see a pattern emerge. Those who work with domesticated animals develop a level of intimate violence with those animals. The intimacy involves getting animals to mate, assisting their births, feeding them, and securing adequate shelter, yet the violence is one also using them for involuntary labour or facilitating their deaths for food or other products. Other animals, wild or feral, can threaten, impinge on, or agitate this process. In such a context, Jesus says his followers are the sheep or cattle, his opponents are a threat to his cattle, and foreigners are a nuisance to his sheep. One has a sense of safety in the herd of fellow followers, danger outside the herd among ideological serpents, wolves, and foxes, and one can spout contempt on those who might interlope and steal a scrap of food from the table – receiving a blessing and healing even if not belonging to the group.

One can appreciate the immediate source and affective power of animalizations to create and maintain group dynamics, but also how this process becomes deeply problematic. As established, the gospel writers present Jesus as very anthropocentric. While all animals have some level of providential care from God, there is a strong sense of speciesism. With that in place, dehumanization is dangerous. Jesus's dehumanizing language does not lead to violence against others, but historically in other cases it has and it does. Once one dehumanizes someone else – either as a threat or in contempt – then one self-justifies treating them the same way one treats other animals (badly). Ultimately, the Jesus of these gospels does not rise above this fray but participates in broader trends of anthropocentrism and follows its logic.

5

Into Gospel Wilds: Divine, Demonic, and Animal

The God of Israel is the God of the desert. If you want to speak to him, then you'll have to go to the desert.

Be careful, God isn't alone out there.

John the Baptist in *Last Temptation of Christ*, dir. Martin Scorsese[1]

In a tableau diffracted across multiple gospels, a spirit-dove comes on or into Jesus and drives him out into the wild, where he encounters the devil, angels, or other animals. This series of interactions starting along the fluid, transitional space of the river and ending in the wild raises questions about how animals, spirits (holy and unclean), and humans relate in terms of the domesticated, the feral, and the wild.

These tracks of doves, humans, angels, demons, and other animals circle around several thinkers under the sign of posthumanism. Lines of posthumanist thinking have opened up ways of engaging the relationship between humans and other animals and how slippery the categories of "human" and "animal" are. Gilles Deleuze and Félix Guattari, Jacques Derrida, and Donna Haraway among others have become central to rethinking animals, animality, humans, and humanity, and the physical and symbolic interactions among them. These posthumanist paths of divine, demonic, and wild musings intersect at the definitional positionality of the civilized against the wild, the undomesticated against the tame, often with colonizing societies defining themselves as "civilized" and those they colonize as "wild." Such a position is variable: different societies define the wild against themselves in different ways and in multiple ways within the same society. This chapter seeks inspiration among these figures to discuss demonic animality, divine animality, and wild companion species, yet I want to frame the discussion with the work of queer theorist Jack Halberstam.

Beginning with children's books and films, particularly Maurice Sendak's *Where the Wild Things Are*, Jack Halberstam has queered the wild, finding it not just in nature, but also aesthetics, politics, theory, and desire.[2] It is an epistemology of disorderliness. Like queerness, wildness is "a challenge to an assumed order of things that refuse and resist order itself. Wildness names simultaneously a chaotic force of nature, the outside of categorization, unrestrained forms of embodiment, the refusal to submit to social regulation, loss of control, the unpredictable."[3] Halberstam emphasizes that it is not a simple binary; wild is not simply the opposite *of* order, it is an intense opposition *to* order: "wildness is the absence of order, the entropic force of a chaos that constantly spins away from biopolitical attempts to manage life and bodies and desires. Wildness has no goal, no point of liberation that beckons off in the distance, no shape that must be assumed, no outcome that must be desired."[4] It is the embrace of a non-teleological chaos, an ever-shifting existence that has no final form; it is fluid; it is fire. It has no certain future; time is uncertain; all is improvised. The wild dissolves binaries and oppositions; in its non-teleology, it can both repress and liberate, shock and bore. It perpetually becomes. It even threatens the division between wild and domesticated order as it absorbs order within itself.[5] Beyond Halberstam, I will also argue order relies on it, and the wild's destructive potential is a source of order's own renewal.

Halberstam's queer wilding has elements that are ill-fitted for the gospel narratives, such as his emphasis on desire; nonetheless, Halberstam's account has much to offer. To begin, as stated, wildness is not merely a binary opposite of order; it is the opposition to order that dissolves binary oppositions. Halberstam writes, "we must find a way around the treacherous binary logics that set the wild in opposition to the modern, the *civilized*, the cultivated, and the real."[6] While order defines itself against shifting forms of the wild to reinforce order, the wild can destroy order. Wild threats to social order appear in the form of the demonic, wild animals, and even the divine interloping into domesticated spaces. Therefore, stories will often rely on this division to blur it, undermine it, and sometimes reinforce it. We will see this in figures who straddle the line between domesticated and wild, such as the (Holy) Spirit or possessed humans, who become divine-human or demonic-human assemblages. Halberstam further writes, "the wild does not simply name a space of nonhuman animality that must submit to human control; it also questions the hierarchies of being that have been designed to mark and patrol the boundaries between the human and everything else."[7] While Jesus may be driven out into the wild, the wild always already exists around us.

Wildness is contextual. Different societies rely on different models of the distinction between wild and domesticated; therefore, we cannot assume our modern "post-domestic" life will resonate easily with the domesticated era of the gospel accounts and must realize that both our contemporary and the ancient epistemologies of wildness are and were multiple. For example, modern sentimentality around pets and the pet industry do not resonate with gospel stories. Domestic animals appear in the gospels for eating, working, and sacrifice rather than companionship, though domesticated or feral dogs eat scraps from the table (Matt. 15:21–8; Mark 7:24–30). Finally, Halberstam's understanding of zombified life and zombie antihumanism will become pertinent when discussing the dehumanizing impacts of spirit possession.

While reframing using Halberstam's work, this chapter does not leave behind Deleuze and Guattari, Derrida, and Haraway yet draws them into new entanglements, combining those things that tend to be pushed outside of civilization but inextricably intertwined with it: the divine, the demonic, and wild animals. While I will discuss domesticated animals, it is the repeated entanglements of the feral and wild – untamed – and the divine, the demonic, and, to a lesser degree, the angelic that interest me. While wild animals and the divine and demonic realms are untamed and, to some degree, untameable by humans, Jesus – and other special humans – harness and redirect this wild energy to (temporarily) tame the demonic and wild through exorcism. Any lengthy exorcistic account tends to emphasize a lack of humanity or loss of socially accepted behavior from the possessed; they are dehumanized by the demonic just as one could become feral by the animalistic. Let us, therefore, leave domesticated orderliness with its hierarchies and distinctions behind and enter the wild.

This chapter repeatedly returns to the different accounts of Jesus's baptism and temptation on the edges of the wilds and spins its webs out from there into dove-like divine animality with Jacques Derrida, wild animals as companion species with Donna Haraway, and the wild pack of demonic animality assembled with Deleuze and Guattari, and their recurrent queered entanglements with one another.

DIVINANIMALITY BETWEEN DOMESTICATED AND WILD

Most thinking about divinanimality derives from readings of Jacques Derrida's *The Animal That Therefore I Am* and *The Beast and the Sovereign*. While starting with his pet cat staring at his naked body, Derrida springs into a series of meditations into contemporary philosophy from Genesis through Descartes. According to Derrida, the divine and animal share the quality of "ahuman." They represent the "excluded, foreclosed, disavowed, tamed, and sacrificial foundation" of the symbolic order of "the human order, law and justice."[8] Divinanimality is both exterior to and necessary and foundational to order. God, the ultimate sovereign, is the most beastly.[9] Derrida leaves behind actual animals to the figure of animals: the figure of the wolf or the dove.[10] Yet, in *The Animal That Therefore I Am*, Derrida uses the word "tamed" for this referent. Turning to a religious context, "tamed" animals tend to be the norm for sacrifice and consumption through eating, wearing, and working. It is a surprising manoeuvre, since one would expect the divine to transcend this order of eating, wearing, working, and killing. On the one hand, the divinanimal energy is channelled and focused through ritual efforts that become religious, economic, and political mechanisms of a particular society, but behind this channel are vast, untamed entanglements that are not human, not social, not civilized: in a word, wild. By contrast, in *The Beast and the Sovereign*, the untamed wolf becomes the typical referent for the beast and the sovereign. Yet to return to Derrida's phrasing; it is the wild – or its representation or threat – that makes domestication possible; it is, as he says, its "sacrificial foundation." So divinanimality is both the basis for, representation of, and the threat to the domesticated social world.

The ancient world abounds with divine-animalistic confluences. The theriomorphism of Egypt was famous and Zeus could transform into various things, including animals (for example, the swan), though ancient Greek and Roman writers looked down on Egyptian deities rather than Zeus's various guises (Pliny, *Natural History* 2.16). Various deities were associated with and rode on animals, such as Dionysus on a leopard, or the rivalry of southern and northern kingdoms in associating the God of Israel with either a bull or the hybrid beast of a cherub (Exod. 25; 1 Kgs. 6:23–8; 12:25–9; cf. Exod. 32:1–16). Socrates could exclaim "by the dog" (likely Anubis) just as "by Zeus" (*Republic* 399e, 567d, 592a; *Gorgias* 428b5).

In the Hebrew Bible, Ken Stone has noted that domesticated animals provide "positive symbols of care and sustenance," while wild animals were "frightening symbols of danger."[11] Not only does the Hebrew Bible animalize God's care for Israel, who keeps wild animals (Israel's enemies) at bay, but also portrays God as a fierce predator of the divine lion ready to devour Israel (Isa. 31:4; 38:13; Jer. 25:30, 38; 49:19; 50:44; Amos 1:2; 3:4, 8; Hos. 5:15; 11:10; 13:7–8; Joel 3:16 [Hebrew 4:16]; Job 10:16; Lam. 3:10).[12] Turning closer at hand to the gospels, Revelation offers extraordinary examples of divinanimality and demonanimality with Jesus as the beaten, bloodied, yet enthroned lamb who is paradoxically the "lion of Judah" (Rev. 5:5) and has breasts (*mastoi*).[13]

Contrasting these images of divinanimality, the gospels' primary exemplar is the (Holy) Spirit. This spirit frustrates categorization. It is multiformed, fluid, blows where it wants to, is wild and uncontrollable, yet can also appear as a domesticated being fit for sacrifice, disrupting the wild/domesticated binary itself. Much like Derrida's ruminations, the divine animal is both the foundation of tamed and wild; like Halberstam, we must consider the intricate ways wild and domesticated are entangled with one another. An animal fit for sacrifice, a potentially domesticated dove, comes on and possesses Jesus and spurs him into the wild.

First, the spirit is wild. Eco-theologian Jacob Erickson refers to the spirit as "an incarnation of Divine Wilderness."[14] Jesus tells Nicodemus in John 3:8 that the "spirit blows wherever it wants to" (*to pneuma hopou thelei pnei*; my translation). The same word can mean spirit, wind, or breath. The spirit is also "poured out" elsewhere in the Bible (Isa. 44:3–4; Joel 2:28–9; Acts 2:17–18). The spirit, wind, and fire are aligned in Acts 2:2–4. What do the spirit, wind, and fire have in common? Wildness! Uncontrollability, constantly shifting form; without final form, it is nonetheless formative; it can be chaotic, but simultaneously destructive and creative. Elizabeth Johnson writes, "Blowing like wind, flowing like water, flaming like fire, the Spirit of God awakens and enlivens all things."[15] Or Jacob Erickson writes, "The perichoretic movement of the Spirit-breath resists all forms of domestication as it moves, plays, bends, dives, and bursts."[16] Moreover, it doesn't blow in any particular place, where one expects it to, where it is "supposed to"; it blows or blazes wherever it feels like it.[17]

The elemental spirit is associated with water. God's spirit/wind/breath hovers over the waters of creation (Gen. 1:2) and reappears at Jesus's baptismal waters. This animalistic occurrence appears in all three synoptic gospels – and some feral gospels as well. I quote Mark 1:10: "And just as he was coming up out of the water, he saw the skies ripped apart and the spirit descending like a dove on him (*hos peristeran katabainon eis auton*)" (adapted). Immediately, this spirit then drives Jesus out into the wild (*eis ten eremon*): "he was in the wild forty days, tempted by Satan; and he was with the wild beasts (*kai en meta ton therion*); and the angels waited on him" (Mark 1:13 adapted). Matthew and Luke are quick to add that this was the "spirit of God"

(Matthew) or "Holy Spirit" (Luke). They expand the temptation account but remove Mark's references to the wild beasts and the angels tending to Jesus.

The spirit-dove is a "revelation," drawing on the apocalyptic imagery of the "open heaven," when John the Baptist has a vision of the skies being ripped apart *(iden schizomenous tous ouranous)* and the revelation of a divine being (the spirit-dove) (Mark 1:10; cf. Ezekiel 1:1; Rev. 4:1). When bringing Acts 2 into the mix, the (Holy) Spirit is also a mighty wind and can separate into multiple tongues of fire – and perhaps even fluid since it is "poured out" (Acts 2:2–3, 17–18, 33; 10:45). Yet the spirit-dove image is so familiar to Christians today that one does not think about what it could mean that the spirit takes the form of an animal. The dove is perhaps an appropriate animal, since it flies and flying things can – though are not always – be associated with skyward things. Most Christians portray this dove as white, but doves are not always or even primarily white. It is difficult to determine what different gospel authors envisioned.

While the spirit can be associated with fluid wildness, doves or pigeons (*Columba livia*) have a long history of interactions with humans. Likely originating from North Africa and the Mediterranean basin through the Middle East and Central Asia, they are now found throughout the world except Antarctica.[18] From the ancient world to today, they display a range of interactions with humans: some are domesticated, some are "commensal" (non-domesticated but living with humans), and some are wild (like the "rock dove"). Ancient rural Romans kept dovecotes – permanent birdhouses for doves – to keep them around for food and fertilizer.[19] In ancient Israel/Judea, the sacrificial complex demanded that doves be available for use, and, therefore, they were kept for sacrifice and for eating. A large complex at Mareshah was established to raise doves and pigeons on a massive scale by the end of the third century BCE and only stopped being used around the Bar Kokhba Revolt in the second century CE.[20] The dove, therefore, does not only conjure an image of wildness for first-century readers. Doves or pigeons, then as now, could be domesticated, a feral pest, or wild.[21]

Other divine animals in the gospels lean more toward the domesticated, such as the potential "divinanimality" of Jesus himself. In Matthew's screed against the Pharisees, which includes several other animalistic references, Jesus laments: "Jerusalem, Jerusalem, the city that kills the prophets and stones those who are sent to it! How often have I desired to gather your children together as a hen gathers her nestlings under her wings (*hon tropon ornis episunagei ta nossia autes hupo tas pterugas*), and you were not willing" (Matt. 23:37 adapted). Here the metaphor not only crosses species (Jesus as poultry) but also transes gender (Jesus as mother).[22] The Jesus-hen seeks to gather these children-chicks, perhaps shifting from the "lost sheep," but the chicks will not listen, so they are lost. "Nestlings" may be a better – and more accurate – translation of *ta nossia* (cf. Attic: *to neottion*) than "brood" (NRSV), especially to distinguish it from the term used in the same gospel for "brood of vipers" (*gennemata echidnon*), which is something like "those begotten of vipers." This message has a religio-political edge, too, since the "house" or temple will also be forsaken.[23]

Jesus also associates himself with the serpent: "And just as Moses lifted up the serpent in the wild (*kai kathos Moüses hupsosen ton ophin en tei eremoi*), so must the Son of Man be lifted up, that whoever believes in him may have eternal life" (John 3:14–15 adapted; cf. Num. 21:9). We tend to expect serpents to be associated with evil or bad qualities and associate them with outsiders, such as John the Baptist calling his opponents a "begotten of vipers" (Matt. 3:7–10; 12:33–4; 23:33; Luke 3:7–9); but here and elsewhere (Matt. 10:16; P. Oxy. 4009 recto) Jesus refers to wild serpents to refer to the quality of wisdom or prudence, a foreshadowing of his own crucifixion, and to healing and life. In the Numbers story, the people spoke against God, and so the LORD sent poisonous (or fiery) serpents (*seraphim*) that bit the people and many died. The survivors asked Moses to intercede, and the LORD had Moses make a poisonous (or fiery) serpent out of bronze, set it on a pole, and whenever anyone who has been bitten looks at it, that person will live. Jesus, here, associates himself with the bronze serpent. The serpent renews life even as it can take it away. This is an anomalous case, since Jesus identifies with a crafted simulacrum of a wild serpent rather than the serpent itself. There is another subtle shift, moreover, since in Numbers one *looks upon* the serpent and lives; here one *believes in* the serpent and lives.

The Gospel of John entwines Jesus with animality from the start when John the Baptist proclaims: "Look, the lamb of God who takes away the sin of the world! (*ide ho amnos tou theou ho airon ten hamartian tou kosmou*)" (John 1:29; my translation). And again, "Look, here is the Lamb of God! (*ide ho amnos tou theou*)" (1:36; my translation). This ultimately is a reference to the Passover lamb as 19:36 makes explicit: "None of his bones shall be broken." This takes the rules of the Passover lamb in Exodus 12:46 and makes them a prophecy about Jesus's death (cf. Ps. 34:20). Jesus's death is entwined with the Passover lamb's death, which foreshadowed Jesus's sacrifice. While John the Baptist, at first blush, appears to be speaking metaphorically, Jesus's death moves beyond metaphor; it is equivalent to and surpasses the Passover lamb's sacrifice. Jesus is the ultimate lamb. The lamb and Jesus mutually signify one another. This also accounts for the shifts in the death account from the synoptics to having Jesus die on the Day of Preparation, along with all the lambs (19:14; see Josephus, *War* 6.423; Philo, *Spec. Laws* 2.145). From hen to lamb, Jesus's animality is domesticated, and, in the latter, becomes, as Derrida would say, the foundation of the sacrificial order. Yet Jesus-as-serpent disrupts this pattern, a rewilding that threatens and heals simultaneously.

While Jesus's animality has an ordering element, though his serpentine associations bring in the potential of disorderliness that blurs poison and cure, the spirit's dove-like embodiment is, like the wind, more difficult to pin down. The dove is like the Jesus-as-lamb part of the sacrificial order, but doves could be wild, domesticated, or feral. The location of its appearance – the Jordan river in the Judean wilderness – reinforces the indeterminacy. The dove appears in a borderland space that, with John the Baptist, living on the fringes in terms of his camel-hair dress and locust-and-honey diet, symbolizes a wild or de-domesticated space. It hovers at the edges of wandering in the wilderness and dwelling in the land. The divine spirit also flits between wild and domesticated in Isa. 32:15–18, where "a spirit from on high" has the ability to make the wilderness a fruitful field, but also turn a fruitful field into a forest. In both cases, this spirit transforms a place into a lusher environment than before but turns a wild place (the wilderness) into a potentially domesticated place (fruitful field), while turning a domesticated place (field) into a wild place (forest). Such a spirit from on high dances between wilderness and domestication. The spirit-dove diving from on high, likewise, alights at this liquid line in the sand, fluidly, flittingly, flying among the wild and domesticated alike.

It is also not clear what "descending like a dove" (*hos peristeran katabainon*) means. Is it the manner in which the spirit descends that is reminiscent of a dove or did the spirit appear in dove form? That is, how literal is the linkage of spirit and dove? Mark's version is ambiguous, and Edward Dixon has argued – using Homeric and Virgilian parallels – that it is a simile that follows a common mythological topos of the arrivals and departures of gods to and from Olympus in human form. He places great emphasis on Mark's *eis*, that the spirit went "into" Jesus; indeed, a possessed Jesus being driven by the possessing spirit into the wilderness will become significant later.

Nonetheless, while Dixon argues for a commonality between the spirit coming into Jesus and the Greek gods taking human form, in the Greek case the gods take a visible form of whatever they want; in Mark's case, the spirit is coming into an already existing body: Jesus's body.[24] The spirit does not appear as Jesus – as a Greek god appears as a human – but possesses Jesus if it goes "into" him analogously to how other spirits – such as unclean spirits – possess existing human bodies.[25] Moreover, most of these birds Dixon lists from the *Iliad*, *Odyssey*, and *Aeneid* are birds of prey like falcons and eagles – even a "dove-slaying falcon" (*Iliad* 15.237–8) – or generic "birds" rather than something like a dove.[26] The distinction is important, at least in the history of interpretation of food laws, since the tannaitic Rabbis declared that predatory birds are unclean (*m. Hul.* 3:6), whereas a dove is clean for both consumption and sacrifice.[27] Dixon is likely correct, however, that the bird simile is not to be taken completely literally for Mark. It describes the *manner* of its movement rather than its *form*.[28]

Dixon may be correct about Mark, but neither Matthew nor Luke understood it as a simile. Matthew notes that the spirit-dove descended and added that it "came upon him" (*katabainon hosei peristeran kai erchomenon ep' auton*; Matt. 3:16). The coming upon is sometimes translated as "alight," which takes the dove analogy into account, but literalizes it in the process. If "alight" is a correct rendering, this movement seems less likely if the spirit was anthropomorphic; if it was a simile, it is becoming extended in Matthew's usage. The language of "coming upon," however, does more work for Matthew, because it aligns Jesus more clearly with the Hebrew Bible and second temple Jewish traditions. In the Hebrew Bible and the Septuagint, the spirit regularly "comes upon" chosen leaders, though not necessarily with the sense that it is bird-like (Judg. 3:10; 6:34; 11:29; 13:25; 1 Sam. 10:6; 11:6; 19:20; cf. Num. 24:2).[29] In Isaiah 11:2 Septuagint, the spirit will "rest upon" the future Davidic king. God will also put his spirit upon his servant (Isa. 42:1; cf. 61:1). In *Testament of Levi* 18:7, the "spirit of understanding and sanctification" will rest on the messianic priest (cf. *T. Jud.* 24:2). These passages, like Matthew, tend to prefer *epi* (upon) instead of Mark's *eis* (into).[30] Mark's passage suggests possession; Matthew's connects Jesus to the tradition of the Judges. Dixon, however, is correct that neither Mark nor Matthew clearly presents the spirit's descent as a literal, embodied bird. But the connection of the descent and coming upon / resting upon with Mark's bird simile begins to empty the simile of its metaphorical nature, increasing its literalness.

Luke, however, removes all ambiguity, saying "and the holy spirit descended upon him in bodily form like a dove" (*katabenai to pneuma to hagion somatikoi eidei hos peristeran ep auton*; Luke 3:22). Whether the spirit merely looked like a dove or moved like a dove in Mark, in Luke it is embodied as a dove: "in bodily form (*somatkoi eidei*)." Indeed, Dixon fails to mention all the times that the gods do appear in animal form. Zeus does not just descend like an eagle, but sometimes appears *as* an eagle, or a swan, or a bull, and so on, or as rain or other forces of nature – like the Holy Spirit does! Luke, however, is unique in this clarity; Fitzmyer refers to the addition of "in bodily form" as a "characteristically Lucan feature."[31] So why make the dove embodied? Does Luke have an obsession with spiritual embodiment? Again, Fitzmyer suggests: yes! He indicates that elsewhere the gospel tries to make extraordinary realities tangible; it is, recall, the only gospel that has the post-resurrection Jesus explicitly eat (Luke 24:41).[32]

Finally, John 1:32, while omitting Jesus's actual baptism and any temptation narrative, retains the spirit-dove's descent: "I [John the Baptist] saw the Spirit descending from the sky like a dove, and it remained on him" (adapted). In this way, John remains closer to Matthew and less to Luke, as the spirit alights upon and remains.

The Holy Spirit, the spirit, or God's spirit does not have recurrent bird-like features in the biblical tradition before this. It hovers over the waters of creation like a bird (Gen. 1:2; cf. Deut. 32:11). Like Mark, the manner in which the spirit hovers over the waters of creation is birdlike but without the form of a bird. Doves themselves have significance in the biblical tradition, but not as forms or movements of the divine. Two of the three birds Noah sent out from the ark were doves – the other was a raven (Gen. 8:6–12). Other than the doves that Noah used (Gen. 8:10–12), it is unclear what existing significance that dove would have had at this point. Unlike a raven, the dove is a clean animal and can be used in sacrifice. Only one post-biblical Jewish tradition associates the spirit's descent with a dove: Babylonian Talmud, Tractate Hagigah 15a. Yet this isolated instance is fairly late to be helpful to reading the canonized gospels. The biblical traditions, however, draw on a larger reservoir of ancient Near Eastern and Eastern Mediterranean traditions, which, in turn, represent female deities of love and war with doves in their iconography, including Ishtar, Astarte, Anat, and Aphrodite, though this would be a more distant echo for the gospels.[33] By contrast, birds can also be compared to Satan in the gospels (Mark 4:3–4, 14–15; cf. Matt. 13:3–4, 19; Luke 8:5, 11–12).

The Proto-Gospel of James presents the pre-pubescent Mary living in the temple of the Lord, where she was cared for like a dove, being fed from the hand of an angel (8.1). A dove is also central in the selection of Joseph as her husband as she approached menarche (9.1; cf. Pseudo-Matthew 12:1–2). In these cases, Mary is like a dove or a dove becomes the sign – perhaps signalling the divine presence – of the providential choice of Mary's life partner. Miller, reflecting on ancient Christian dove imagery, writes that the dove became "an enduring Christian emblem of the avian complex of air, freedom, and liberation ever since the Gospels pictured the Holy Spirit descending upon Jesus at his baptism in the form of a dove."[34] The spirit-dove hovers between wind and water, domesticated and wild, yet drives those it possesses to where the wild things are.

WILD COMPANION SPECIES

In the narrative space between baptism and temptation, the spirit-dove – whether possessing or coming upon Jesus – drives Jesus into the wilds. While Matthew and Luke focus on Satan being there, Mark briefly glimpses something broader:

> He was in the wild forty days, tempted by Satan;
> and he was with the wild beasts (*kai en meta ton therion*);
> and the angels waited on him. (Mark 1:13 adapted)

Mark is the only author who mentions wild beasts. Due to our familiarity with Matthew's and Luke's versions, we expect Satan, but not wild beasts or angels. But if you go out into the wild, you will likely encounter beasts. What ties them all together?

In multiple publications, Donna Haraway has spoken of "companion species." She looks at animals not only as categories to think with but as micro-relationships – *sympoiesis* of being- and becoming-with;[35] all animals and living things, including bacteria and plants, are "companion species" of some sort. She writes: "Companion species are relentlessly becoming-with … In human-animal worlds, companion species are ordinary beings-in-encounter in the house, lab, field, zoo, park, truck, office, prison, ranch, arena, village, human hospital, forest, slaughterhouse, estuary, vet clinic, lake, stadium, barn, wildlife preserve, farm, ocean canyon, city streets, factory, and more."[36] Hers is a world of "com- / cum-" or "sym-": it is always "with." She describes her work as "compost" – that is "making" and "unmaking" "with": composing and decomposing all at once with companion (*cum panis*) animals (from microbes to dogs to feral pigeons to spiders) coming together at the table.[37] It is not only "thinking with" animals as categories, but "becoming with" them; living with specific animals and finding the webs of relationships that we spin together with our own and other species.[38]

Haraway has largely illustrated this "becoming with" of companion species with regard to her dog, Cayenne. Halberstam has responded to this primacy of pets in our society, and in theorizing, as their zombification.[39] While zombified life will become important later, I think Haraway partly withstands Halberstam's critique: her list includes domesticated life in various forms as well as wild and those that straddle the two. What does it mean, though, to think of wild animals as companion species rather than a cat (Derrida) or a dog (Haraway)? What might it mean to be "with the wild animals"? Others, such as Terry O'Connor, have introduced the term "neighbour species" to discuss non-domesticated animals that have come to inhabit spaces made by humans, including birds, vermin, urban foxes, and raccoons, among many others.[40] Timothy Morton uses such a term for cats alongside bees.[41] Drawing on O'Connor, Josh Milburn uses this term to refer to non-domesticated animals within human environments to whom we have an ethical responsibility.[42] I am not sure this alternative terminology is necessary. While I will turn to wild animals that occupy domesticated spaces, I also want to discuss how humans go out into their habitats, as Jesus does. Put into Haraway's terms, both places – domesticated spaces and wild spaces – can be "contact zones" for wild animal-human entanglements.[43] Moreover, while it is true Haraway's primary example is her dog, she includes microbes, bacteria, and a wide range of other domesticated, feral, and wild species that are not easily categorized as "intimate" with humans, but with which we are continually entangled in our becoming. That is why she uses the terminology of "companion species" instead of "companion animal."[44] So I want to keep the "with" of Haraway's analysis, while also considering some criticisms of her concepts, so we can think through how one can "be *with* the wild animals."

Focusing on Jesus's "being-with" the wild animals, Richard Bauckham suggests the "ecotopia" of Isaiah 11 is key to understanding this.[45] In this passage, the "spirit" of God rests on the "shoot" that comes from the "stump of Jesse." Moreover,

> the wolf shall live with the lamb,
> the leopard shall lie down with the kid,
> the calf and the lion and the fatling together,
> and a little child shall lead them. (Isa. 11:6)

In the kingdom of God, the wild predator and the domesticated prey will live in harmony. It happens not by the socialized becoming wild, but by folding the wild into the socialized, which is why a "child shall lead them." The wild becomes part of the domesticated, socialized world. As Bauckham puts it, wild animals – particularly the predators – are the "enemies of whom Jesus makes friends."[46] Bauckham sees Mark 1:13 as a foretaste of the Isaianic ecotopia. One may also suggest that Mark 1:13 – as well as Isaiah 11 – envisions a return to Edenic conditions.[47]

This is a possible reading, but a child is hardly a symbol of civilization; in fact, Halberstam rereads Derrida's divinanimality by including the child alongside the divine and the animal as part of the forces of the wild rather than the domesticated.[48] The child is the not-yet-domesticated and, therefore, provides an intermediary between the domesticated and the wild. The child is, however, perceived as vulnerable.

While Bauckham's reading is a possibility, it is fruitful to compare this episode with the other wild animals in the gospel accounts, especially Mark. On the one hand, there are ways in which it is difficult to think of wild animals as companions in Haraway's sense. The wild, wildness, and wild animals usually signal danger to socialized human beings. They stand outside of society and culture. Mary Douglas, for example, notes that in the biblical tradition, cattle and domesticated animals enjoy the blessings of the covenant, especially Sabbath rest and fertility, and "they had to be brought into the social order in order to enjoy the blessing."[49] On the other hand, "the wild beasts have no covenant to protect them." Douglas is partly correct; the Mosaic covenant that guarantees rest only extends to the domestic sphere (Exod. 23:12); God's covenant with Noah extends to all animals, whether domestic or wild (Gen. 9:10, 12, 16). Nonetheless, the same covenant creates a distance between humans and animals, even as they had existed briefly as companions on the ark (9:2). Hosea 2:8, similarly, envisions a future covenant between God and wild animals.

While there are alliances between God and animals, they remain, however, outside of the socialized order. Wild things punctuate, puncture, and disrupt the daily rhythms of domesticated life, imposing on it. Like God, like the demons, and like the angels, wild animals stand apart from and potentially threaten to disrupt daily life.

Wild companion species, therefore, pop in and out of the various gospel stories. Most birds – other than chickens and some doves – would have been considered in some way wild. Snakes and vipers, foxes, wolves, and vultures all appear in the gospels as potentially opportunistic or threatening scavengers and hunters. Fish that one eats would have been wild. The Gospel of Thomas plays on the wild birds and fish, who live in the sky and sea respectively, to argue that the kingdom is neither in the sky or the sea, since, if it were, the birds and fish would precede you (human beings); rather, it is inside of you (Thomas 3). Gospel wild animals have natural comforts: foxes have holes, birds have nests, but the son of humanity has nowhere to place his head (Matt. 8:20; Luke 9:58; cf. Thomas 86). Jesus's itinerant lifestyle is even more wild than the wild animals, who at least have stable homes. Or, for example, Jesus says, "Where the corpse is, there the vultures will gather" (Luke 17:37; Matt. 24:28). In this case, a simple reference to the scavenging activities of vultures is a metaphor for divine judgment on the day when the Son of Man will be revealed. Is God a vulture or just God's judgment? Even so, vultures are part of everyday life when there is something to scavenge.

The gospels, therefore, portray humans within proximity to wild animals in daily life, not just as a threat or as beings who have commonalities with human companions, seeking food and shelter, but as entangled in mundane life. As the animal rights theorists Donaldson and Kymlicka write, "wild animals live all around us, in our homes and cities, airways, and watersheds."[50] They are not "out there" apart from us. As Jesus is in the beginning of the narrative, humans are "with the wild animals" throughout, entangling human-made spaces with wild animals and wild spaces with human animals.

BECOMING-ANIMAL, BECOMING-DEMON, AND ZOMBIE ANTI-HUMANISM

Mark entangles wild animals with unclean and holy spirits, heightening the wildness and highlighting entities typically outside of human control. The spirit, Satan, wild beasts, and angels: these are all beings who exist outside of the socialized human order, but who alternately threaten, energize, or simply and mundanely encroach on that order when seeking food and shelter. Moreover, the wild is a contact zone where good and evil spirits meet along with wild animals. As one can find already in Isaiah 34:14, wildcats, goat demons, hyenas, and Lilith all brush by each other in wastelands. The wild is both a part of yet apart from the domesticated world. And, in the following gospel narratives, this wild energy breaks through and threatens domesticated life through demonically induced diseases, healings, spirit (demonic and divine) possessions, and exorcisms.

The connection between the quotidian yet threatening wild, the demonic, and one's power to control them shows up in otherwise weird ways in the gospels, but understanding their entanglements clarifies these passages. For example, Jesus says elsewhere,

> See, I have given you authority to tread on snakes and scorpions and over all the power of the enemy; and nothing will hurt you. (Luke 10:19)

> And these signs will accompany those who believe: by using my name they will cast out demons; they will speak in new tongues; they will pick up snakes in their hands, and if they drink any deadly thing, it will not hurt them: they will lay their hands on the sick, and they will recover. (Mark 16:17–18)

The extraordinariness of these passages is in controlling things that are uncontrollable, a power beyond the domestic. Luke's version links treading on snakes and scorpions (venomous animals that a good parent would never feed or give their child!) with power over the enemy, the enemy being Satan and demonic forces. Mark, likewise, links the ability to encounter deadly snakes with power over demons, speaking in tongues, drinking poison, and healing the sick. What connects these things? The demonic, the ability to heal and exorcise, wild animals, and venom? Again, the Isaianic ecotopia may lurk behind these passages. Note especially Isaiah 11:8: "The nursing child shall play over the hole of an asp, / and the weaned child shall put its hand on the adder's den." Here even the serpent will not harm the most vulnerable of humans. Yet again, as Halberstam has pointed out, the child stands against the civilized, adult world. The child is not (yet) socialized, not (yet) tamed.[51] In some ways, children stand in tension between dangerous and vulnerable; in other ways, they have an epistemological kinship of entities that exist along the edges of socialization. Yet children do not play a part in these animal accounts in the gospels as they do in the Isaianic ecotopia. More to the point, there is no ecological harmony in these gospel passages either; instead, the humans threaten the wild animals rather than the other way around, an inversion.

I would like to recontextualize the serpents and scorpions the way Luke and Mark do: with demonic possession. Jesus gives his followers authority over the forces beyond human life that potentially endanger that life and, otherwise, would normally be beyond human control. These forces can possess, debilitate, and kill. Jesus allows one to exorcise, heal, and not be harmed.

In this case, our interlocutors will be Deleuze and Guattari's discussion of animality and Jack Halberstam's zombie anti-humanism. Unlike Derrida and his pet cat, Deleuze and Guattari prefer the wild pack of wolves, though they sometimes may think of the collective wolf.[52] One may recall they differentiated between three types of animals: (1) sentimental, regressive, individual animals of much of the pet industry; (2) paradigmatic or mythic animals; and (3) demonic pack animals that are always a multiplicity.[53] The sentimental animals have been central to much animal studies theorizing, including Derrida's cat and Haraway's dog. These, for the most part, do not play a part in the gospel tales. Paradigmatic and mythic animals find a place in Jesus's parables and aphorisms. But for this case, it is significant that Deleuze and Guattari align the wild multiplicity of animals with the demonic: after all, they observe, "Beelzebub is the Devil, but the Devil is lord of the flies."[54] They even allude to the episode of the Gerasene demoniac about to be discussed: "what interests us are modes of expansion, propagation, occupation, contagion, peopling. *I am legion*."[55] So Derrida aligns the animal with the divine; Deleuze and Guattari, swarms or packs of wild animals with the demonic. One does not become part of the pack, what they call "becoming-animal," by filiation or heredity, though, but by contagion; I would add possession to this list. They also note that animals become rhizomatic in pack form, in their assemblages.[56]

Keeping this multiplicity in mind, something else that combines venomous serpents and scorpions, drinking poison, and the demonic register is the specter of death and, even, the undead. When situating demon possession among wild things, Halberstam's concept of zombie anti-humanism is relevant for the demonic dehumanization we see in the gospel accounts. Like Legion, zombies' power lies in numbers.[57] Wildness does not only seek to dissolve the binaries imposed by domesticated orderliness by invading that order through unbounded and uncontrollable vitality – like weediness – but also the chaos of death: "As much as wildness speaks of life, liveliness, dynamism, vitality, and excess, it also raises the specter of death."[58] Moreover, as mentioned, for Deleuze and Guattari, the demonic "becoming-animal" occurs not by filiation or heredity, but by contagion and occupation, and so does zombified life.[59]

Zombification is Halberstam's critique of a streak within humanism and posthumanism that brings the co-evolution of different animal lives – and all wildness – into the "economy of voracious human consumption."[60] Zombification is the cultivation of life as human prostheses and dependence in modern capitalist appetites. Coming from the Haitian word "zombi," meaning "spirit of the dead," the word emerged in the conditions of slavery with the fear of being re-enslaved after one's death. It evolved through filmic traditions to be a threat to white order, always containing a residue of its racialized origins.[61] Even given its specific modern trajectory, if we think of zombification as the fading of the boundary between the domestic and the wild, the creation of a category between life and death, and as a form of objectification that is a "living death," as Halberstam has described modern zombification, then, when placed alongside the wolf pack of the demonic, it seems a partly fitting conversation partner for possession.[62] It is such a zombified life – rather than the fully wild – against which non-zombified humans "insist on our own humanity."[63]

Looking at the Hebrew Bible, Ken Stone has noted the entwinement of the desolation of cities, rewilding of those cities with wild animals, and potential demonic presences, including Lilith and "goat creatures" in Isaiah 13 and 34, both of which blur "the line between real animals and mythical creatures."[64] In this case, instead of a possession, wild animals and evil presences haunt particular places, as the wild encroaches on and threatens the domesticated, turning cities into a wilderness.[65]

While demon possession and exorcism recur frequently in the gospels, there are few actual exorcisms. While Mark mentions exorcism throughout (3:15; 3:22–30; 6:7; 9:38–41; 16:9; 16:17), Mark records only four exorcism accounts. There are two extensive exorcisms: the Gerasene demoniac (Mark 5:1–20; cf. Matt. 8:28–34; Luke 8:26–39) and the epileptic boy (Mark 9:14–29; cf. Matt. 17:14–21; Luke 9:37–42). The other two in Mark include an exorcism in a synagogue (1:21–8), which has little comment, and the Syrophoenician woman's daughter (7:24–30), in which one never actually meets the daughter – it is a "distance" miracle. The story of the Gerasene demoniac, however, is one of the most descriptive scenes in Mark and Luke (Matthew makes it a much shorter story and doubles the number of demoniacs). The level of description slows down the narrative and draws the reader in.

Focusing on Mark and Luke, I will follow Mark and note where Luke makes significant alterations for the present discussion.[66] As noted, Mark offers a higher level of description in this narrative than in the rest of that gospel. The set-up to the confrontation between Jesus and the demon(s) inside the man includes several nouns that capture the scene. After Jesus steps out of the boat, the word "tombs" shows up three times, "chain" or "chains" three times, "shackles" once, "stones" once, and "mountains" once. The scene has been set. The excess of description – at least for Mark – and the repetition of terms, especially tombs and chains, is reminiscent of what Halberstam says of the wild as "monstrous, excess" yet also "extravagance, freedom, unspeakable desires, death, life and illegible territories in between."[67] The man lives along the edges of civilization and culture, also along the edges of the living and the dead. In this way, he exemplifies "zombie anti-humanism," by collapsing distinctions between life and death, present and future, and, therefore, the hierarchies that sustain society.[68] While Luke limits the number of nouns in the opening scene (one sees "tombs" and "chains" only once each, for example), Luke otherwise emphasizes this outsider situation, noting that not only did he live among the tombs, but he also did *not* live in a house (Luke 8:27). He dwells solely among the dead. Moreover, he is clothed in broken chains and shackles. He is desocialized; he is feral. That his demonization, which is also a desocialization, is also a dehumanization is further suggested by the verb usage.

Mark's verbs are violent: the possessed man "wrenched apart" and "broke in pieces" the chains and shackles; he could not be "restrained." He has nonhuman strength. The possessed man is also "always howling" and "bruising himself." The word translated here as "howl" is *krazo*, which can mean a human cry but is more of a scream, a howl, an expression beyond intelligible, translatable social speech. It also has animalistic overtones, used in post-Homeric Greek for the "croak" of ravens and frogs.[69] Halberstam notes, regarding the feral, "the feral, indeed, is situated beyond human language."[70] While Halberstam reframes feral expression in terms of sex and desire, here it is a death drive, almost one of a wounding. This super-strong feral man screams, screeches, or bawls in unintelligible sounds. Luke further emphasizes his desocialized, dehumanized, and feral state, since he adds that he had not worn clothes for a long time (Luke 8:27). While Luke omits the mountain, he notes that the man would break his bonds and the demon would drive him "into the wilds" (*eis tas eremous*).

This unnamed man is an inverse mirror of Jesus. A spirit possesses both Jesus (in Mark) and the man. The (Holy) Spirit drives Jesus into the wilderness, where he meets the devil, and in Mark also the wild animals and angels. Similarly, a demon pushes the man into the wilds. The wilds or wilderness (or desert) is the place of the uncanny, the nonhuman and non-socialized, where spirits, holy and unholy, and feral and wild animals dwell. Spirit possession has become entwined with desocialization, dehumanization, and animalization. These elements cannot be fully unravelled; they are entangled.

Act 2 of this scene is the actual exorcism, which I will return to shortly. Act 3 is the man's reintegration into society. In this, the people find the formerly possessed man "clothed and in his right mind." While Mark did not emphasize the man's nakedness earlier as Luke did, he now retroactively indicates it by remarking that the man is now "clothed," having his human faculties restored to him. The demon leaves, and the man re-enters a socialized status: he wears clothes; he is "in his right mind." Presumably, he would stop hanging out around tombs and return to a house. While the people begin to fear Jesus and ask him to leave, the formerly possessed man begs to accompany Jesus, and the man proclaims what Jesus has done for him in the Decapolis.

In acts 1 and 3, we see the relationship between demon possession and animalization (and not just any animalization but feral animalization) alongside desocialization. Act 2 highlights the relationship between demonanimality and animality. In the confrontation between Jesus and the demon, one learns that the name of the demon is "Legion; for we are many" (Mark 5:9). Deleuze and Guattari emphasized that the animalistic demonic is many, a swarm or a pack. They write, "a becoming-animal always involves a pack, a band, a population, a peopling, in short, a multiplicity."[71] Like their rhizome, Legion swarms as multiplicity in unity. Likewise, for Halberstam, the subversive power of zombies is in their multiplicity.

In Mark, Legion begs not to be sent out of the country; in Luke, Legion begs not to be sent back into the abyss (Luke 8:31). Instead, they ask Jesus to send them into a herd of swine, Jesus permits them to do so, and the swine rush down a bank and drown in the sea, a simulacrum of an abyss. Mark says about two thousand pigs died; Luke omits the number. It is a double possession, then: possessing the human and then the pigs. The "becoming-animal" of both the human by the demons and the demons themselves as they enter the pigs occurs, as Deleuze and Guattari would say, by occupation, even infection, rather than by filiation and heredity.[72] It is a multiplicity that becomes another multiplicity. After the demons turn a man into a feral animal, they possess domesticated animals. The monstrous threat, thereby, has been named, domesticated, and neutralized. Halberstam writes, "we have fashioned monsters to embody what we cannot name, to frame what we have come to fear, and to banish what we cannot tolerate."[73] Demon possession and exorcism, together, embody the monsters both conjured and banished.

There have been post-colonial and anti-imperial readings of this episode, since the demon uses the name of "Legion," a contingent of the Roman army, which would have been occupying the land at the time. Fittingly, the Legion X Fretensis was involved in fighting Jewish insurgents during the Jewish War and its insignia was a boar.[74]

Perhaps kosher readers and hearers of this story would get a laugh from the fairly Roman demon(s) being degraded to possess an unclean animal and promptly dying.

Additionally, the destruction of the pigs has proven a sticking point for ecological readings. Ecological readers remark on how pigs are the most intelligent of all animals humans eat.[75] Critics from the philosopher Peter Singer to the biblical studies scholar Hector Avalos have remarked on Jesus's indifference to nonhuman life and the unnecessary suffering these pigs underwent.[76] Indeed, Jesus's attitude towards pigs mirrors that towards dogs: they are unclean and unworthy (Matt. 7:6). Even Richard Bauckham, who sees Jesus as eco-friendly, has trouble with this passage, seeing it as evidence that the world remains unharmonious and unredeemed even as Jesus tries to usher in harmony and redemption.[77]

Beyond post-colonial and ecological readings, something else is happening here; there is, first, a resonance between the uncleanness of the animals (pigs) and the uncleanness of the spirits (demons). As such, alongside post-colonial understandings, one should not be surprised from a zombified perspective that the demonic and the animal are both situated in terms of their foreignness, since Jesus is in a Gentile city and pigs were a Gentile food. Jesus sends the foreign, invading demons into foreign pigs within a foreign city. Moreover, the possession itself also signifies the threat of the dissolution of the boundary between civilized and wild, human and demonic, domesticated and feral, and even living and dead. The exorcism, however, temporarily neutralizes this threat.

What happens to the demons mirrors and inverts what happens to the man. The demons do not enter wild boars, but domesticated pigs. As the man leaves his demonically feral animal state and returns to domesticated order, the demons shift from their wild status and are transferred into domesticated animals. He is restored to life; they return to the abyss and forces of death. Losing their freedom, their wildness, though, the demons choose extinction. The zombified threat of feral and wildness has been tamed, domesticated by a spirit-possessed Jesus who was also driven into the wilds.

ENTANGLING THE DIVINE, THE DEMONIC, AND THE WILD

God is of the wilds, but God is not alone out there; the wild is not just a place, but a condition, an epistemology of the extraordinary, the untamed, the fantastic, the monstrous, the mysterious, and the unknown. The Greek term for "wild animal" is *to therion*, the same term used for "monsters," facilitating the slippage from "wild beasts" to "monstrous beasts."[78] In Haraway's terms, it is a "contact zone" between humans, wild animals, God, the devil, angels, and demons. It is undomesticated by definition, but the domestic cannot exist without it; the domestic needs it to define itself. Yet, the wild is not just the opposite of domestic, but opposes the domestic. It seeks to dissolve the domestic into itself. It impinges upon, infiltrates, and ultimately becomes entangled with domesticated daily life as the wild and the domesticated interact and interrupt one another in mundane, dangerous, surprising, and uncanny ways such as spirit possession and exorcism, demon-induced disease and healing, and, therefore, becomes the source of extraordinary, fearful, awe-inspiring energies.

The spirit hovers between domesticated, feral, and wild, appearing as a potentially domesticated dove, yet possesses and drives one into the wild. Wild animals become entangled in one's daily life and in extraordinary moments of life, necessary for our mutual becoming, as they come into the domesticated contact zones and we go out to wild contact zones. The demonic causes more unease. As societies seek order by domesticating and taming the wild, possession returns the domestic back into the feral; it is the wild turning the domestic (back?) into itself. It flagrantly dehumanizes, zombifies, and makes one feral, living on the borderlands of life and death, domestic and wild/foreign.

The gospel wilds may be the populated demons, the devil, the (Holy) Spirit, and other beasts, but thinkers from Derrida to Halberstam are correct to note that the wild is the founding condition of the domestic, and that to which the domesticated must repeatedly return and face its potential dissolution, renewal, or transformation.

6

Reshaping Gospel Animality in the Filmic Imagination: *Son of Man*

As the opening titles roll on a blank screen at the beginning of Mark Dornford-May's film *Son of Man*, one hears sea birds. The first shot is a close-up of a locust, which we briefly hear. Then we meet Jesus: black, bald, and clean-shaven. He wears white with a blue stripe with his skin covered in white clay. He holds a reed. We also see Satan: a black man with a serpent tattoo on his face; he wears black pants and a black trench coat with a red t-shirt. He holds a sceptre of a crooked goat's leg and foot. Much has been made of this opening scene as a dislocated temptation narrative that is resumed later in the film, setting the parameters of the film in terms of magical realism, framing what follows within the cosmic struggle between good and evil.[1] Indeed! But what of the locust, the serpent tattoo, the goat foot, and the birds? What is the role, significance, or meaning of these animals within the texture and interplay of text, image, and sound?

In this final reflection on animals and animality in the gospels, I spin out some of the ways filmic retellings of the (mostly) domesticated gospels have filled in gaps, relied on, adapted, and transformed the animals and animality of the ancient gospels, focusing primarily, but not exclusively, on Dornford-May's *Son of Man*.

Film intensifies the tensions of animal absences and presences in the gospels discussed in the introduction. Filmmakers must make an audio-visual decision about whether and how to fill in the narrative gaps of missing animals or to augment the narrative in new ways with animals, continuing the tradition started in the earliest feral gospels, such as the Proto-Gospel of James.[2] One could exclude animals completely, but this may accentuate the gospel absence, especially if the filmmaker removes animals in those rare occasions when the gospels draw attention to their presence. Filmmakers may seek to create an aura of verisimilitude to the filmic account by adding animals that we imagine to be present in the ancient gospel accounts (having Mary ride a donkey; having the Magi ride camels) but can also activate and undermine certain evaluative codes, using animals as symbols for divisions among humans, demons, and angels.

Mark Dornford-May's film *Son of Man* (2006) brings these evaluative codes into focus. Filmed in South Africa, *Son of Man* is set in modern-day Judea, Afrika.[3] Though the film is better known for sound editing and music, among his many uses of animals in this film Dornford-May uses animals and animality in socially and spiritually significant ways, particularly to demarcate corrupt political figures under Satan's influence from those who seek justice.

Given the increased complexity of image and sound, the entanglements of human and nonhuman animals likewise become complex. On the one hand, the filmic urgency of representation in image and sound is to fill in gaps with animals, reintegrating animals as a part of daily life for Jesus and his interactions with others. In this way, the film represents social circumstances of humans brushing up against wild, feral, and domesticated animals throughout the film through insects, birds, dogs, and cattle. In the film, humans use animals for food, work, and clothing, though not for sacrifice. On the other hand, building on the discussion in chapter 5, one finds a dominant strain of demonic, more precisely satanic, animality throughout. What is startling in this film is that, even with abundant quotidian animal presences, Satan's presence is indicated by singular animals throughout in a way that Jesus's presence is not. Given Deleuze and Guattari's concept of demon animal packs, it is surprising to see demon animality here reduced to singularity and anomaly, though Deleuze and Guattari were also interested in the anomalous. Here it is the exceptional demon animal that captures attention: Satan himself. But if animals are repeatedly, though not exclusively, associated with Satan's presence throughout the film and not Jesus's or angelic presences, then what message is the film sending about animals and animality? At the end of the film, there is an emphasis on all humans being made in the divine image and, in the context of a film that undermines racist retellings of the gospels and the film's own South African context, it is an important message. It is, however, from an animal studies perspective an unsettlingly anthropocentric one that excludes nonhuman animals, who are left out of God's image at best or aligned with Satan at worst.

SATANIC ANIMALITY

Bringing this film into dialogue with previous chapters, Deleuze and Guattari would seem to be the most resonant conversation partners. Their demonic animality of the pack that even refers to Beelzebub the Lord of the Flies, something this movie seems to dwell on as well, however, does not quite resonate. Satan is not part of a pack, though he can incite a mob; he is a lone wolf. One may be tempted to turn to Derrida's work on divinanimality, and, I think, there may be much to say here. But one must make a shift: it is the inversion of divine animality but follows much of the same basic patterns.

Like God, both Satan and the animal in the film can represent the "excluded, foreclosed, disavowed, tamed, and sacrificial foundation" of the symbolic order of "the human order, law and justice."[4] If this is Satan's world, then Satan is its sovereign; as its sovereign, he stands outside the law, as does the animal, while also shaping the actions of those in charge. Satan also attracts animal symbols more than any other figure in the film. As with the previous chapter, I object to the word "tamed." Satan is not completely tame in this film, though not wild either. Jesus knocks him down a sand dune at the beginning of the film, indicating that Satan may no longer have as much free rein. He is, perhaps, wounded. But Satan is the force that interacts with and guides the local powers that be: Caiaphas and Annas. He shapes the violent actions of the film and sets up the sacrificial foundation for the local state: state-sponsored violence against innocent children at the beginning and Jesus at the end. This violence is the foundation of law, but *without* justice.

Son of Man's prologue prefigures the temptation narrative, here reimagined as a Xhosa rite of adult circumcision,[5] before circling back to Mary's pregnancy. We begin with non-synchronous sounds of birds, a close-up and sound of a locust, Satan's serpent tattoo, and finally his goat-hoof staff. This sequence signals to the viewer that animals in this film will play a symbolic role and one should pay attention when they appear.[6]

As stated, most of the animal sounds and sights in the prologue surround Satan throughout the film. They signal Satanic influence – or that something bad is about to happen – and accompany Satan's two kinds of manifestations throughout. We see through them Satan's counterclaim to Jesus's claim: "This is my world."[7] Not all animals in this film are associated with evil, but many have strong associations with the prince of the power of this world.

I will first trace the animalistic representations associated with Satan throughout the film, bringing them into dialogue with biblical, traditional, and other filmic traditions, before turning to other animal sights and sounds that do not have such strong symbolic associations but bring to the surface mundane entanglements of human and non-human animals in terms of eating, farming, and work animals.

Before doing so, I should note that there are two major ways Satan manifests. I call the first the "spiritual Satan." This Satan wears the black pants and coat with a red shirt, has hair on top of his head, has a serpent tattoo, always carries the goat staff, and is accompanied by the sight or sound of a locust. Only angels, Jesus, and the viewer can see this version of Satan. The other Satan, which I will call "Satan incarnate," is completely bald, wears a red plaid flannel shirt, and also carries the goat-hoof cane. He physically interacts with human characters in the film, usually found to be hanging out with Caiaphas and Annas.[8] Both manifestations of Satan with the animals associated with them nudge human acts of violence throughout the film.

SATAN AND THE SERPENT

Strikingly, as the most obvious animal association with Satan in the Christian tradition, the serpent only appears on the facial tattoo of the "spiritual Satan" and is only fully visible in a couple of scenes. The serpent identifies Satan before his fall (down a sand dune) and before he manifests himself in the world, imprinting his true identity outside of regular space and time. We only get a good look at the serpent tattoo once more later in the film. When Jesus has all his disciples give up their guns, Judas has a flashback of his childhood when he was forced to shoot people who had bags over their heads. At the end of this flashback, we see someone pull off their own bag only to reveal the grimacing face of Satan with his serpent tattoo, indicating he has been shaping Judas for a very long time.

Of course, the serpent has an old association with Satan. Although the serpent in the Garden of Eden was originally just a serpent, it did not take long for some Jews and mostly Christians to associate a serpent with evil if not the greatest evil.[9] In the filmic imagination, the serpent appears in a complex way in Martin Scorsese's *The Last Temptation of Christ*, where it takes on dual associations with Mary Magdalene and with Jesus's temptation in the desert, where the serpent – a cobra – has Mary Magdalene's voice. The serpent claims to be Jesus's spirit and to have created Eve. Scorsese's film repeatedly associates Mary Magdalene with serpents and reptiles, whether in Jesus's imagination or physically. Her henna tattoos could give a sense of snakeskin, while a serpent on the door and a lizard above the door mark her place as one of sex work. Also, two cobras show up in Jesus's room at the monastic desert community, speaking in Mary Magdalene's voice, saying, "I forgive you." In Mel Gibson's *The Passion of the Christ*, the gender-ambiguous Satan confronts Jesus in the Garden of Gethsemane, having a serpent slither from under their robes, and Jesus crushing its head with his foot (an allusion to Gen. 3:15).

Dornford-May, however, dispenses with serpentine imagery after the earliest scenes. It serves to identify the "spiritual Satan" early on and, afterwards, seems to have served its purpose. Alongside Satan's penchant for wearing red throughout the film, the combination of colour and serpentine imagery could conjure the red dragon (Rev. 12). If that is the case, then Mary would be the "woman clothed with the sun," given her prominent place at key points in this film, especially as she appears at the end of the film to sing away the violence and protest imperial rule.

THE LOCUST AND THE PLAGUE OF VIOLENCE

Much more so than the serpentine imagery, Dornford-May draws attention to the locust, which is the first image in the film and reappears throughout the film. Sometimes you see it; most of the time you just hear it. One interpretation takes the locust as a symbol of John the Baptist because it is a lone locust, John the Baptist ate locusts (Matt. 3:4; Mark 1:6), and it heralds the coming of Christ. The locust does herald something throughout the film, but not Christ.

Within the texture of the film, the locust proclaims the coming presence of Satan.[10] It nearly always accompanies the "spiritual Satan" rather than "Satan incarnate."[11] Directly after the prologue we meet Mary at a school where there has been a massacre of children by an insurgent army. She, seeking to escape detection, enters a classroom and lies with the dead children, playing dead. As she hides, we see the feet of someone appear; as the sound of locusts rises on the soundtrack we see a cloven goat foot, revealing that Satan is the force behind this bloody massacre.[12] As the wise men hit one of Herode's checkpoints one begins to hear locust sounds slowly increase on the soundtrack, as the wise men draw near to potential danger. As baby Jesus sleeps, we hear the sound of a locust and see spiritual Satan locking eyes with the angel Gabriel. Next, a baby angel gives Joseph a vision. The entire village leaves as we see a close-up of a locust, which, again, we hear briefly. Along the road, Jesus, Mary, and Joseph run into a group of slaughtered children. The soundtrack crescendos along with the sound of several locusts. Mary turns Jesus's face away at first, and, after an abrupt cut to spiritual Satan,[13] indicating he is the unseen force behind all of this, she then forces Jesus to look while the sound cuts out completely.[14] Again, a locust anticipates evil and violence. When Judas leaves at night to start collaborating with Caiaphas and Annas, we see a shot of Satan and hear the sound of a locust. At the Garden of Gethsemane, we hear the sound of a locust, then see Satan as he and Gabriel stare each other down, and we see him silhouetted with his goat staff. After they beat Jesus, they throw his dying body in a car and we hear the sound of a locust and a smiling spiritual Satan looking through the window. Clearly the locust serves as a herald, but only to destruction, massacre, and violence. But why is it there?

Satan has been associated with insects since the first century CE if not longer, where he acquired the label "Beelzebub," or "Lord of the flies" (Matt. 10:24–7; Mark 3:22; Luke 11:15–19). The name Beelzebub itself is older, identified in 2 Kings 1:1–18 as the God of the Philistine city of Ekron. The similar title of Beelzebul or "Lord of heaven" appears as a prince of demons in the *Testament of Solomon* 6.2–7. The iconographic tradition has not developed this association as it has serpentine symbolism, but the filmic imagination has regularly included insects to herald demonic or Satanic presence. Most famously, in *The Exorcist*, William Friedkin had his sound technicians record the buzz of bees enclosed in a bottle to create a subliminal buzzing noise repeated throughout the film.[15] In Kevin Smith's *Dogma*, one hears buzzing sounds just before the "triplets" – three demonic teenagers on rollerblades – appear. One can also see it in a more subdued way in *The Passion of the Christ*. As the demonic children rush Judas out of town, swarming around him like insects goaded on by Satan themself, the children suddenly disappear, and we see flies buzzing around Judas's head. In this case, you see the source of the flies: a dead horse along the side of the road, which is where Judas finds a rope to hang himself.

Son of Man, however, is unusual for its choice of not just flies, but of specifically locusts. If we can dismiss the association with John the Baptist's diet and focus on negative locusts in the Bible, then we see them as the bringer of plague followed by death and destruction (Exod. 10:12–20; Joel 1.4, 2.25; Rev. 9.1–11).[16] But it also has a local African context. If one googles "plague of locusts in modern history," most of the hits will be plagues that have descended on various parts of Africa, including some very nasty ones in 2020, including Southern Africa, where this film was made. It is a biblical image of destruction, to be sure, but one that resonates in modern African – and of course other – contexts.

THE GOAT-FOOT: OR, SATAN'S SCEPTRE

In addition to the earliest two scenes of the film – the prologue and Mary attempting to escape a massacre – where we see Satan and a goat foot, a man wearing red flannel can be spotted carrying a goat foot throughout the film at key points. Just after we see spiritual Satan pull a bag off his head in Judas's flashback, we see "incarnate Satan" wearing his red plaid flannel shirt carrying the crooked goat-foot staff and dragging a woman caught in adultery as he douses her with gasoline and reaches for his lighter.[17] He squares off with Jesus, who parallels him by wearing a blue flannel shirt. It is a striking juxtaposition from scene to scene as we see the face of spiritual Satan and then cut to incarnate Satan, alongside the juxtaposition coding bad things with red and good things with blue, a colour code set by the opening scene.[18]

After Jesus exorcises a demon from a girl, we see incarnate Satan holding his goat staff and smoking a cigarette as he watches Judas's footage of the event. He's also present with his staff when Jesus confronts Caiaphas and Annas, and sits next to Pilate just before he "washes his hands." As noted the "spiritual Satan" stands silhouetted with his goat staff at the Garden of Gethsemane, but the action then cuts to "incarnate Satan" also with the staff among the mob coming to get Jesus. When Caiaphas and Annas echo Satan's temptation in their offer to give Jesus power, the flannel-clad Satan stands holding his hoof staff. While Jesus's body is being carried to the unmarked field, we see spiritual Satan walking through a field full front toward the camera in a dominating posture with his goat foot and then cut to incarnate Satan wearing flannel and holding the goat foot waiting for Jesus's body to bury it in the field.[19] There are, indeed, several juxtapositions between "spiritual Satan" and "incarnate Satan" throughout the film, strengthening their association.

I have to admit this imagery has been trickier for me to track down. I have seen a source note that it has South African importance, but without explaining what exactly that importance is.[20] I can, however, discuss goat feet and Satan in Euro-American traditions. Biblical sources do not associate Satan with a goat. There is, however, some devaluation of a goat compared to sheep, when one separates the sheep from the goats in a scene of judgment where to be a goat is to be condemned (Matt 25:31–46). As we shall see below, there are positive or neutral goat images in the film; traditional Jesus filmic representations of Satan also avoid goat imagery.

Nonetheless, the European Christian tradition at some point merges the imagery of Pan (the goat-footed, goat-horned lesser god of Greek tradition) with the devil, such as the figure of Baphomet, who has a humanoid body, but goat-like horns, head, and legs. Popular representations of Satan from Anne Rice's *Memnoch the Devil* to the *Simpsons* in various Halloween specials all include goat legs and horns. Even if television shows and movies that flirt with the supernatural eschew the legs, they at least show the horns.

Short of a fantastic vision of Satan as half man, half goat, then, *Son of Man* with its third-cinema realism brings in the goat imagery as a staff rather than as Satan's actual legs. The dismembered goat leg connects the "spiritual Satan" with his incarnate counterpart throughout as they influence and incite state-sponsored violence that brings about Jesus's death.

Satan attracts various animals in the film. The serpent is tattooed on his very face, being part of his very identity, part of his very body. The locust heralds Satan and his violence as he influences the leaders of this world. The goat-hoof is his sceptre as he tries to maintain his sovereignty, as he tries to defend his claim, "This is my world!"

AMBIVALENT BIRDS

As birds flit between wild and domesticated, they also fly between various kinds of representation throughout the film. The first sound we hear in the film are sea birds, likely gulls. We do not see them, but we hear them throughout the prologue. In the scene directly after the prologue, militia men in yellow t-shirts chant three words that are not subtitled: "The gang! The birds! The birds!" as the men psych themselves up for violence against the birds – or victims – they seek to flush out.[21] In this case, birds are the innocent victims of violence. It is an animalization of victims by their murderers as they murder; an act of dehumanization precedes and coincides with acts of violence, as discussed in chapter 4. One can faintly hear them as Joseph and Mary walk along the beach just following the Annunciation scene, but they are mostly drowned out by Mary's singing and the sound of waves. Just before Joseph and Mary are led to the stable, there is a strange shot of birds flying in the sky.

There is also a menacing shot of vultures circling above the cross. While birds have been either positive (connected to angels) or neutral throughout (largely background noise), here they take on a more threatening posture as they threaten to swoop down upon the dead body of Jesus on the cross.[22] Shots and sounds of birds, especially birds of prey, occasionally arise in Jesus films. *Jesus Christ Superstar*, which largely eschews animals in the film (as does *Godspell*), has some strange interscene shots of birds of prey just before the meeting of the council on the scaffolding. The juxtaposition suggests the council are such birds of prey about to attack.

As with other things, in *The Last Temptation of Christ*, birds of prey operate more ambiguously: they represent Jesus's divine side attacking and clawing into him when his divine part (or God) tries to speak with him in a striking case of divinanimality, creating a split in Jesus's psyche. This occurs in a voice-over monologue at the beginning of film; also when Jesus walks along a shoreline, one hears the screech of a bird of prey and then him falling to the ground as he is attacked by God. These "attacks" only go away when he accepts who he is and his mission.

In *The Passion of the Christ*, while Jesus prays in the garden, one hears the sound of a vulture (or another bird of prey) with a parallel cut to Judas. At the public trial before Pilate, there is a super slow motion shot of a dove – representing the Holy Spirit – flying above

Jesus in another moment of divinanimality. Also, in *The Passion of the Christ*, a crow pecks out the bad thief's eyes on the cross – perhaps a bit of verisimilitude (why wouldn't birds begin to be attracted to the exposed flesh?) and a bit of symbolism, because it only attacks the bad thief.[23]

In addition to actual birds, angels in *Son of Man* – as they have been portrayed for millennia from Persia to Europe in literature, art, etc. – have white bird feathers. Feathery wings of birds signify angelic presence in ubiquitous ways in art and films, though I do not recall any "popular" Jesus films in which angels appear with such frequency and with feathers – though without wings as such – as in *Son of Man*. If one steps just outside the Jesus-film tradition, however, they come into clearer view. For example, *Dogma*'s angels have enormous feathered wings, though they try to keep them hidden when travelling incognito on earth.[24] *Son of Man*'s birds are victims of violence, neutral parts of the setting, menacing, and angelic.

DAILY ANIMALS

Finally, Dornford-May also "fills in the narrative gaps" with animals but translates these "gaps" into their South African context, entangling Jesus with animals throughout his life in his daily interactions. Mostly these are working animals, the animal prostheses that allow humans to do more than they could on their own, though some are food or are being raised for food or clothing, and some are wild or feral. No nonhuman animals are sacrificed in the narrative of the film; only humans are.

Jesus grows up in a rural setting surrounded by animals. It begins before he is born. One sees Mary being brought to "Bethlehem" in a donkey cart, drawn by two donkeys – something, I think, that might be more realistic than having her ride directly on a donkey's back as is often depicted.[25] The shepherd boys keep a flock of goats, so goats are not entirely associated with evil, and one brings a baby goat to meet the baby Jesus.[26] A baby goat comes face to face with the baby human. Living goats provide a counterpoint to the dismembered dead goat hoof of Satan.[27] We also hear and see a cow. Angelic children wander over to Jesus from their visit to the shepherds along with a flock of ducks. The Magi come riding horses rather than camels or rather than walking. Later in the film, we see women preparing chickens to eat. All of these cases are those of a world that is definitely squarely in the time and place of domesticity; none fit with Bulliet's discussion of post-domesticity. Jesus grows up around working animals – donkeys and horses. He grows up with animals that provide food, particularly milk, such as the cow and goats. The ducks may also be part of this context of being kept around for food. The chickens are prepared on screen for food.

There are other kinds of animals who have more freedom. Throughout we hear dogs barking, sometimes warning of the danger of Herode's men searching for babies before the massacre of the innocents or just as part of the general background noise. When Jesus gives his first major speech to his disciples, a dog dutifully sits outside the door. We regularly hear crickets at night.

These animals bring us into the context of rural South Africa but also remind us how the ancient world behind the representation of the gospels was likely brimming with the sights, sounds, and smells of animals.[28] Like the gospel narratives, animals provide food, clothing, and labour for humans in the film.

ANIMALS AS SOCIAL AND SPIRITUAL CODES IN SIGHT AND SOUND

Upon reflection, *Son of Man* does not just "fill in" narrative and interpretive gaps; it does not simply add animals where we expect to find them but where they are lacking in the gospels, as films such as *King of Kings* mostly do; it uses them in strategic and symbolic ways, more in line with *The Last Temptation of Christ*. But even when similar motifs are used from the Christian traditions or from filmic traditions, Dornford-May, for the most part, adapts them in very specific ways. By framing the entire movie through the temptation narrative and a series of embedded animalistic motifs,

Dornford-May strategically uses animals as an audio-visual symbolic code to demarcate those under Satan's thrall from those who fight against injustice.

Of course, *Son of Man* does use animals for verisimilitude, such as for the rural setting: we see birds, goats, ducks, cows, donkeys, dogs, and more goats. Animals are presented without much emphasis or additional attention as food and labour, though not sacrifice, in a setting full of domesticated working animals and animals raised for food and food products.

But Dornford-May also uses animals as a symbolic code throughout. Most animalistic motifs surround Satan. The serpent identifies Satan in the prologue with extra clarity, connecting his very body, his very self with the serpent on his facial tattoo; the locust heralds Satan-influenced violence; the goat-hoof is his sceptre as he claims authority over this world and especially its violence.

While some commentators speak of Satan's ineffectuality in this film,[29] or that he seems to just "grease the wheels" here and there, once one brings the two forms of Satan and all of the animal cues together, Satan is as omnipresent as a plague of locusts. I cannot think of another Jesus film where Satan has such a presence – not even *The Passion of the Christ*, which inserts Satan more so than previous films, or *The Last Temptation of Christ* when Satan manifests as a creepy tween girl. Satan lurks as in previous films, but also manifests and directly interacts with the world, guiding it towards destruction and violence. The combination of spiritual lurking and physical presence is a rarer combination found in this film. As we have spoken of divine and demonic animality, satanic animality sometimes mirrors and sometimes undermines the logics behind divine animality, while shifting demon animality away from the pack of legion to the singular – yet still split – figure of Beelzebub himself.

While good or neutral characters in the film regularly interact with animals, and animals fill the screen and soundtrack of the film from beginning to end, other characters are not "marked" by animals in the same way as Satan's manifestations are, except maybe the angels with their feathers. We should ask why other characters are not "marked" animalistically. Why can animality only be neutral or evil? What attitudes towards animals and animality is the filmmaker reflecting or shaping in the audience?

In the inversion of divine animality and perhaps intensification of demon animality, this film reflects, as White and Singer would argue in different ways, broader Christian anthropocentrism and speciesism. This is reinforced by the film's ending. It concludes with a quotation from Genesis 1: "Let us make man in our own image and after our likeness." While democratizing all humans, regardless of race, in the image of God (something that is quite significant in the South African context of the film), animals are left out of the divine image to reflect Satan instead.

This augmentation of the gospel narrative doesn't start with the filmic imagination; rather the filmic imagination is part of a long tradition extending from the apocryphal gospels of late antiquity, especially the Proto-Gospel of James, and the visual artistic tradition. These traditions also fill in the gaps and develop animal-based codes. But films have a greater hermeneutical urgency to fill in these gaps and develop these codes in a way that written texts do not. We are called to see and hear concurrently, stimulating and guiding our own beastly imaginations in the process.

Concluding Queer Entanglements with Gospel Beasts

What did Noah do with hermaphrodite animals? What did Noah do with transsexual animals?

Isabella Rossellini, "Seduce Me – Noah's Ark"[1]

And Say the Animal Responded?

Jacques Derrida, *The Animal That Therefore I Am*

A TRANS POSTHUMANITIES

In the fall of 2021, I returned to teaching face-to-face classes. I had come out as trans to my partner and kids, but I was not out publicly. I was having a one-on-one meeting with a nonbinary student who had a pride flag sticker on their laptop that said "PETA 2." I asked them what that meant. I knew what PETA was, but what was PETA 2?[2] At first, they said something like, "Oh, well, I just thought it looked cool." Then something in the room shifted. They perhaps saw something in my eyes or instinctively realized at some visceral level that I, too, was queer but in hiding. Or maybe they just realized I was looking for something more. They said something like: animals are taken for granted, abused, abandoned, and marginalized. So are queer folks. What I began to notice after that meeting was that while cisgender heterosexual people often labelled queer people as beastly or, alternatively, unnatural in an act of name-calling that attempted to create social boundaries between "us" straight humans and "those" queer animals (or monsters), this could also signal solidarity between queer people and animals.[3] It was a queer assemblage among those pushed to the edge by a cisheteronormative and anthropocentric society. I came out publicly as transgender a few weeks later. This event did not trigger my coming out, but it was caught up along a broader series of events that had been leading inexorably to my social and embodied gender transformation.

As I transition my life is taking a new direction, and likewise this conclusion is not an ending, but a new beginning. It is an invitation to further consider the issues raised beyond the confines of its pages or my own parameters, categories, and ways of organizing that I have learned in the act of writing this book. I will be looking, as my student has prompted me to do, along the multiple entanglements of animals, animality, and queerness, but with a trans sensitivity to the potential ways that change, transformation, and becoming are emerging, and are enabled, redirected, or resisted.[4] Trans and genderqueer people have been studying nonhumans for years, including nonhuman or partly human animals, cyborgs, gods, demons, and monsters. Some have worked on how the culturally driven gender binary does not just harm trans and intersex humans, but also disguises the gender diversity of nonhuman animals, many of whom have more than two sexes and genders, and many species of which can change sex and gender.[5] Our animal bodies are fluid and changing, individually and phylogenetically, throughout our lives and in evolutionary time.[6] One of Donna Haraway's students, Sandy Stone, was inspired by Haraway's "Cyborg Manifesto" to write her "Posttranssexual Manifesto."[7] Halberstam has repeatedly investigated monsters, the inhuman, and the anti-human.[8] Even Karen Barad has brought trans embodiments into diffractive dialogue with their theory of "agential realism."[9]

As a trans person, I do not want to look only at those who fall between, live beyond, or challenge by their very existence the gender binary, or only at how the gender binary not only does violence against trans and intersex people, but also against those whom it purportedly supports; I also want to touch on themes of becoming, transformation, concealment, and revelation. Through transgender posthumanism, I wonder: When human animals touch, brush against, or intra-act with nonhumans, what elements of humans crystallize, ossify, or harden, and what elements melt, thaw, and resolve themselves into a dew as they become entangled with one another?[10]

If Deleuze and Guattari sprouted rhizomes as the guiding conceptual metaphor, and if Haraway decomposed her theory as compost, I have repeatedly spun a spider's web with its perpetual maintenance, various connections, and entanglements. I see the words "entanglement," "entangled," and other permutations everywhere from sociology and physics to philosophy of religion and theology.[11] The term originates from a letter penned by Edwin Schrödinger to Albert Einstein to characterize the emergent theorizations of quantum mechanics.[12] As Catherine Keller and Mary-Jane Rubenstein write, "We are materializations entangled in other materializations; we happen in our mattering."[13] There are many entanglements between humans and other animals. As Haraway writes, "Critters are always relationally entangled rather than taxonomically neat."[14] Or, in another place, "Living and dying on earth is tangled turtles all the way down."[15] As posthumanists, nonhumanists, and new materialists emphasize in their own distinctive ways, humans are not the only actors. As Barad repeatedly emphasizes, we only exist in our "intra-actions." Central to their "agential realism" is this concept of "intra-action," which they define as "the mutual constitution of entangled agencies."[16] They write, "Individuals do not preexist their interactions; rather, individuals emerge through and as part of their entangled intra-relating."[17] Elsewhere, they write, when bringing agential realism into conversation with trans embodiments, "Matter is promiscuous and inventive in its agential wanderings: one might even dare say, imaginative."[18]

These entanglements resemble what queer eco-theologian Jacob Erickson calls "larval divinity"; it is "divinity in drag." As many trans women, I have often referred to my transition in terms of becoming a butterfly: I regularly call my pre-transition life my caterpillar phase, and, as I continue to transition, I am in my chrysalis phase. For Erickson, "incarnation occurs in the midst of complex material agencies, luring them on in mutual process of transformation." But, inspired by Barad's concept of "intra-action," this is more of an "intra-carnation"; Erickson continues: "the divine and creatures enflesh together, are wrapped together, open possibilities of becoming differently, are fundamentally indeterminate, and appreciate responsibility to the multiplicity of creaturely masks. Drag shows, carnivals, burlesque only occur in the creative flow and intra-active participation of performer and spectator. And those masks quite often become blurred or change roles."[19] From a trans perspective, what are the intra-active becomings of these entanglements? The larval – or chrysalis – stage shows that this process is "always an unfinished memory, a trace, a gestating, changing possibility of metamorphosis."[20] That is, perpetual potentialities of becoming haunt our narratives at every turn, whether these metamorphoses are embraced or feared.

My categories of eating animals, prosthetic animals in wearing animals and working animals, sacrificing animals, animalizing humans, divine and demonic animality in ancient gospels and in filmic adaptations, and other issues that have cut across categories, such as the domesticated, feral, and wild, have all touched on intra-active bodily becomings and the ethical stakes of such entanglements. But what if, to paraphrase Derrida, the animals responded? What then would be the intra-actions of our mutual becoming? I will focus these questions by returning to a series of binaries that this analysis initially assumed, built on, and then slowly began to unwind: predator and prey in eating meat, wild and domesticated, and insider and outsider. These categories cut across multiple chapters at once, offering different, sometimes oblique, ways to approach the issues as I turn around in the web once more and continually disentangle and reentangle these threads in new ways as Penelope wove and unwove and rewove her tapestry (*Odyssey* 22.122–48).[21]

WE ARE MEAT

We began our discussion with various forms of consuming nonhuman animals through eating, working, wearing, and sacrificing animals. What animals we eat, what animals we use for work, and what we animals we wear repeatedly refracts through various social dimensions of class, gender, ethnicity, and religious markers. Let's begin again there and find a new strand along the queerly tangled web for consideration. Eating in particular is a sensuous action as one tastes, smells, and touches the body, matter, or flesh of another. It is also the absorption of other living and nonliving things, whether plants, fungi, animals, or minerals. It transforms others into oneself, impacting and altering one's own embodiment, even at the tiniest levels. You are not just you. Humans are also composed of other life, such as bacteria, within you, as well as non-life, including metals and minerals. What is you and what is not you? Donna Haraway reminds us that only about 10 per cent of the cells of our bodies have human DNA; everything else consists of the genomes of bacteria, fungi, and other life.[22] "You" are a composite of lives. Our bodies are the meeting place of multiplicities. As Keller and Rubenstein write, "Rather, things – actual entitled – are multiplicities, assemblages, hybrids, resonance machines, sonority clusters, intra-actions, complexities, and viscous porosities – all terms that variously express the insight that each cell, organism, vegetable, and photon is irreducibly composed of what Karen Barad would call an 'intra-active' host of others."[23] Some of this other life is necessary to live; other forms of life within you will make you sick or kill you; others you simply expel. Humans absorb calories from outside of us through plants, animals, and fungi as we are in perpetual becoming.

Humans are omnivores, predators who can subsist, survive, and flourish without consuming meat. The consumption of animals – *whether* one eats animals and *which* animals one eats – is marked in the gospels and in our own lives. As we saw with eating fish, the fatted calf, a goat, locusts, and pigs, among other potential animal products, you can learn about a person by what they eat; their food choices often correlate with other social markers, including political orientation, gender identity and expression, economic status, religious identity, and geographical location. When I used to teach my Sexuality & Christianity course, I would point to gendered assumptions about eating: men eat meat, steak, and heavy foods; women eat salads and light foods.[24] Of course, this is not really true in our daily lives, but there is a performative element to eating that overlays the absorption of calories. Meals are a social event.

At this point, however, I want to push against our comfort with eating, our comfortable complicity with the transformation of living animals into lifeless meat. I am not simply talking about vegetarianism or veganism. I am now thinking beyond the original question of whether Jesus would eat an animal or whether Jesus enabled others to eat animals. Instead, I am thinking about eating as something uncanny, as one ingests life and incorporates it within oneself. Then again, humans are not the only animals that eat other animals in the gospels. Foxes, vipers, dogs, and pigs – all mentioned in the gospels – can and do eat other animals. Humans are not the only predators; and humans are not only predators. Humans can also become meat.[25] Our flesh, muscles, and organs can be eaten; our material bodies can provide vital calories for other animals. Jesus calls his followers to eat his meat and drink his fluids, especially in John 6:52–65. Jesus's meat and Jesus's fluids give not just life, but Life. "Does this offend you?" (John 6:61).

At least one feral gospel tradition, moreover, speaks of a human eaten by an animal. In Thomas 7, which exists in Coptic and Greek fragments (P. Oxy. 654.40–2), one hears the voice of Jesus and the hunger of a predator: "Jesus said, 'Blessed is the lion which a human will eat, and the lion becomes (*shope*) a human. And cursed is the human which the lion will eat and the lion shall become (*nashope*) a human'" (translation mine). Some people think the last line has been corrupted and should read: "And the human becomes a lion" to retain the structure of the first part of the saying.[26] I will retain the original saying.[27] Lions only appear here in the Thomas traditions, and the issue of eating only shows up in one other place in the Gospel of Thomas in saying 11.[28] Nonetheless, the issue remains eating animals, but which animal eats which? Not only do humans eat the lion – a top predator – but lions also eat humans. The choice of a lion in this saying seems odd. While humans can eat lions, humans usually do not eat lions. In the Roman period, it was considered a mark of a lack of civilization to eat lions.[29] In the passage, Jesus uses eating to signify something else. But what is this something else? What do the components of eating, lion, and human mean? And, especially drawing on trans studies, how does eating relate to becoming (*shope*)?

Many scholars look to the Greek philosophical tradition stemming from Plato (*Republic* 436A–441C; 588B–589B). The lion is a metaphorical being here, representing one's animalistic passions that must be brought into control by the quintessentially human element – one's mind.[30] So the "human" represents reason/mind and the lion represents passions. To be fully human, the human/reason must maintain dominance over the animal (lion)/passions; otherwise, if the animal nature becomes dominant, one will simply become animalistic and beastly.

The metaphor for reason and passions relies on a few assumptions: that only humans have the capacity for reason among living things, for example. But probably the most important assumption is that humans should be dominant in nature, but aren't. The choice of a wild, powerful animal, such as a lion, rather than a domesticated animal illustrates the difficulty of maintaining this "dominance." Nonetheless, if we add a touch of historical context, one would see the "reassertion" of such "dominance" throughout the Roman Empire in the *venationes* (wild beast hunts) held in various amphitheaters throughout the Mediterranean world, including in Jerusalem (Josephus, *Ant.* 15.8).[31]

While biblical traditions included the potential, but unattained, lion consumption of human meat in the story of Daniel (Dan. 6:10–24; cf. Greek Daniel 15:23–40) or even God as a predatory lion who threatens to rip apart and devour his people at any time (Hos. 13:7–

8; cf. 11:10), one should also consider the contemporary Roman context: part of the executions in the Roman amphitheaters could (but did not always) include prisoners being attacked and eaten by animals. That is, in the Roman Empire in the context of the amphitheatre, one could see someone dominating (though not eating) a lion (in the *venationes*) and a lion eating a human (in the midday executions).[32] These scenes became popular in ancient Christian accounts of martyrs and saints, including the Apocryphal Acts of the Apostles.[33] The scenes of animals, including animals fighting humans and other animals and animals eating humans in the arena, were even a favorite artistic motif, found in a variety of mosaics.[34]

As humans become eaten in a formalized and ritualized manner, one finds entanglements with traditions of sacrifice, the central institution in which other animals were consumed in a ritualized and formalized manner. As Keith Hopkins notes in his classic study of gladiators: "In gladiatorial contests and in wild beast shows, the Romans came very close, even at the height of their civilisation, to performing human sacrifice."[35] Just as one eats animals, so other animals eat humans; just as humans consume animals through sacrifice, so are humans consumed together with other animals in sacrifice.

Combine the Roman setting with the Greek philosophical tradition and all of the anthropocentric assumptions – and potential fears and challenges to those assumptions represented by the lion – then one gets a powerful metaphor. But as noted in chapter 4, metaphors are never merely metaphors. Thomas 7 exceeds its own assumptions. Central to the saying is transformation and becoming (*shope*). Andrew Crislip places the saying within the broader discourses of ancient Christian becoming, in particular, the becoming of the resurrection.[36] For those invested in a physical, fleshly resurrection in the early Christian world, the state of a body eaten by animals in the arena would be of preeminent concern: how can ingested bodies be raised?

More critically, this saying polices the boundaries of proper and improper becoming. If one follows the emendation, it seeks to enable one kind of becoming (becoming human) and warn against another kind (becoming beastly). If one leaves the saying as it is, when the human eats the lion, the lion is blessed to become part of the human; when the lion eats the human, the human is cursed as, again, the lion becomes human. The only movement is from beast to human; not human to beast. In this case, it is a variance of becoming based on who incorporates whom. In the first, you are who eats you (which is good); but in the second you are what you eat (which is bad). It combines consumption and becoming; it is an animalistic transformation as the human and animal feed one another. The lion becomes human – and perhaps the human becomes lion – in a mutual consumption that blurs humans and animals into an uncanny humanimality as both are simultaneously predator and prey.[37]

WHAT KIND OF CRITTER ARE YOU?

Whatever the lion and human represent in the Gospel of Thomas, eating both constitutes and reconfigures the lines of predator and prey, but also wild (lion) and domesticated (human). These predator/prey and wild/domestic dichotomies intra-act with each other under the manifold manners of consumption – not just eating, but otherwise using. Our post-domesticity culture, as Richard Bulliet calls it, has an obsession with consumption. There is, of course, the continued consumption of animals by humans that extend the human as animal, the animal prosthesis to the human. The animal prosthetics are increasingly replaced today by tech prosthetics, as human and animal and machine become increasingly entwined in new ways in biotechnologies and AI. The human-animal assemblage is shifting to the human-machine assemblage or actually the human-animal-machine assemblage.[38] Humans still use other animals for clothing (wool, leather) and for physical and emotional assistance, even as other prosthetic extensions have moved increasingly into the laboratory.[39]

Returning to the wild/domestic binary, the topics of the domesticated, feral, and wild have impacted this analysis in retrospect far more than I initially realized it would. The human-animal-consumption linkages just discussed – eating animals, wearing animals, making animals work for you – has, mostly, examined domesticated animals. Domestication looms large in the sacrificial complex as well.

But there are areas where domestic and wild blur, especially in eating animals, and where the wild impinges on the domestic and where the domestic relies on the wild, against which it defines itself. In the gospels, we have examined wild birds, ravens, wolves, fish, vipers, scorpions, demons, and the divine, who stand apart from and invade the sheep, oxen, donkeys, hens and roosters, pigs, and humans. The feral dog crosses between wild and domesticated, and, as Mary Douglas might say, as a category blurrer, is the unclean yet familiar thing, a potential pet, scavenger, or something that might bite back, like a foreign woman seeking Jesus's help.[40]

Possession – whether divine or demonic – also becomes entangled in blurry boundaries between wild, feral, and domesticated. The demonic and the divine simultaneously reside in the wild as wild – they are uncivilized. They animalize, de-domesticate, de-civilize the human through possession; possession by a holy or an unclean spirit dehumanizes, animalizes, and even sometimes divinizes. Divine possession obtained in the wilderness can rejuvenate and heal the civilized through the boundary-crossing Jesus, but the divine element itself remains untamed. The demonic, however, may be transformed (back?) into domesticated animals (pigs!) through exorcism, but the divine cannot; the divine remains marked as undomesticated and wild.

BACKTALK:
DRAG PERFORMANCES OF MONSTROUS ASSEMBLAGES

As the divine and demonic wear and ventriloquize humans, the divine or demonic performance threatens the difference between performer and costume, between possessor and possessed. Legion speaks through the Gerasene demoniac; likewise, the spirit ventriloquizes humans (Matt. 10:20; Mark 13:11; cf. Luke 12:12).[41] That's why Jesus exorcises by the spirit; the spirit is fighting the possession competition (Matt. 12:28). If the "spirit blows wherever it wants to," then equally, "thus it is for all who are born of the spirit" (John 3:8). The spirit leaves the imprint of wildness upon those who are of the spirit, those whom the spirit inhabits or possesses, whether human, animal, wind, water, fire, or some other entity or element.[42] When imprinted with the "wild," the possessor of spirit becomes changed, something feral, something not-quite or no-longer human. The possessor of spirit transforms, becomes, and, in the process, both attracts and repels others who remain locked in existing categories.

Much like the human body is already an amalgam of multiple organisms with their own DNA, the possession of a human or animal by a god or demon creates an amalgamated divine-demonic-human-animal body. Or as Alphonso Lingis more evocatively writes, "Our bodies are coral reefs teeming with polyps, sponges, gogonians, and free-swimming macrophages continually stirred by monsoon climates of moist air, blood, and biles."[43] It externalizes the intra-active beings in and among us. The result of this multiplicity becomes monstrous.

One can find posthumanist, queer, and trans readings of the "monster," just as one can of nonhuman and partly human animals, cyborgs, gods, and demons. Discourses and affects of monsterizing others shares many elements with animalizing others. The monster, much like Mary Douglas's discussion of category transgressions of "dirt," is "an embodiment of difference, a breaker of category, and a resistant Other known only through process and movement."[44] Similarly, Halberstam writes, "The monster always represents the disruption of categories, the destruction of boundaries, and the presence of impurities and so we need monsters and we need to recognize and celebrate our own monstrosities."[45] I will return to the surprise ending here of celebrating our own monstrosities later. Monsters are not just profane but can be sacred, though they are regularly feared: think of the living creatures or Cherubim in Ezekiel 1, which are amalgams of a human, eagle, ox, and lion.[46]

While there are some patterns of monstrosity across cultures (e.g., gigantic size, blending of categories, shapeshifting, etc.), there is no single defining trait of a monster; specific forms of a "monster" can only be local: if it is "a form suspended between forms that threatens to smash distinctions," and some such distinctions are culturally specific, then the monster must also be culturally specific.[47] It may not even be society-wide; in fact, "monstrosity is in the eye of the beholder."[48] An entity that may not fit neatly in one culture's taxonomy may fit perfectly fine in another's.

Like animalizing humans, monsterizing humans dehumanizes to justify horrific behaviour towards them. The processes of animalization and monsterization are often linked. One may remember that the Greek term for "wild animal" – *to therion* –can also signify a monster. Historically this has included monsterizing different ethnicities, races, and cultures to justify conquest. It is also used to justify violence against LGBTQIA+ people. As Hebrew Bible scholar Esther Hamori writes in her own account of biblical monsters, "Describing people as monsters, as aberrations and somehow not perfectly human, serves to rationalize persecution, oppression, racism, and murder. From medieval Christian monsterization of Jews and Muslims to the present-day monsterization of gender nonconforming people, people with disabilities, Black people, and more, people have characterized those who differ from them as monstrous, sometimes to horrific ends."[49] Just like animalization, monsterization operates to determine in-group and out-group status, justify exclusion, and even elimination.

The "monster" is a spectre that has repeatedly been raised with regard to queerphobic or transphobic people: like the category-crossing possessed of god or a demon or a feral animal, trans people who cross and blur socially enforced gender categories are cast as "monsters" or "freaks."[50] We are also, to a small extent, shapeshifters. Such a dehumanization is supposed to put us in our place as simultaneously less than and more than human, less than deserving of equal consideration. As we challenge categories, others try to put us back in our old boxes or create new ones to re-domesticate us. But, as Jeffrey Cohen writes, citing John 1, "The monster is difference made flesh, come to dwell among us."[51] Queerness and transness, like monstrosity, resembles the divine spirit of wildness that comes to dwell among the domesticated: while others seek to re-domesticate us by labelling us as "monster," we can both challenge and reinvigorate as we dwell among others.[52]

But, just as Derrida asked the question – "And Say the Animal Responded?" – so Susan Stryker has lent her voice as Frankenstein's monster speaking back.[53] Noting that the central chapters of Mary Shelley's masterpiece comprise an extended speech of the creature speaking back to his creator, Stryker also speaks back to those who construct trans people as monstrous, reclaiming the terms: "I want to lay claims to the dark power of my monstrous identity without using it as a weapon against others or being wounded by it myself. I will say this as bluntly as I know how: I am a transsexual, and therefore I am a monster."[54] Stryker's reclaiming of monstrosity is a reflection of her transgender rage. Many trans people do not want to be characterized in such a way: we just want to exist. Instead, I, for example, try to represent transgender joy to those around me. But the rage has a point. Others have, like Stryker, embraced the term and speak back to the creators and maintainers of categories that trans people disrupt.[55] Commenting on Stryker's transgender rage, Barad writes, "Monstrosity, like electrical jolts, cuts both ways. It can serve to demonize, dehumanize, and demoralize. It can also be a source of political agency. It can empower and radicalize."[56] One can harness the strength of the monster, "to transform despair and suffering into empowering rage, self-affirmation, theoretical inventiveness, political action, and the energizing vitality of materiality in its animating possibilities."[57]

In a parallel manner, Mitzi Smith, a womanist Bible scholar, talks about women of colour speaking back to white patriarchy in what is called "sass" and "talk back," using the story of the Syrophoenician woman as a prime example of "sass" – a foreign woman triply marginalized (as a woman, as a foreigner, as a "little dog") speaking to a Jewish human man.[58] To the centre that privileges men over women, white people over everyone else, straight people over queer people, and humans over animals, defining us as peripheral and, in some cases, monstrous, we speak back.[59] As Smith writes, "Womanist sass is a legitimate contextual language of resistance."[60]

What all of these threads have in common is someone at the margins speaking back to those in the centre. Frankenstein's monster, living in frozen mountainous wilderness, talks back – at great length – to his creator who had abandoned him. Susan Stryker talks back to those who call trans people "monsters."

What happens when the dog barks back, the Syrophoenician woman talks back, or the possessed – those amalgams of human and beyond-human spirit – speak? Is it discernable, understandable, and to whom? Do we speak with the tongues of angels or with the grunts of animals? Is there a discernible difference between them? I grew up Pentecostal, and the "tongues of angels" I heard in a service were not more comprehensible than other nonhuman sounds I have heard. More importantly, a monstrous prophet or prophetic monster does not have to speak to give a message; we merely have to exist, appear, and show up. A "monster" is a *monstrum*; like a sign or miracle (*miraculum*), we "show" something, we "reveal" something.[61]

The act of "coming out" is an apocalypse: we reveal who we really are when we come out, but, simultaneously, others reveal to us and, sometimes for the first time, to themselves who they really are when they respond to us. We reveal the taxonomies that ensnare us in their nets to be illusions, the lines between male and female – like those of human and animal, divine and human, and divine and animal – to be gossamer, changeable, porous, and permeable. As Stryker-qua-monster says to the cis person: "You are as constructed as me."[62] As Barad comments, "Materiality in its entangled psychic and physical manifestations is always already a patchwork, a suturing of different parts."[63] If difference is, as Cohen writes, "mutable rather than essential," we "bear witness to the fact that it could have been constructed otherwise."[64] We are the prophets of the otherwise possible.[65]

As Barad, Keller and Rubenstein, and Haraway, among others, remind us: we are all always composites. As trans theorists remind us, we are all always becoming.[66] The spirit-possessed and the trans person are not monsters because of their multiplicity, because all beings are multiplex entities; neither are the spirit-possessed and trans people monsters because we transform, because we are all always becoming.[67] There is nothing essentially monstrous about us – we are not inherently monsters. We are called monsters because we *reveal* to others who *they* really are. This revelation is frightening to those who cling to the old categories, but it has the potential for innovation and transformation as the gospel wilds do.

Queer and transgender people have been regularly yet paradoxically animalized: we are accused of being beastly and unnatural in the same breath.[68] In the gospels, animalizing humans through out-group and in-group animalizations attempted to create affective boundaries based on religious disputes, class differences, or even gender, using predominantly feral and wild animals for out-group animalizations (vipers, dogs) or predominantly domesticated animals for in-group animalizations (sheep, cattle), creating affects of fear, contempt, and comfort. This was a tendency rather than a strict rule, since the disciples would also be "wise as serpents" and outsiders could be goats. Both manoeuvres sought to tame, domesticate, create, or reinforce human social groups, bringing them into taxonomic control. To call an opponent a viper, or a foreign woman a dog, is to assert one's authority or superiority over them and create or reinforce their outsider status.

But one can talk back. Yet the wild animal and the feral animal cross and blur boundaries, transforming the domesticated humans into the liminal, feral, and wild. When blending these animalization with the divine and demonic, a new potential opens up. The divine and the demonic and the wild have the potential to challenge the civilized and domesticated or have the power to transform it and revivify it. The monster does not just frighten; it also educates and renews.[69] Since monsters expose our taxonomies as something that always could be otherwise, along with Halberstam, we can find a way to celebrate our own monstrosities for this revelatory role.[70] As Barad writes, "The promise of monsters is a regenerative politics, an invitation to explore new ways of being in touch, new forms of becoming, new possibilities for kinship, alliance, and change."[71] In that spirit, I will second Stryker, who writes, "I challenge you to risk abjection and flourish as well as have I."[72]

BEGINNING ANEW

Donna Haraway's companioned composting alongside the Derridean and Deleuze-Guattarian rhizomatic lines of flight she critiques as well as those who critique her (e.g., Halberstam) have been persistent conversation partners for me alongside the domesticated and feral gospels the past several years. As I bid adieu to these entanglements of humans, animals, gods, and demons eating, working, wearing, killing, and possessing in the admixtures of wild, feral, and domestic to explore other becomings, I conclude with the words of one of Haraway's pupils, Sandy Stone, who long ago wrote: "But, although *individual* change is the foundation of all things, it is not the end of all things. Perhaps it's time to begin laying the groundwork for the next transformation."[73] So, let's begin again.[74]

Notes

INTRODUCTION

1 My analysis of biblical and related sources relies on the texts in their original language. However, biblical citations refer to the New Revised Standard Version (NRSV). I have indicated instances where I have adapted the translation.

2 Mostly "unowned" domesticated cats kill between 1.3 billion and 4.0 billion birds in the lower forty-eight states of the United States each year: Loss, Will, and Marra, "The Impact of Free-Ranging Domestic Cats." As Milburn (*Just Fodder*, 3) writes: "What guardian of a free-roaming cat doesn't have a story of waking up to 'gifts' of dead or dying animals? These animals, too, matter."

3 Milburn (*Just Fodder*, 4, 147–54, 157, 181) discusses when a human has an obligation to intervene in predator/prey relationships; cf. Regan, *Case for Animal Rights*, 361.

4 Hobgood-Oster, *Holy Dogs and Asses*, 4.

5 Calaway, *Sabbath and the Sanctuary*.

6 Cf. the "methodological bricolage" of Hobgood-Oster, *Holy Dogs and Asses*, 1–20.

7 Barad, *Meeting the Universe Halfway*, 33.

8 Ibid., ix.

9 Lingis, "Animal Body, Inhuman Face," 166.

10 This subtitle is taken from Johnson, *Ask the Beasts*, who, in turn, took it from Job 12:7.

11 Derrida, *Animal That Therefore I am*, 23.

12 Cf. the discussion by Hobgood-Oster, *Holy Dogs and Asses*, 6.

13 Cf. Derrida's penchant for using "beast" (*bête*) in both *The Animal That Therefore I Am* and *The Beast and the Sovereign*.
14 All translations in this paragraph are my own and far more literal than most standard translations to make a point. For ease of reading for non-specialists, I have transliterated words in Hebrew, Greek, and Coptic into an accessible English spelling rather than a formal transliteration system.
15 Berkowitz, *Animals and Animality in the Babylonian Talmud*, 47; Firmage, "Zoology (Fauna)," 1152, 1156.
16 This is depicted in Neil Gaiman and Terry Pratchett's *Good Omens*, where the angel Aziraphel and the demon Crawley/Crowley, who keep bumping into each other throughout the ages, are watching the animals be shepherded into the ark with one unicorn running the wrong way.
17 For example, Alfred Ely Day, an alumnus of Illinois College, taught geology at the Syrian Protestant College in Beirut (renamed the American University of Beirut) in the late nineteenth and early twentieth centuries and contributed to the *International Standard Bible Encyclopedia* (1915) with several entries on the natural history of the Levant. This encyclopedia was designed to fight the emergence of higher criticism of the Bible in the US. Day was a geologist who specialized in oyster fossils along the coastline of Lebanon.
18 "Animals in the Bible," *Wikipedia*, retrieved 8 January 2024, https://en.wikipedia.org/wiki/Animals_in_the_Bible; Firmage, "Zoology (Fauna)," 6:1109–67; quotation 1109.
19 Darwin, *Descent of Man*, 39.
20 Ibid., 101.
21 Ibid., 105; cf. Montaigne, "But when, among the most moderate opinions, I meet with arguments that set out to prove how closely we resemble the animals, how largely they share in our privileges, and how feasible are the comparisons between us and them, I certainly forswear a great deal of our presumption, and willingly resign that imaginary sovereignty over other creatures we are supposed to have" ("On Cruelty," 189).
22 Note the final clause in this book, "Man still bears in his bodily frame the indelible stamp of his lowly origin" (Darwin, *Descent of Man*, 405).
23 Schaefer, *Religious Affects*, esp. 43–50, 147–77. Building on the work of

Jane Goodall, Schaefer writes that "starting with animals in the study of religion prompts us to think about emotion and, as a corollary, that thinking about animality and emotion together gives us new ways of exploring human religion" (4).

24 Johnson, *Ask the Beasts*.

25 White, "Historical Roots of our Ecologic Crisis," 1203–7; see an analysis of this and other of White's writings by Riley, "A Spiritual Democracy of All God's Creatures," 241–60.

26 Earth Bible: Reading the Bible from the Perspective of Earth, last accessed 10 January 2024, https://www.webofcreation.org/Earthbible/earthbible.html.

27 For a survey of ecological readings of the Bible, see Horrell, *The Bible and the Environment*; Horrell, Hunt, Southgate, and Stavrakopoulou, *Ecological Hermeneutics*; Horrell, Hunt, and Southgate, "Appeals to the Bible in Ecotheology and Environmental Ethics," 219–38; Harrison, "Subduing the Earth," 86–109; Bauckham, "Joining Creation's Praise," 45–59; Orr, "Armageddon Versus Extinction," 290–2; Flannery, "Senators, Snowballs, and Scripture."

28 See the combination of ecological and post-colonial ("ecolonialism") perspectives in Nilsen and Solevåg, "Expanding Ecological Hermeneutics." Ecological considerations are also Virginia Burrus's starting point in *Ancient Christian Ecopoetics*.

29 Bauckham, "Reading the Synoptic Gospels Ecologically," 70.

30 See Singer, *Animal Liberation*, 1–23; Regan, *Case for Animal Rights*; *Defending Animal Rights*. For discussions of Singer in biblical and adjacent fields, see Koosed, "Humanity at Its Limits," 3–4; Seesengood, "What Would Jesus Eat?," 238–40; Berkowitz, *Animals and Animality in the Babylonian Talmud*, 9–10, 94–9; Linzey, *Animal Theology*, 28–30; see further discussion of Singer and Singer's critics in Bulliet, *Hunters, Herders, and Hamburgers*, 27–34. Regan is less frequently cited among biblical studies scholars, though he does address the impact of Genesis 1–3 in *Defending Animal Rights*, 7–9. For further readings among animal rights ethicists, see Donaldson and Kymlicka, who in *Zoopolis* have one of the strongest cases for animal rights, treating domestic animals as co-citizens, wild animals as having sovereignty, and all those in between (wild animals adapted to human environments) as denizens or resident aliens; and Milburn, *Just Fodder*. Milburn has a nice summary

of the field (*Just Fodder*, 6–7). For a critique of both Singer and Regan, see Wolfe, *Animal Rites*, 21–43, 69–70.

31 Bentham, *Principles of Morals and Legislation*, 310–11n1. In this footnote, he notes the neglect of the treatment of animals in European legislation and how the European treatment contrasts with Hindu and Islamic law, which gives some attention to animals. Bentham removes the ability to reason or speak from the realm of considerations for morality and replaces it with the ability to suffer. He also notes that the treatment of animals parallels the treatment of human slave populations. He writes,

> The day has been, I grieve to say in many places it is not yet past, in which the greater part of the species, under the denomination of slaves, have been treated by the law exactly upon the same footing as, in England for example, the inferior races of animals. The day *may* come, when the rest of the animal creation may acquire those rights which never could have been withholden form them but by the hand of tyranny. The French have already discovered that the blackness of the skin is no reason why a human being should be abandoned without redress to the caprice of a tormentor. It may come one day to be recognized, that the number of legs, the villosity of the skin, or the termination of the *os sacrum*, are reasons equally insufficient for abandoning a sensitive being to the same fate. What else is it that should trace the insuperable line? Is it the faculty of reason, or, perhaps, the faculty of discourse? But a full-grown horse or dog is beyond comparison a more rational, as well as a more conversable animal, than an infant of a day, or a week, or even a month, old. But suppose the case were otherwise, what would it avail? The question is not, Can they *reason*? nor, Can they *talk*? but, Can they *suffer*? (emphasis original)

Cf. Montaigne's reflections that "Natures that are bloodthirsty towards animals show a native propensity towards cruelty" ("On Cruelty," 187).

32 Kant saw animals as means merely to serve the interests of humans; see Regan, *Defending Animal Rights*, 13, 17.

33 Gaard, "Living Interconnections with Animals and Nature," 1–12; Birkeland, "Ecofeminism," 13–59; see in general the collected volumes of Gaard, ed., *Ecofeminism*; Diamond and Orenstein, eds., *Reweaving the World*.

34 For example, Adams, *Sexual Politics of Meat*, xxvi–xxvii, 178; Gruen, "Dismantling Oppression," 60–90.

35 See Adams, *Sexual Politics of Meat*.

36 Ibid., xxi.

37 Donovan, "Animal Rights and Feminist Theory," 167–94.

38 Some scholars prefer "nonhumanism" or "non/humanism" instead of "posthumanism" since any definition of who or what counts as "human" is exclusionary by nature; see Giffney and Hird, "Queering the Non/Human," 1–4.

39 For a selection of posthumanist thought, see the edited volume by Wolfe, *Zoontologies*; Wolfe's own book *Before the Law* is a masterful composition on posthumanism and law that interacts intensely with the works of Jacques Derrida; see also his *Animal Rites*.

40 Derrida's work, *The Animal That Therefore I Am*, nonetheless, has retained a sense of heterogeneity between self and other, and humans and animals. It has not blurred the boundaries as much as it has complicated them. For the impact of these works on biblical studies, see, for example, Koosed, ed., *Bible and Posthumanism*; Strømmen, *Biblical Animality after Jacques Derrida*, esp. 20–34. See also the brief remarks by Burrus, *Ancient Christian Ecopoetics*, 85–7; Miller, *In the Eye of the Animal*, 6–9.

41 Derrida, *The Animal That Therefore I Am*, 27–9; see Wolfe, *Animal Rites*, 67.

42 See especially their essay, "1730: Becoming-Intense, Becoming-Animal, Becoming-Imperceptible …" in *A Thousand Plateaus*, 232–309. George Aichele (*Tales of Posthumanity*) develops his discussion of posthumanism in conversation with the works of Deleuze and Guattari more so than Derrida. See also Burrus, *Ancient Christian Ecopoetics*, 130–1. Others have brought the animality of Derrida and the institutional insights of Foucault together into "zoo studies": McDonald and Vandersommers, *Zoo Studies: A New Humanities*.

43 Deleuze and Guattari, *Thousand Plateaus*, 26–38; cf. Derrida, *Beast and the Sovereign*, 1:1–2, 63–96; Detienne and Svenbro, "Feast of the Wolves."

44 Deleuze and Guattari, *Thousand Plateaus*, 240–1.

45 Ibid., 6–7.

46 Koosed, "Humanity at Its Limits," 5, and Seesengood, "What Would Jesus Eat?," 243–4, briefly interact with Haraway.

47 Haraway, *When Species Meet*, 19–27; Burrus, *Ancient Christian Ecopoetics*, 126.

48 Haraway, *When Species Meet*, 22; emphasis original; see Schaefer, *Religious Affects*, 214.

49 For a critique of Haraway's "pet love" and questioning the social and economic conditions that lead to such pet love, see Halberstam, *Queer Art of Failure*, 36–7; Halberstam, in turn, relies upon Nast, "Critical Pet Studies?," 894–906.

50 And continues to impact scholarly engagements with animals and animality, even in the title of Miller's book, *In the Eye of the Animal.*

51 Wolfe, *Animal Rites*, 169.

52 Haraway, *When Species Meet*, 3.

53 Deleuze and Guattari, *Thousand Plateaus*, 243–8.

54 Haraway, *When Species Meet*, 27–35; she has harsher words for Deleuze and Guattari than for Derrida. Haraway writes, "Despite keen competition, I am not sure I can find in philosophy a clearer display of misogyny, fear of aging, incuriosity about animals, and horror at the ordinariness of flesh, here covered by the alibi of an anti-Oedipal and anticapitalist project" (*When Species Meet*, 30); cf. Schaefer, *Religious Affects*, 184.

55 Baudrillard, *Simulacra and Simulation*, 137.

56 Deleuze and Guattari speak of "becoming" throughout their work, but especially, *Thousand Plateaus*, 237–9. They write, "Each multiplicity is symbiotic; its becoming ties together animals, plants, microorganisms, mad particles, a whole galaxy" (250).

57 Bataille, *Theory of Religion*, 17.

58 Ibid., 17–25.

59 Ibid., 27–30.

60 Ibid., 32–3.

61 Ibid., 39.

62 See Miller's remarks in *Eye of the Animal*, 18.

63 Wolfe, *Animal Rites*, 1, 7–8.

64 See Singer, *Animal Liberation*, 185–212, where he traces speciesism from biblical (mostly Genesis), Greek (mostly Aristotle), ancient, and medieval Christian traditions, into humanist and Enlightenment movements. He does note some kindly views towards animals sporadically found in the prophets, especially Isaiah, but that Genesis's decla-

ration that humans are made in the image of God and have dominion over the earth and animals predominates in the history of Western Christian attitudes towards animals. See Berkowitz's discussion of Singer's blame in *Animals and Animality in the Babylonian Talmud,* 96–9; Koosed, "Humanity at Its Limits," 3–4; Seesengood, "What Would Jesus Eat?," 240–1; Derrida, *Animal That Therefore I Am*, does not "blame" so much as engage Genesis 1–4 intermittently throughout, though mostly in the first part of the essay (1–51). Strømmen, *Biblical Animality after Derrida*, 10–17; Strømmen, "Beastly Questions and Biblical Blame," 13–28, more extensively discusses how these and other thinkers blame the bible for Euro-American anthropocentrism.

65 See Miller, *Eye of the Animal*, 51; cf. Strømmen, *Biblical Animality after Derrida*, 18.

66 Cf. the voluminous scholarship cited by Berkowitz, *Animals and Animality in the Babylonian Talmud*, 21–6.

67 See Bataille, *Theory of Religion*, 42, where he refers to the farmer as an object: "The farmer is not a man: he is the plow of the one who eats the bread. At the limit, the act of the eater himself is already agricultural labor, to which he furnishes energy."

68 Bulliet, *Hunters, Herders, and Hamburgers*; cf. Bulliet, *Camel and the Wheel*, 2–3.

69 For the very long co-evolution and perhaps intra-active mutual domestication of the human and the dog (*canis familiaris*), see Hobgood-Oster, *Holy Dogs and Asses*, 81–4.

70 Baudrillard, *Simulacra and Simulation*, 135.

71 Halberstam, *Wild Things*, 147–74.

72 For a historical study of such phenomena from a medieval perspective, see Bynum, *Metamorphosis and Identity*; otherwise, see Freud, "The Uncanny," 121–62. Freud's "uncanny" is both "at home" and "not at home"; it is both familiar and strange. It is the familiar that is unfamiliar, or the unfamiliar that is strangely familiar. A typical example is the return of something familiar – something repressed either individually or socially – in a new setting (e.g., ghost stories in an age of scientific knowledge); it can be the flash of recognition of something familiar that is unexpectedly out of place, creating a sudden defamiliarization. This can lead – like a lot of mystical discussions of God – to a simultaneous awe and fear, a simultaneous attraction and repulsion. See Derrida,

Beast and the Sovereign, 1:246, 266, for a similar sense with a discussion of a snake.

73 See, for example, Singer, *Animal Liberation*, 95–157. Singer writes, "The use and abuse of animals raised for food far exceeds, in sheer numbers of animals affected, any other kind of mistreatment. Over 100 million cows, pigs, and sheep are raised and slaughtered in the United States alone each year; and for poultry the figure is a staggering 5 billion" (95); see LeDuff, "At a Slaughterhouse, Some Things Never Die," 183–97.

74 Though Haraway has her own moments of diving into the Genesis discussions. Speaking of the sixth day in Genesis 1, she writes, "I think the sixth day is where the problem of joint mundane creaturely kinship versus human exceptionalism is sharply posed right in the first chapter of Jewish and Christian monotheism. Islam did no better on this point … In this feast, there are no companion species, no cross-category messmates at table. There is no salutary indigestion, only licensed cultivation and husbandry of all the earth as stock for human use. The posthumanities – I think this is another word for 'after monotheism' – requires another kind of open" (*When Species Meet*, 245).

75 Haraway, *Staying with the Trouble*, 5; "becoming with" also serves as a major theme in *When Species Meet*, especially 3, 16–17, 27–35.

76 Haraway, *Staying with the Trouble*, 13; cf. *When Species Meet*, 4–5.

77 Haraway, *Staying with the Trouble*, 11–12, 32, 55, 101–2; *When Species Meet*, 15–19, 134–6, 208, 245, 285–301. For an adjunct to "companion species," see *When Species Meet*, 253–4; cf. Derrida, *Animal That Therefore I Am*, 10–11, for a discussion of "being-with" versus "being-after-it."

78 Haraway, *Staying with the Trouble*, 11–12, 55, 169–70n3.

79 Haraway, *When Species Meet*, 5, 205, 242; cf. discussion of Haraway in Strømmen, *Biblical Animality after Derrida*, 4–6, who focuses more on Haraway's earlier work; cf. also Wolfe, *Animal Rites*, 3.

80 Haraway, *Staying with the Trouble*, 131–2.

81 As Berkowitz also does with the Rabbis (*Animals and Animality in the Babylonian Talmud*) and Miller does with ancient Christianity (*In the Eye of the Animal*); also Hobgood-Oster, *Holy Dogs and Asses*, 129–46.

82 Ehrman and Plese, trans., *Apocryphal Gospels*, 61.

83 For fuller analysis of this passage, see Bovon, "Suspension of Time."

84 As noted by Hobgood-Oster, *Holy Dogs and Asses*, 17–18. Compare the popular view that Paul fell off his horse on his way to Damascus, even though the biblical texts never mention him riding a horse; Kahl, "Reading Galatians," 27–43. She indicates, however, that the horse is a fitting image to the story even in its absence.

85 On the association with horses and the Roman military in ancient imperial visual culture, see Kahl, "Reading Galatians," 27–8. Cf. Acts 10:1–48, in which Peter converts a centurion. A couple of important points: Simon (Peter) is called a tanner (instead of a fisherman) – both of his professions in the New Testament relate to animal products; in this case, he is working with animal skins at the beginning of the story. He equivocates but has his dream about all "foods" being declared clean. But this is not literally about "food," but Gentiles! Gentiles are literally what they eat: unclean food.

86 I am thinking of the feminist historical reconstructivist project of Schüssler Fiorenza, *In Memory of Her*; Berkowitz draws a assemblage of animals and other "others": "Animals sit at the edge of personhood, like a variety of human characters – women, children, slaves, foreigners" (*Animals and Animality in the Babylonian Talmud*, 38); cf. Hobgood-Oster, *Holy Dogs and Asses*, 42.

87 Hobgood-Oster productively brings together feminist and ecological critiques of Christianity's andro- and anthropocentrisms as well as Christian racism, all of which undergird patriarchy; see Hobgood-Oster, *Holy Dogs and Asses*, 4, 6.

88 See discussion of this passage in Berkowitz, *Animals and Animality in the Babylonian Talmud*, 63–88.

89 See Bulliett, *Hunters, Herders, and Hamburgers*, 5–10.

90 See Berkowitz, *Animals and Animality in the Babylonian Talmud*, 5–8; Spittler, *Animals in the Apocryphal Acts of the Apostles*, 133–40.

91 See Spielman, "Playing Roman in Jerusalem," 1–24.

92 Bauckham, "Reading the Gospels Ecologically," 73; Bauckham notes the frequency with which Jesus refers to flora and fauna is greater compared to Paul (73–4).

93 If daily animals are missing from the gospels, then it is important to consider what Sean Freyne, following Horden and Purcell, calls the "micro-ecologies" of the three regions of Galilee. See, for example,

Freyne, *Jesus Movement*, 93; cf. Bauckham, "Reading the Synoptic Gospels Ecologically," 70–5.

94 This pericope includes both, since Jesus sends his disciples out as sheep amidst wolves.

95 Or John's identification of Jesus as the Lamb.

96 See Deleuze and Guattari, *Thousand Plateaus*, 235.

97 Berkowitz, *Animals and Animality in the Babylonian Talmud*, 3.

98 This idea came from a conversation with James McGrath at the book exhibit at the 2019 SBL.

99 See Berkowitz, *Animals and Animality in the Babylonian Talmud*, 14.

100 Derrida, *Animal That Therefore I Am*, 29.

CHAPTER ONE

1 See Milburn, *Just Fodder*, 28.

2 Douglas, "Deciphering a Meal," 61.

3 Douglas, "Deciphering a Meal"; see Douglas, *Purity and Danger*, 42–58, where she discusses Levitical classification as a form of imitating God's holiness; Durkheim, *Elementary Forms*, 127–40, 338–40.

4 Adams, *Sexual Politics of Meat*, xxiv.

5 Bataille, *Theory of Religion*, 39.

6 Seesengood, "What Would Jesus Eat?," 230.

7 Magness, *Stone and Dung*, 46, 48–9, 212n70, 213n78, 213n86; Magness, *Archaeology of Qumran*, 117–21.

8 Crossan, *Jesus*, 66–70; see Smith, *From Symposium to Eucharist*; Taussig, *In the Beginning Was the Meal*.

9 An exception – though not one focused on the gospels – is James Davidson's discussion of cuisine in classical Athens in *Courtesans and Fishcakes*.

10 Taussig, *In the Beginning Was the Meal*, 26–32.

11 Crossan, *Historical Jesus*; Crossan, *Jesus*, 66–70; Smith, *From Symposium to Eucharist*, 237–9. For a summary of dining practices from Qumran to the Jesus movement, see Magness, *Stone and Dung, Oil and Spit*, 77–84.

12 Taussig, *In the Beginning Was the Meal*, 48–9, 82–4.

13 Schüssler Fiorenza, *In Memory of Her*, xlii–lv, 128–30; Schaberg, *Resurrection of Mary Magdalene*, 74–7.

14 On Paul's vegetarianism, see Seesengood, "What Would Jesus Eat?," 235–6.

15 Taussig, *In the Beginning Was the Meal*, 41–2, 72–3, 168–70; Smith, *From Symposium to Eucharist*, 173–217.

16 See Strømmen, *Biblical Animality after Jacques Derrida*, 67–89, who focuses on eating in Acts 10, and how the animals eaten get forgotten in the discussion.

17 Smith, *From Symposium to Eucharist*; Taussig, *In the Beginning Was the Meal*; see Gold and Donahue, *Roman Dining*.

18 See discussions in Purcell, "The Way We Used to Eat," 11–13.

19 The classic case here being Singer, *Animal Liberation*, especially 159–83. For Jesus as vegetarian, see Linzey, *Animal Theology*, 125–37.

20 Ehrman and Plese, trans., *Apocryphal Gospels*, 213.

21 For a discussion of ancient and modern vegetarian interpretations of John the Baptist, see Kelhoffer, *Diet of John the Baptist*, 134–93.

22 See discussion and critique by Kelhoffer, *Diet of John the Baptist*, 19–21.

23 Bernard, trans., "Life and Martyrdom of John the Baptist," 257.

24 Ehrman and Plese, trans., *Apocryphal Gospels*, 215.

25 Avalos, *Bad Jesus*, 333–4.

26 Linzey, *Animal Theology*, 135–7; see Horrell, *Bible and Environment*, 62–3.

27 Singer, *Animal Liberation*, 173.

28 For what John the Baptist eats, see Kelhoffer, *Diet of John the Baptist*.

29 Kelhoffer, *Diet of John the Baptist*, 127–8.

30 Ibid., 108–18.

31 Ibid., 129–32.

32 Ibid., 37–9.

33 Ibid., 81–99.

34 For an ancient discussion of bees and honey, see Pliny, *Natural History* 11.11–74; 21.70–4; trans., John Healy, *Pliny the Elder*.

35 Kelhoffer, *Diet of John the Baptist*, 43–6, 49–56; cf. Burnside, "At Wisdom's Table," 225–6, 233–6.

36 See discussion in Magness, *Stone and Dung, Oil and Spit*, 37, 39–40.

37 See, for example, discussion in Kelhoffer, *Diet of John the Baptist*, 107–8.

38 Kelhoffer, *Diet of John the Baptist*, 60–80.

39 Ibid., 122–3.

40 Ibid., 121–7.

41 See additional discussion of locusts and bees in Firmage, "Zoology (Fauna)," 1150.

42 Crawley, *Blackpentecostal Breath*, 3; Crawley, *Lonely Letters*, 88, 202.

43 Some have nothing to do with eating, such as the case when the disciples find a coin in a fish's mouth to pay taxes (Matt. 17:24–7).

44 Crossan, *Jesus*, 174–8.

45 Taussig, *In the Beginning Was the Meal*, 149–52; 167–8.

46 Firmage, "Zoology (Fauna)," 1146–7.

47 See discussion of synthetic meat and "eating well" in Wolfe, *Before the Law*, 95–7.

48 Davidson, *Courtesans and Fishcakes*, 27–8.

49 Ehrman and Plese, trans., *Apocryphal Gospels*, 26–7.

50 Cf. Peter's miracle in Acts of Peter 13; Spittler, *Animals in the Apocryphal Acts of the Apostles*, 148–54.

51 See discussion in Avalos, *Bad Jesus*, 333–4.

52 Klawans, "Was Jesus' Last Supper a Seder?"

53 Magness, *Archaeology of Qumran*, 114–5.

54 For discussion, see Crossan, *Jesus*, 66–70.

55 A note on translation: NRSV has "oxen," but the word *tauroi* can denote "bulls" or "oxen." Oxen would make it clear the animal was originally trained to be a work animal but may have been castrated. Bull denotes any adult male bovine.

56 Luke lacks the quoted part. In Luke's version, one person says he just purchased five oxen and needs to test them out and they do not kill the slaves (just turn them down).

57 In Luke, the king has the slave invite the poor, crippled, blind, and lame. Matthew's version stands in tension with the fish-sorting parable. Before the good and bad are sorted: here, because those originally invited responded negatively, the good and bad are invited and mixed together.

58 For Luke, the second issue is less of a concern, since it never says the King slaughtered animals; instead, we find a comment that one of the people who cannot make the feast has purchased some new oxen – the tractors of the ancient world – and wants to try them out. It provides a flash of verisimilitude (see chap. 2). Luke's version also shows up in the middle of Jesus having such a dinner and commenting on dinners in general; Luke has, therefore, organized a long segment of

the narrative with Jesus going to dinner and commenting on how the dinner is run, and then ending with a parable about a dinner.

59 On the domestication of cattle, pigs, and goats indigenous to Israel see Firmage, "Zoology (Fauna)," 1115, 1127, 1130–5.

60 Purcell, "The Way We Used to Eat," 12–13; Wilkins, "Land and Sea," 34–41, 44.

61 See Magness, *Stone and Dung, Oil and Spit*, 32–6.

62 See Singer, *Animal Liberation*, 174–6. Singer does not object to free-range eggs, but he does object to eggs derived from intensive factory farm operations.

63 See Warren, *Food and Transformation*; cf. Ginzburg, *Ecstasies*, 108.

64 *T. Abr.* 4 (Rec. A); Pseudo-Matthew 3.3; Warren, *Food and Transformation*, 9–11.

65 See Crossan, *Jesus*, 170–4.

66 See an attempt in Horsley, *Jesus and Empire*, 110.

67 Douglas, *Purity and Danger*, 42–58.

68 See Bulliet, *Hunters, Herders, and Hamburgers*, 17; ironically, he notes the increase of meat consumption coincides with the increasing numbers of elective vegetarians (those who are vegetarian from individual choice rather than from cultural tradition).

69 Firmage, "Zoology (Fauna)," 1120.

70 See Firmage, "Zoology (Fauna)," 1116

71 Freyne, *Jesus Movement*, 95.

72 For fish as a luxury item in fifth-century BCE Athens, see James Davidson, *Courtesans and Fishcakes*; see also Plato, *Republic* 404b–c. Davidson portrays the classical Greek love of fish as an obsession or craving. For the Roman period, see Wilkins, "Land and Sea," 34–41. For the local Palestinian context in the Roman period, see sources in Magness, *Stone and Dung*, 210n39; Firmage, "Zoology (Fauna)," 1147.

73 The argument being that in the blood is the "*nefesh*" or life, but this life was likely thought to be an air/blood amalgam; see Whitekettle, "A Study in Scarlet"; on the Qumran community, see Magness, *Stone and Dung*, 37–41.

74 This is also true in Greek sacrifice; see Davidson, *Courtesans and Fishcakes*, 12.

75 Socrates (as Plato presents him) gives an account of a sufficient city in which people are largely vegetarian, but, when pressed by Glaucon,

allows in the luxurious city meat-eating as well as many other unnecessary things (*Republic* 2, 372a–3c).

CHAPTER TWO

1 Quoted in Firmage, "Zoology (Fauna)," 1128.
2 Haraway, *Staying with the Trouble*, 16; see further discussion of working animals on 129.
3 On the "secondary products revolution" of animal domestication, see Firmage, "Zoology (Fauna)," 115–6.
4 Hobgood-Oster, *Dog's History of the World*, 3, 108.
5 Haraway, *When Species Meet*, 55; see 55–62 more generally.
6 Hobgood-Oster, *Dog's History of the World*, 4.
7 Broadie and Rowe, *Aristotle: Nicomachean Ethics*, 8.11 (1161b).
8 See also the comparison of domesticated animals and slaves by Donaldson and Kymlicka, *Zoopolis*, 74; yet, for them, it is more of a history of servitude that is to be overcome in co-citizenship.
9 Donaldson and Kymlicka, *Zoopolis*, 134–42.
10 Hobgood-Oster's analysis of dog burials alongside owners suggests that dogs have been tools but also more than tools for humans (*Dog's History of the World*, 40).
11 See criticisms of Haraway in Halberstam, *Wild Things*, 119, 149, 160.
12 For the health benefits for humans and the health deficiencies for dogs of this relationship, see Hobgood-Oster, *Dog's History of the World*, 59–78, 105–23.
13 Halberstam, *Wild Things*, 116, 149–55.
14 Ibid., 116 (emphasis original).
15 Donaldson and Kymlicka, *Zoopolis*, 141.
16 See Hobgood-Oster, *Dog's History of the World*, 105–23.
17 Ibid., 4.
18 Halberstam, *Wild Things*, 119, 149–51.
19 Wolfe, *Before the Law*, 13.
20 See the discussion of the difficulty of categorizing working animals and livestock between persons and things in Rabbinic literature in Beth Berkowitz, *Animals and Animality in the Babylonian Talmud*, 153–78; cf. Derrida's question of whether the "beast" is a "who" or a "what" in *Beast and the Sovereign*, 1:61–2, 140–1.

21 Reeve, trans., *Plato: Republic* 2, 370b–c.

22 Cf. Wolfe, *Animal Rites*, 178.

23 Rees, "Women Rule Over Them," 165–6.

24 McKay, "Dress Deployed as an Agent of Deception," 38.

25 Ibid., 41–2.

26 Rees, "Women Rule Over Them," 165–6; cf. McKay, "Dress Deployed as an Agent of Deception," 45.

27 For priestly garments, see Exod. 28–29; Lev. 6:10; 16:1–4; Ezek. 44:17–18.

28 The term is *ketonet passim*, which is difficult to translate (Gen. 37:1–4, 12–28). The only other person in the Hebrew Bible to wear a *ketonet passim* is Tamar, noting that this was the type of garment that princesses of Israel wore (2 Sam. 13). Joseph's and Dinah's genders were switched in the womb by God according to the rabbis (see *b. Ber.* 60a; cf. *Pseudo-Jonathan* to Gen. 30:21). For Joseph's other gender-nonconforming qualities, see *Gen. Rab.* 84.7. In this case, the *ketonet passim* is what Alfred Hitchcock would call a "MacGuffin" – an object that sets the plot in motion but is quickly dispensed with; see Truffaut, *Hitchcock*, 138.

29 See the collected essays in Finitsis, ed., *Dress and Clothing in the Hebrew Bible*; Finitsis, ed., *Dress Hermeneutics and the Hebrew Bible*; Upson-Saia, Daniel-Hughes, and Batten, eds., *Dressing Judeans and Christians in Antiquity*; and Upson-Saia, *Early Christian Dress*; Daniel-Hughes, *Salvation of the Flesh in Tertullian of Carthage*; Sebesta and Bonfante, eds., *World of Roman Costume*; and Edmondson and Keith, eds., *Roman Dress and the Fabrics of Roman Culture*. Croom, *Roman Clothing and Fashion* focuses primarily on stage of life and gender. For ancient Roman Palestine, see Edwards, "Social, Religious, and Political Aspects of Costume in Josephus," 153–9; Roussin, "Costume in Roman Palestine," 182–90.

30 Note the *Martyrdom of Perpetua*, where she has a vision of a tall shepherd with gray hair in paradise (likely God or Christ), milking a sheep and giving Perpetua fresh cheese that tastes sweet; see Warren, *Food and Transformation*, 136–7.

31 On the domestication of sheep and prevalence of wool over linen in ancient Palestine, see Firmage, "Zoology (Fauna)," 1114–6; cf. Borowski (*Every Living Thing*, 178), who assumes linen would have been the norm based on climatic conditions. Borowski surprisingly does not appear to be familiar with Firmage's work.

32 Firmage, "Zoology (Fauna)," 1126–7.
33 Donaldson and Kymlicka, *Zoopolis*, 136.
34 The purple was also supposed to have apotropaic properties for Roman children; see Olson, "Appearance of a Young Roman Girl," 141.
35 Magness, *Archaeology of Qumran*, 196.
36 While not the only clothing materials – there were luxury materials such as silk – wool and linen were the most dominant with wool being the most widely used; see Croom, *Roman Clothing and Fashion*, 19, 24–5.
37 See Pliny, *Natural History*, 8.189–97; 19.2; Firmage, "Zoology (Fauna)," 1115–6, 1126–7; cf. Borowski, *Every Living Thing*, 178–9.
38 Magness, *Stone and Dung*, 108–10; Edwards, "Costume in Josephus," 156–8.
39 More generally, see Goldman, "Roman Footwear," 101–29.
40 Goldman, "Roman Footwear," 122.
41 Magness, *Archaeology of Qumran*, 195; Magness, *Stone and Dung*, 111–20; Roussin, "Costume in Roman Palestine," 183; Spoelstra, "Apotropaic Accessories," 70.
42 Magness, *Stone and Dung*, 112.
43 Though it seems unlikely they would put such a luxurious item on a soon-to-be crucified man; for a discussion of murex and the dying of wool with it, see Pliny, *Natural History* 9.125–47; Firmage, "Zoology (Fauna)," 1148–50.
44 This identification between John the Baptist and Elijah and Elisha through clothing becomes overdetermined in the *Life of John the Baptist by Serapion* where Gabriel gives John the Baptist the scapular worn by Elijah and the belt worn by Elisha (3.11–12). On hairiness, beastliness, angelification, and overall liminal status, see Upson-Saia, "Hairiness and Holiness in the Early Christian Desert," 155–72.
45 See Crossan, *Jesus*, 46–7. Other people sometimes have discussions about their clothing, but mostly their outer cloaks. When Jesus calls the blind Bartimaeus to him, Bartimaeus throws off his cloak (Mark 10:50). On "Palm Sunday," the disciples threw their cloaks on the colt as a makeshift saddle, while the people also laid their cloaks on the road (Mark 11:7–8; Matt. 21:7–8; Luke 19:35–6; missing in John's account).
46 Cf. the "Hymn of the Pearl" in the Acts of Thomas; Ephrem the

Syrian's "Hymns of the Pearl," which are part of his *Hymns of Faith*; see Batten, "Paradoxical Pearl," 243.

47 See Upson-Saia, *Early Christian Dress*, 37.

48 For the history of pearl harvesting, trade, and values attached to pearls – from monetary to spiritual – see Batten, "Paradoxical Pearl," 233–50. On the characterization of "un-Roman," "foreign" adornments more generally, see Upson-Saia, *Early Christian Dress*, 15–32. Other animal products in the gospels include cloth and wineskins (Mark 2:21–2; Matt. 9:16–17). Wineskins were made from sheep or goat skin. See Davidson, *Courtesans and Fishcakes*, 40. Finally, there is the Isaiah scroll Jesus reads from in the synagogue in Nazareth (Luke 4:16–20). Scrolls could be made from either papyrus or animal skin ("parchment"), though there is the rare case of the "copper scroll" at Qumran; in general, however, while papyrus was relatively cheaper than parchment, animal skin lasts longer and would be more appropriate to the regular readings of the synagogue. Of the scrolls recovered from Qumran, for example, the vast majority are parchment; only about one hundred texts (13 per cent of the total) were made from papyrus. The "copper scroll" is actually made of bronze. See Magness, *Archaeology of Qumran*, 32–3.

49 Daniel-Huges, *Salvation of the Flesh in Tertullian of Carthage*, 8.

50 Pointed out by Burke and Landau, *New Testament Apocrypha*, xxviii; for a discussion of date and provenance, see Vuong, *Gender and Purity*, 31–59, 193–239.

51 Cf. Latin Infancy Gospels (Arundel Form) 61–4.

52 Cf. Latin Infancy Gospels (Arundel Form) 87.

53 Cf. Latin Infancy Gospels (Arundel Form) 112, 116.

54 See, for example, the Legend of Aphroditianus (Heyden) and Revelation of the Magi (Landau), both of which can be found in Burke and Landau, *New Testament Apocrypha*, 3–38.

55 Way ("Donkey Domain," 110–11) argues that the Hebrew term means "male equid."

56 For the domestication and imagery of donkeys, see Bulliet, *Hunters, Herders, and Hamburgers*, 143–73.

57 For a critique of this standard translation, especially "colt," see Way, "Donkey Domain."

58 Deutsch (*Hidden Wisdom*, 15) sees its literalism as a typical example of rabbinic interpretation.

59 Bauckham, "Reading the Synoptic Gospels Ecologically," 80–1; Horsley, *Jesus and Empire*, 131.
60 Bauckham, "Reading the Synoptic Gospels Ecologically," 81.
61 Stratton, "Magic, Abjection, and Gender," 161.
62 Firmage, "Zoology (Fauna)," 1137–8.
63 Bulliet (*Hunters, Herders, and Hamburgers*, 153–9) discusses Balaam and other cases in the region where the donkey has a spiritual connection in ancient Israelite religion, Judaism, Christianity, and Islam. He postulates a pre-Abrahamic connection between the ass and the spirit.
64 See Miller, *Eye of the Animal*, 51–6.
65 Firmage, "Zoology (Fauna)," 1138–40.
66 See discussion in Metzger, *Textual Commentary*, 90.
67 See Clement of Alexandria, *Who Is the Rich Man Who Shall Be Saved?* See the discussion of how ancient Christians dealt with this among other New Testament stories of poverty and wealth in late antiquity by Brown, *Through the Eye of a Needle*.
68 Horsley, *Jesus and Empire*, 123.
69 See Liddell and Scott, s.v., κάμιλος.
70 See Pliny, *Natural History* 8.1–32. While not indigenous to the region, people were aware of them, though it is not clear whether a first-century person in Roman Palestine would have seen one. See Firmage, "Zoology (Fauna)," 1140–1.
71 Firmage ("Zoology (Fauna)," 1110) also notes that the hippopotamus survived in marshlands surrounding the Jordan River until the Iron Age, but still before our period.
72 For the domestication and use of camels, see Bulliet, *Camel and the Wheel*.
73 Finley, *Ancient Economy*, 126; see also Firmage, "Zoology (Fauna)," 1129–30.
74 Matthew's version does not include this excuse (Matt. 22:1–14).
75 Everson, ed., *Aristotle: the Politics and the Constitution of Athens*, 1.1253b–4b.

CHAPTER THREE

1 Smith, *Religion of the Semites*, 213–440; Durkheim, *Elementary Forms*, 127–140, 338–54; Hubert and Mauss, *Sacrifice: Its Nature and Function*; Detienne and Vernant, *Cuisine of Sacrifice*.

2 Douglas, *Purity and Danger*, 115–16.

3 Girard, *Violence and the Sacred.*

4 Ibid., 8.

5 Bataille writes, "Sacrifice is the antithesis of production" and "in sacrifice the offering is rescued from all utility" (*Theory of Religion*, 49).

6 Bataille, *Theory of Religion*, 43–61. Whether one accepts Bataille's theory, one must admit the intimacy of a priest slicing an animal's flesh with a quick movement of a blade as hot, sticky blood pours out, even if it is not the kind of intimacy Bataille imagined. As Seesengood writes, "Flesh is too visceral for words; it is image, smell, taste, and touch. It is my left hand, resting on the still warm carcass, my right pressing a blade against it; it is the moment before the cut, the pressure of the skin pushing back against the blade, surprising in both its firmness and its pliability" ("What Would Jesus Eat?," 227).

7 Sherwood, "Cutting Up Life," 247.

8 Jay, *Throughout Your Generations Forever*, xxiii.

9 For a defense of sacrifice as a form of humility and securing peace in the land in the context of ecological hermeneutics, see Morgan, "Sacrifice in Leviticus," 32–45.

10 Note Montaigne's revulsion: "For my part, I have never been able to watch without distress even the pursuit and slaughter of an innocent animal, which has no defence [*sic*] and has done us no harm" ("On Cruelty," 186).

11 In the New Testament writings, this is most clear in the Letter to the Hebrews; see Calaway, *Sabbath and Sanctuary*, 139–77.

12 For example, Linzey, *Christianity and the Rights of Animals.*

13 Avalos (*Bad Jesus*, 333–43) cites the Passover meal of Luke 22 as well as Matthew 8 as evidence that Jesus supported sacrifice.

14 A point emphasized by Horsley, *Jesus and Empire*, 85. On Jesus's condemnation of the temple and priesthood, see further 86–98.

15 For issues surrounding the attitudes of Jesus, early Christians, and Galileans towards the temple, see the essays in Charlesworth, ed., *Jesus and Temple.*

16 Especially *Purity and Danger*; most of these theories emerged before her *Leviticus as Literature*, which engages the biblical scholarship that had built on her early work.

17 As part of the broader issue of purity rules; see Douglas, *Purity and Danger*, 42–58.

18 Milgrom, "Israel's Sanctuary," 390–9.

19 Gane, "Privative Preposition מן"; Milgrom, "Preposition מן"; Gane, *Cult and Character*; Nihan, *From Priestly Torah to Pentateuch*, 166–95; Calaway, *Sabbath and the Sanctuary*, 85.

20 This is in his commentary on Leviticus; see discussion by Klawans, *Purity, Sacrifice, and the Temple*, 27–32.

21 He lays this out with particular clarity in *Purity, Sacrifice, and the Temple*, 49–73; see discussion in Calaway, *Sabbath and Sanctuary*, 85–7.

22 I have refrained from discussing Walter Burkert's argument that sacrifice originated in the hunt; this seems unlikely for much of the biblical evidence, which focuses on domesticated animals and leaves hunted animals – even when permitted to eat – outside the sacrificial system. Though Burkert does have his followers among biblicists, such as Firmage, "Zoology (Fauna)," 1113. If Burkert is correct in his reconstruction of hunting as the origin of sacrifice, sacrifice had become so transformed that hunting does not provide any clear meaningful contribution to how sacrifice would have been understood. Bulliet (*Hunters, Herders, and Hamburgers*, 121–42) also follows the hunting-as-origin-of-sacrifice theory, noting, in particular, that there is often evidence of sacrifice in many societies pre-domestication. He sees the transition to domestic animals following in the trail of human sacrifice. He, therefore, largely sees a progression of hunting, human sacrifice, and domesticated animal sacrifice. In fact, he sees that sacrifice is the origin of domestication rather than domestication the origin of sacrifice. That is, the keeping of live animals for regularized sacrifice – rather than the occasional sacrifice of the hunt – led to the domestication of those animals kept for sacrifice. Therefore, the widespread equation of domesticated animals for sacrifice is due to the wild ancestors of those animals being herded to supply the sacrifice rather than the other way around. For an interesting juxtaposition of a modern autobiographical account of deer hunting, ancient sacrifice, and Jesus's eating, see Seesengood, "What Would Jesus Eat?" By contrast, note Sherwood's note that sacrificial systems necessarily create a distinction from other death activities, including hunting and murder ("Cutting Up Life," 248).

23 Jay notes that Isaac's "taste for game must be understood in sacrificial terms … Isaac's refusal to sacrifice led to his loss of control of his line of descent" (*Throughout Your Generations Forever,* 104).
24 Seesengood, "What Would Jesus Eat?," 232–4.
25 Klawans, *Purity, Sacrifice, and the Temple*, 58–62.
26 Ibid., 75–100.
27 YHWH is the name for God in the Bible that is usually translated as LORD in all caps.
28 See Calaway, *Sabbath and Sanctuary*, 92–5, 126–37, 168–75, 196–7; Klawans, *Purity, Sacrifice, and the Temple*, 145–74.
29 He is referring to 1 Sam. 21:1-6. Priests were allowed to eat the bread of the presence once new loaves were presented, but Jesus jumbles the account. While David and his companions seek bread from a priest and the priest gives them the bread of the presence, there is no indication that David and his companions entered the temple at Nob. Moreover, the priest lays out ritual regulations for consuming the bread – David and his companions can eat of the bread if they have kept themselves away from women and, therefore, are more pure. David ensures these conditions have been met.
30 This idea came from a conversation with James McGrath at the book exhibit at the 2019 SBL. Crossan (*Jesus*, 34) also hints at this in his reading of Josephus's account of John the Baptist. See Klawans, *Sin and Impurity*, 138–43.
31 Klawans, *Purity, Sacrifice, and the Temple*, 222–41.
32 Coloe, *God Dwells with Us*.
33 Klawans, *Purity, Sacrifice, and the Temple*, 237.
34 Firmage, "Zoology (Fauna)," 1145.
35 Though Luke's version is also pretty positive, while Matthew's is quite negative.
36 See Klawans, *Purity, Sacrifice, and the Temple*, 214–22, esp. 222.
37 Crossan, *Jesus*, 83.
38 Avalos (*Bad Jesus*, 337–9) sees the "gift" language as reflecting the general background of sacrifice being built upon tribute owed to kings.
39 Crossan, *Jesus*, 84.
40 See Avalos, *Bad Jesus*, 334–5.
41 Luke 13:1: "At that very time there were some present who told him about the Galileans whose blood Pilate had mingled with their sacrifices."

42 High levels of meat consumption are a post-domestic phenomenon.
43 Also Latin Infancy Gospels (Arundel Form) 76.
44 Neyrey, "John," in *New Oxford Annotated Bible with Apocrypha*, 1893, note to John 6:51–9.
45 Ehrman and Plese, trans., *Apocryphal Gospels*, 215.
46 See DeConick, *Thirteenth Apostle*, 123–4; Pagels and King, *Reading Judas*, 67–9.
47 Pagels and King, *Reading Judas*, 59.
48 See DeConick, *Thirteenth Apostle*, 134–48.
49 DeConick, *Thirteenth Apostle*, 5; emphasis original.
50 Kotrosits, *Rethinking Christian Identity*, 144.
51 Becker and Reed, eds., *Ways That Never Parted.*

CHAPTER FOUR

1 Doniger, "Making Animals Vanish"; Miller, *Eye of the Animal*, 50; Wolfe (*Animal Rites*, 101) also uses the terminology of animalization; Millar ("Species and Ethnicity in 1 Samuel 15") discusses animalizations in conjunction with ethnic othering in biblical materials.
2 See the discussion by Fernandez, "Persuasions and Performances."
3 Geerz, "Deep Play," 418.
4 Ibid., 419–20.
5 While a more recent development in biblical studies, several scholars have brought affect theories into dialogue with ancient biblical materials. Runions ("From Disgust to Humor") is credited with the first publication bringing affect theory and biblical materials together. Kotrosits's work (*Rethinking Early Christian Identity*; *How Things Feel*) has been helpful for me to navigate the swirling sensations of affect theory; see Cottrill, "Reading of Ehud and Jael"; Koosed, "Moses: The Face of Fear"; Knust, "Who's Afraid of Canaan's Curse"; Kotrosits, "Seeing Is Feeling"; Waller, "Violent Spectacles and Public Feelings." The affect theorists that resonated most with me and my work have been ones that intersect with queer theory: Cvetkotvich, *Archive of Feelings*; Ahmed, *Cultural Politics of Emotion*; and Sedgwick, *Touching Feeling*. I have also consulted Massumi, *Parables for the Virtual*; Stewart, *Ordinary Affects*; Schaefer, *Evolution of Affect Theory*; Gregg and Seigworth, eds., *Affect Theory Reader*. One of the divisions within affect

theory is how affects relate to emotions: do they include emotions or are they distinct from or opposed to emotion? An example of one who thinks emotions and affects are distinct if not opposed is Massumi, *Parables for the Virtual*; an example of how they are entangled is Ahmed, *Cultural Politics of Emotion*. While I am an interloper in my reading of affects, in my sources I largely encounter bodily sensations, impressions, feelings, and emotions as continually sliding into one another to the point that they are difficult – if not impossible – to disentangle.

6 Schaefer, *Religious Affects*, 99–100.
7 My language reflects Ahmed, *Cultural Politics of Emotion*, 8, 14.
8 Stewart, *Ordinary Affects*, 128.
9 Schaefer, *Religious Affects*, 108.
10 Ahmed, *Cultural Politics of Emotion*, 4, 10.
11 Ibid., 8.
12 See Knowles, "Serpents, Scribes, and Pharisees," 174.
13 Fernandez writes, "The metaphorical predication can be self-fulfilling. The king can be told so often he is a lion that he comes to believe it. He roars at his subjects and steadily stalks those he thinks are enemies to his interest. He finally springs upon them in fell and summary justice. In the privacy of our experience we are usually not sure who we really are. A metaphor thrust upon us often enough as a model can become compelling" ("Persuasions and Performances," 54).
14 Haraway, *When Species Meet*, 18; cf. Chen, *Animacies*, 95.
15 Wolfe, *Animal Rites*, 7–8, 37.
16 Adams, *Sexual Politics of Meat*; see Wolfe, *Animal Rites*, 105.
17 Slaves were regularly thought to be "domesticated animals" that were broken to the harness. See earlier, Plato, *Republic* 430c, in which slaves and animals are mentioned in the same breath as roughly equivalent.
18 See the analysis of "savagers" by Schaefer, *Religious Affects*, 120–46.
19 See Koosed, "Moses: The Face of Fear," 429.
20 Ahmed, *Cultural Politics of Emotion*, 68.
21 Ibid., 63.
22 Ibid., 65.
23 Knowles ("Serpents, Scribes, and Pharisees," 166) writes,

"Notwithstanding the plausibility of such language on the lips of John and Jesus alike, these terms are singularly appropriate to Matthew's own task of situating his community in relation to that of Pharisaic Judaism in the immediate aftermath of the first Jewish war."

24 Schaefer, *Religious Affects*, 131.
25 Ahmed, *Cultural Politics of Emotion*, 50.
26 Knowles, "Serpents, Scribes, and Pharisees," 167–8.
27 Ibid., 168–9.
28 Kahl, "Reading Galatians," 21–2, 33 plate D.
29 Derrida, *Animal That Therefore I Am*, 107–18; *Beast & the Sovereign*, 1:237–8, 244.
30 See discussion in Horrell, *Bible and Environment*, 90–5.
31 See Detienne and Svenbro, "Feast of the Wolves," 148–63; Deleuze and Guattari, (*Thousand Plateaus*, 26–38) are also obsessed with the wolf; see also Derrida, *Beast and Sovereign*, 1:1–2, 63–96.
32 Ahmed, *Cultural Politics of Emotion*, 72.
33 Ahmed writes, "borders need to be threatened in order to be maintained" (*Cultural Politics of Emotion*, 87).
34 I originally thought of this episode as "disgust," but as I read the affect literature on disgust, I realized something else was going on in this passage; Jesus has a haughtiness that makes him turn away from the woman with contempt rather than disgust. By comparison with disgust, contempt seems vastly undertheorized. Schaefer ("Visions of Contempt") gets close but is more about shame and dignity; for disgust, see Ahmed, *Cultural Politics of Emotion*, 82–100.
35 Lerner, "A Dogmatic Jesus," 50.
36 See the analysis by Cotter (*Christ of the Miracle Stories*, 137–60), who focuses on Mark's version and a reconstructed pre-Markan version.
37 Also noted by Smith, *Womanist Sass and Talk Back*, 37.
38 Lerner, "A Dogmatic Jesus," 51.
39 See Cotter, *Christ of the Miracle Stories*, 148–54; Shinall (*Miracles and the Kingdom of God*, 67–8) tries to mitigate the offensiveness by noting how women or lower classes chasten emperors or Rabbi Judah the Prince (Dio Cassius 69.6.3; Macrobius, *Saturnalia*

2.4.27; *b. B. Bat.* 8a). R. Judah the Prince only opens the storehouse of food for those learned in Torah; Jonathan ben Amram, pretending to be unlearned, asks for food and Judah rebuffs him. Jonathan replies, "Give me food, for even a dog and raven are given food." From then on, Judah allowed both learned and unlearned to take food from his storehouse.

40 See dog insults throughout both epics (e.g., *Iliad* 1.158–9; 1.225–7). The *Odyssey* is one of the few ancient Greek works that positively portrays a dog with Odysseus's faithful dog, Argos (*Odyssey* 17.290–319). Dogs were also considered useful as hunting dogs. Cf. the dogs of Patroklos that were sacrificed on their dead master's funeral pyre (*Iliad* 23.170–6).

41 See Haraway, *When Species Meet*, 45–67.

42 See Spittler, *Animals in the Apocryphal Acts of the Apostles*, 141–5.

43 Firmage, "Zoology (Fauna)," 1143; for a discussion of ancient Mediterranean dogs, see Hobgood-Oster, *Holy Dogs and Asses*, 84–9.

44 Stone, "Dogs of Exodus," 43–4; Hobgood-Oster (*Dog's History of the World*, 49) reflects on the liminality of dogs as well, here as mediators or guardians between the world of the living and the afterlife.

45 Quoted in Casson, *Libraries in the Ancient World*, 14.

46 See Betz, "Jewish Magic in the Greek Magical Papyri (*PGM* VII.260-71)," 58–61; for continued associations of dogs with the demonic, see Johnston, "Rising to the Occasion," 176–7, 180; Firmage, "Zoology (Fauna)," 1144.

47 For analysis, see Hobgood-Oster, *Dog's History of the World*, 61–9.

48 Crossan, *Jesus*, 123–58; cf. Horsley, *Jesus and Empire*, 28, 30.

49 See Graver, "Dog-Helen and Homeric Insult," 41–61.

50 See Segal, *Paul the Convert*, 140–3.

51 This may be part of eschatological speculation in which wild animals are driven out so that people can live in peace and safety (Ezek. 34:25; Isa. 35:9; Lev. 26:6; Horrell, *Bible and Environment*, 91–2). Though these texts usually focus on animals such as lions and dogs that are not "wild" but domesticated (or feral), they likewise seem to have no place in the idealized sacred space of the Dead Sea Scrolls or Revelation.

52 Note the discussion of animal sacrifice in modern Greece in which the unused parts must be buried so that the dogs do not get them; Georgoudi ("Sanctified Slaughter in Modern Greece," 190) cites the gospel tradition of not giving to the dogs what is holy.
53 See Magness, *Stone and Dung, Oil and Spit*, 46; *Archaeology of Qumran*, 120.
54 Cited from Cotter, *Christ of the Miracle Stories*, 152–3.
55 Lerner, "A Dogmatic Jesus," 53.
56 Cotter, *Christ of the Miracle Stories*, 153.
57 Vernant, "At Man's Table," 47.
58 Ibid., 66–7.
59 Smith, *Womanist Sass and Talk Back*, 28–45.
60 Ehrman and Plese, trans., *Apocryphal Gospels*, 269–71.
61 Deleuze and Guattari, *A Thousand Plateaus*, 240 (emphasis original); cf. Baudrillard, *Simulacra and Simulation*, 134–5.
62 See discussion in Magness, *Stone and Dung*, 50–2.
63 This is the reading of Davies and Allison, *Matthew 1–7*, 647–77; see Carter, *What Are They Saying*, 95–6.
64 Betz (*Essays*, 15n76) suggests that the "swine" may be a veiled critique of Epicureans. If so, it is so veiled as to be unrecognizable. Indeed, he elsewhere states that this passage is "clothed in images and metaphors clear only to the initiated" (*Essays*, 93).
65 DeConick, *Original Gospel of Thomas*, 263–5; *Recovering*, 121–3, 242–3.
66 Schaefer, *Religious Affects*, 131.
67 Broadie and Rowe, *Aristotle: Nicomachean Ethics*, I.5 (1095b20).
68 Kant, "What Is Enlightenment?," 1–2.
69 Haraway, *Staying with the Trouble*, 96; see further 204n89; *When Species Meet*, 33–5.
70 Cf. *2 Clem.* 5:2–4.
71 See Broadie, "Philosophical Introduction," 46–54.
72 For a discussion of this and other ways rabbinic literature aligns scholars with serpents, see Knowles, "Serpents, Scribes, and Pharisees," 170–4.
73 Explored by DeConick, *Voices of the Mystics*.
74 See Barton, "Reading the Prophets," 46–55.
75 See Dell, "Significance of the Wisdom Tradition," 56–69.

76 See discussion in Lohr, "A Jewish Teaching," 31–4.
77 Lohr, "A Jewish Teaching," 34–6.
78 See the second appendix in the posthumously published Foucault, *Confessions of the Flesh*, 302–14, where he covers biblical, Christian, Egyptian, Mesopotamian, and some of the Greek references to shepherding as leadership.
79 Recalled in Aristotle, *Nic.* 8.11 (1161a15).
80 For a study of Matt. 11:25–30, see Deutsch, *Hidden Wisdom*; see further, Mitchell, "Matthew 11:30."
81 Deutsch, *Hidden Wisdom*, 42–3.
82 For the translation of "beneficial" rather than "easy," see Mitchell, "Matthew 11:30," 325–40. I have followed suit in translating Thomas 90, which similarly uses the Graeco-Coptic term *ouchrestos*; otherwise, my translation largely matches most others.
83 Douglas, *Purity and Danger*, 55.
84 Deutsch, *Hidden Wisdom*, 115–6.
85 Discussed by Deutsch, *Hidden Wisdom*, 40–3.
86 Similarly, Kant ("What Is Enlightenment?," 2) speaks of the "yoke of tutelage," which one must throw off to think for oneself.
87 Cf. *Barn.* 2.6; for more expansive uses of "yoking" in Tannaitic Rabbinic literature, see Deutsch, *Hidden Wisdom*, 126–8, 133–5; Mitchell, "Matthew 11:30," 330–1; for further reflections on "yoking" in linguistic and personal human-animal entanglements, see Haraway, *Staying with the Trouble*, 110–14.
88 Cf. *1 Clem.* 16.17; Mitchell, "Matthew 11:30," 331–3.
89 This recounting follows the translation by Nickelsburg and VanderKam, *1 Enoch*, 124.
90 See Thiessen, *Contesting Conversion*, 91–2, 136–7.
91 Douglas, *Purity and Danger*, 55.
92 Others have *probaton* ("sheep"); others still have all three; see Metzger, *A Textual Commentary*, 138–9.
93 See, for example, Bauckham, "Reading the Synoptic Gospels Ecologically," 76.
94 See Horrell, *Bible and Environment*, 66–7.
95 Avalos (*Bad Jesus*, 343–5), by contrast, sees this as an abdication of stewardship, noting that Jesus seems to be ignorant about how humans alter habitats and destroy food sources for animals.

96 Point made by Bauckham, "Reading the Synoptic Gospels Ecologically," 76.
97 Berkowitz, *Animals and Animality in the Talmud*.

CHAPTER FIVE

1 I published an earlier version of this chapter as "Into Gospel Wilds: Divine, Demonic, and Animal," *Bible & Critical Theory* 19, nos. 1–2 (2023): 1–19.
2 Halberstam, *Wild Things*, ix.
3 Ibid., 3.
4 Ibid., 7.
5 Ibid., 26, 31.
6 Ibid., ix (emphasis original).
7 Ibid., 5.
8 Derrida, *Animal That Therefore I Am*, 132; *Beast and the Sovereign*, 1:17, 49–50, 126–7.
9 Derrida, *Beast and the Sovereign*, 1:50; cf. Aristotle, *Nic.* VII.1 (1145a24–33).
10 Derrida, *Beast and the Sovereign*, 1:1–31.
11 Stone, *Reading the Hebrew Bible with Animal Studies*, 116–17.
12 Pyper, "Lion King," 59–74; Stone, *Reading the Hebrew Bible with Animal Studies*, 116–39.
13 Gieschen, "Lamb (Not the Man)"; Kotrosits, "Seeing Is Feeling."
14 Erickson, "Apophatic Animal," 95.
15 Johnson, *Ask the Beasts*, 138.
16 Erickson, "Apophatic Animal," 97.
17 Johnson, *Ask the Beasts*, 139–40.
18 O'Connor, *Animals as Neighbors*, 101.
19 Ibid., 103, 115.
20 Firmage, "Zoology (Fauna)," 1144–5.
21 O'Connor, *Animals as Neighbors*, 101–15.
22 For "transing," see Strassfeld, "Transing Religious Studies"; *Trans Talmud*, 114–15; Stryker, Currah, and Moore, "Introduction."
23 Horsley, *Jesus and Empire*, 88–91.
24 Dixon, "Descending Spirit and Descending Gods," 770–2.
25 Cf. Dixon, "Descending Spirit and Descending Gods," 778–9.

26 Ibid., 767–9.
27 Cf. Douglas, "Deciphering a Meal," 77.
28 Dixon, "Descending Spirit and Descending Gods," 723n52.
29 Levison, *Boundless God*, 33–52.
30 Dixon, "Descending Spirit and Descending Gods," 764.
31 Fitzmyer, *Gospel According to Luke*, 480.
32 Ibid., 484; Craddock, *Luke*, 51.
33 Johnson, *Ask the Beasts*, 139; cf. Fitzmyer, *Gospel According to Luke*, 483–4.
34 Miller, *Eye of the Animal*, 33.
35 Haraway, *When Species Meet*, 3, 16–17, 27–35; *Staying with the Trouble*, 5.
36 Haraway, *Staying with the Trouble*, 13; cf. *When Species Meet*, 4–5.
37 Haraway, *Staying with the Trouble*, 11–12, 32, 55, 101–2; *When Species Meet*, 15–19, 134–6, 209, 245, 285–301; cf. Derrida, *Animal That Therefore I Am*, 10–11.
38 Haraway, *When Species Meet*, 5, 205, 242; Strømmen, *Biblical Animality*, 4–6.
39 Halberstam, *Wild Things*, 147–74.
40 O'Connor, *Animals as Neighbors*.
41 Morton, *Dark Ecology*, 49.
42 Milburn, *Just Fodder*, 82–106; cf. his other terms of neither fully wild nor domesticated animals: "animal thieves" (107–34) and "animal refugees" (135–55); see also the "liminal animal denizens" of Donaldson and Kymlicka, *Zoopolis*, 210–58.
43 Haraway, *When Species Meet*, 216–7.
44 Haraway, "Cyborgs to Companion Species," 301–2; cf. Stone, *Reading the Hebrew Bible with Animal Studies*, 28–9.
45 Bauckham, "Reading the Synoptic Gospels Ecologically," 79–80; cf. Horrell, *Bible and the Environment*, 65–71.
46 Bauckham, "Reading the Synoptic Gospels Ecologically," 80.
47 Cf. Philip L. Tite, "An Encomium on John the Baptist," in *New Testament Apocrypha: More Noncanonical Scriptures*, ed. Tony Burke and Brent Landau, vol. 1 (Grand Rapids: Eerdmans, 2016), 217–46. Miller, *Eye of the Animal*, 153; Stone, *Reading the Hebrew Bible with Animal Studies*, 124–5.
48 Halberstam, *Wild Things*, 125–46.

49 Douglas, *Purity and Danger*, 55; cf. Stone, *Reading the Hebrew Bible with Animal Studies*, 155–6.
50 Donaldson and Kymllicka, *Zoopolis*, 8.
51 Halberstam, *Wild Things*, 125–46.
52 Deleuze and Guattari, *Thousand Plateaus*, 26–38; cf. Derrida, *Beast and the Sovereign*, 1:1–2, 63–96; Detienne and Svenbro, "Feast of Wolves."
53 Deleuze and Guattari, *Thousand Plateaus*, 240–1; see Wolfe, *Animal Rites*, 169–71.
54 Deleuze and Guattari, *Thousand Plateaus*, 239.
55 Ibid., 239 (emphasis mine).
56 Ibid., 6–7.
57 Halberstam, *Wild Things*, 162–6.
58 Ibid., 37.
59 Deleuze and Guattari, *A Thousand Plateaus*, 241.
60 Halberstam, *Wild Things*, 119.
61 Ibid., 162–6.
62 Ibid., 149.
63 Ibid., 151.
64 Stone, *Reading the Hebrew Bible with Animal Studies*, 126.
65 Ibid., 125–9.
66 Klutz, *Exorcism Stories in Luke-Acts*, 82–151.
67 Halberstam, *Wild Things*, 147.
68 Ibid., 167.
69 Liddell and Scott, s.v. "*krazo*."
70 Halberstam, *Wild Things*, 79.
71 Deleuze and Guattari, *Thousand Plateaus*, 239.
72 Ibid., 241–2.
73 Halberstam, *Wild Things*, 148.
74 Shinall, *Miracles and the Kingdom of God*, 66.
75 Haraway, *When Species Meet*, 297; Singer, *Animal Liberation*, 119.
76 Singer, *Animal Liberation*, 191; Avalos, *Bad Jesus*, 328; cf. Horrell, *Bible and the Environment*, 65.
77 Bauckham, "Reading the Synoptic Gospels Ecologically," 81.
78 Liddell & Scott, s.v. "therion."

CHAPTER SIX

1 Giere, "This is My World!," 21–5; Tatum, "*Son of Man*'s 'Son of Man,'" 90–1; Tatum, *Jesus at the Movies*, 277; Staley, "Intertextual Reading of Two Jesus Films," 97–8; Baugh, "The African Face of Jesus in Film," 127. On "fantastic realism" or "magical realism" in these opening scenes, see Zwick, "Between Chester and Capetown," 110, 112, 115.

2 On the necessity of gap-filling in Jesus – and other biblical films – see Reinhartz, *Bible and Cinema*, 65–6; Flesher and Torry refer to the gap-filling and amplification of biblical narrative in film as "targumic." See Flesher and Torry, *Film & Religion*, 15–38; Flesher and Torry, "Filming Jesus: Between Authority and Heresy."

3 Webster, "Teaching *Son of Man*," 158: "Instead of focusing on the geography and exotic animals as in the older Hollywood tradition, recent African filmmakers tend to focus on distinctive individuals set within their broader social, cultural, and political contexts." She continues to discuss filmic techniques that tend toward the realist techniques often preferred by Third Cinema – longer takes, eye-level shots, mid-range to capture groups rather than individuals, largely eschewing close-ups – and puts these techniques in the context of Third Cinema globally and especially in Africa. And she looks at where *Son of Man* diverges from these tendencies as well (158–9).

4 Derrida, *Animal That Therefore I Am*, 132; *Beast and the Sovereign*, 1:17, 49–50, 126–7.

5 For a discussion of this "translation" of baptism into the Xhosa circumcision ritual, see West, "The *Son of Man* in South Africa?," 3–4; Giere, "This Is My World!," 25–7.

6 Others have noted a lion's roar here and elsewhere in the film; Walsh, "A Beautiful Corpse," 195. After several viewings, I do not hear it. I do, however, hear thunderclaps and wonder if that is what others are identifying as roars.

7 See Giere, "This Is My World!," 22–33.

8 There are some variances of readings of Satan throughout the film: some see a variety of characters who carry the symbols; others see

them as all Satan. Zwick ("Transformations of the Gospel in *Son of Man*," 114–15) sees the repeated behind-the-scenes appearances of Satan as something that ties it to *The Passion of the Christ*, which also introduces Satan "greasing the wheels" throughout the film. Baugh ("African Face of Jesus in Film," 127) also notes the strange, perhaps unique, repeated appearances of Satan throughout the film. Aichele ("Film as Betrayal," 208) also notes Satan's repeated appearances, but notes that Satan does not seem to drive the action or conflict, but merely "greases the gears." Giere calls him the "Satan-figure" – a slight slippage from "Satan." Tatum's chapter on this film in *Jesus at the Movies* (274–93) recognizes it is largely one figure (played by the same actor), but also has some slippage between Satan and Satan-figure, and even sometimes puts quotes around the phrase "Satan-figure." Staley ("What Hath New York City to Do with Khayelitsha?," 97n7) thinks a number of characters carry the goat-hoof cane. While the difference does not matter for my analysis – the hoof identifies each figure who carries it with Satanic powers – we may think of the various appearances of the hoof-carrier under slightly different guises as manifestations, incarnations, avatars, or simulacra of Satan. On the other hand, in a of couple articles, Adam Porter has identified the ability to change one's appearance as a characteristic typology of Satan-like figures (who are not necessarily Satan) in popular films: Porter, "Satanic but Not Satan"; "Satanic Humans."

9 For example, Revelation 12:9, 14, 15; 20:2; History of the Rechabites 20.3; Greek Life of Adam and Eve 16.5, 17.4; Justin Martyr, *1 Apology* 28.1; *Dialogue with Trypho* 45; Irenaeus, *Against Heresies* 3.23.3; 4.40.3. The references to the serpent in Jewish sources are found in Pseudepigraphical works that have a Jewish origin but were preserved by Christians and have Christian editing. One cannot find such an association in the Hebrew Bible, Rabbinic, and later Jewish works. In Revelation the reference to the "great serpent" may refer to the Leviathan, the primeval chaotic watery being, especially given its watery associations. The pseudepigraphical and second-century Christian sources make the Edenic serpent Satan's mouthpiece, while others say that Satan took the form of a serpent; some even say both (Irenaeus). See Wright, *Satan and the Problem of Evil*, for a discussion of all these sources.

10 For the locust as like John the Baptist, see West, "*Son of Man* in South Africa?," 4.
11 It marks the presence of the spiritual Satan in the world, whereas Satan incarnate already has a physical presence.
12 Punt ("Agency in *Son of Man*," 53) writes: "Does the slaughter of the innocents take on special meaning in Africa, with the entrance of Satan's boots hinting at both his complicity and satisfaction about the deed? Imperial agency appears not only to be expanded beyond the 'suits' but is also connected to Satan's appearance."
13 Rohrer-Walsh and Walsh, "Mary and the Mothers," 168; Tatum, *Jesus at the Movies*, 279.
14 Jesus dismisses the angel that has accompanied/protected him. And then the film cuts to the circumcision ritual as partly seen in the prologue.
15 See Flesher and Torry, *Film & Religion*, 179.
16 Staley suggests allusions to Joel 1:4; 2:25 or Revelation 9:1–11 to destructive, swarming locusts, though also throwing Mark 1:6 (John the Baptist's diet) in the mix for good measure; "Intertextual Reading of Two Jesus Films," 97. It could also be from a more well-known referent to the eighth plague of Egypt (Exod. 10:12–20), though, in this case, the plague is brought by God against the world rather than by Satan. Or, in the filmic imagination, looking beyond Jesus films, Imhotep revives this among several other plagues in the film *The Mummy*. Likewise, see Tatum, *Jesus at the Movies*, 277.
17 The woman is identified as Mary Magdalene only in the credits.
18 Being "necklaced," as this is called in South Africa, is usually for political and not sexual reasons; see discussion in West, "*Son of Man* in South Africa?," 10–11.
19 Another man shoots Jesus and they all bury him. Incarnate Satan steals dead Jesus's boots. This is the last shot of anything directly associated with Satan; his work is finished.
20 See West, "*Son of Man* in South Africa?," 3–4. Adejumobi ("Empire and Utopia," 77) notes that – just as Jesus bears African spiritual social markers (such as the white-chalked face and body) – so "Satan bears cultural markers that are markedly distinct and foreboding (for example, the goat-hoofed cane)."
21 In Xhosa, the words are "Mabutho! Izinyoni! Izinyoni!": the "birds"

are the victims they must "flush out" and kill; Nkadimeng and Baugh, "Strategies of Sound," 44.

22 Runions ("*Son of Man* and Resistance to U.S. Imperialism," 182) writes, "The hanging body of Jesus becomes a symbol of state and vigilante violence and a rallying point for protest. Vultures circle, evoking the rapacious and predatory nature of imperialism and its lackeys."

23 Of course, one does not need to use vultures and hawks or other large birds of prey to create terror, as Hitchcock's *The Birds* demonstrates.

24 Angels don feathered wings in the film adaptation of *Angels in America* as well.

25 West ("*Son of Man* in South Africa?," 6–7) writes: "not only did the donkey cart clearly locate the film in the rural and peri-urban areas of the Eastern and Western Cape, where the donkey is a primary means of transporting goods, but the donkey of the entry of Jesus into Jerusalem is redeployed here! Matthew's two donkeys are acknowledged (Mt. 21.2), and the 'unused' donkey of Mark (11.2) and Luke (19.30) is reworked into a well-used donkey!" This is also briefly mentioned in Tatum, *Jesus at the Movies*, 278.

26 See Tatum, *Jesus at the Movies*, 278.

27 West, "*Son of Man* in South Africa?," 7.

28 Other discussions of these "verisimilitude" animals: "'Today we are united, we are one people' is the angels' refrain, and this, the images make clear, includes the animals. African people are their communal and holistic way of life are celebrated, even if the reality of poverty remains" (West, "*Son of Man* in South Africa?," 7). When Jesus leaves his mother looking for work, we hear men singing in background, "We men are going to look for cattle/calves" – sung in Zulu rather than Xhosa. Building a herd is a symbol of economic prosperity and dignity (even if not literally raising cattle) – seeking economic stability (West, "*Son of Man* in South Africa?," 9). As Nkadimeng and Baugh write, "One of the distinguishing characteristics of the life of poor, rural people in South Africa, however, is the presence and sounds of animals, with the corresponding belief that animals are sensitive to the powerful human and transcendent realities that surround them (compare Ps. 148.7, 10)" ("Strategies of Sound," 45).

29 Punt, "Agency in *Son of Man*," 51.

CONCLUSION

1 Isabella Rossellini, quoted in Erickson, "Irreverent Theology," 56. This is referring to a video one can watch online: "Seduce Me – Noah's Ark," dir. Isabella Rossellini, 19 March 2012, doublewidemedia, http://www.youtube.com/watch?v=3WBr7aVADtU.

2 When I searched the peta2 website (www.peta2.com), I did not find anything related to LGBTQIA+ or queer social movements. Last checked 25 May 2023.

3 Erickson ("Irreverent Theology," 59) refers to the "twin ghettoization of LGTBQ voices and the earth"; for queer people being compared to animals for racist and dehumanizing purposes, see Chen, *Animacies*, 93–8, 102–6; for non-queer people to be queered and bestialized simultaneously to make them in/human to justify violence, see Runions, "Queering the Beast," 79–110; *Babylon Complex*, 179–212.

4 For both "queer animality" and trans considerations, see Chen, *Animacies*, 89–155 (chaps. 3–4). Chen writes, specifically using the prefixal "trans-" "as a way to explore that complexity of gender definition that lies between human gender systems and the gendering of animals" (*Animacies*, 137). Deleuze and Guattari in *Thousand Pleateaus* (esp. 232–309) have an emphasis on becoming that trans theorists have already appropriated, such as Crasnow, "'Becoming' Bodies."

5 Roughgarden, *Evolution's Rainbow*; Hird, "Animal Trans," 227–47; Parisi, "Nanoengineering of Desire," 290–3; Hayward, "Spider-women," 255–78.

6 Schaefer, "Precopulatory Sexual Cannibalism and Other Accidents."

7 Stone, "A Posttransexual Manifesto."

8 Halberstam, *Skin Shows*; *Wild Things*; "Animating Revolt/Revolting Animation," 265–81.

9 Barad, "Transmaterialities," 387–422.

10 Echoing Shakespeare's *Hamlet*, act 1, scene 2.

11 See, for example, Bender, *New Metaphysicals*, 12–18, 44–7; especially Barad, *Meeting the Universe Halfway*; Keller and Rubenstein, eds., *Entangled Worlds*.

12 Keller and Rubenstein, "Introduction: Tangled Matters," 4.

13 Ibid., 1.

14 Haraway, *When Species Meet*, 330n33.
15 Haraway, "Foreword," xxv.
16 Barad, *Meeting the Universe Halfway*, 33.
17 Ibid., ix.
18 Barad, "Transmaterialities," 387.
19 Erickson, "Irreverent Theology," 72; for another take on queer eco-biblical criticism, though one with less reference to animality, see Tipton, "A Backward Glance for a Queer Utopian Future."
20 Erickson, "Irreverent Theology," 73.
21 My tangled metaphors here also owe a bit to Haraway's conceptual "cat's cradle" to speak of the creative knots and patterns of science studies, feminist and anti-racist projects, and cultural studies; Haraway, "A Game of Cat's Cradle."
22 Haraway, *When Species Meet*, 3–4; Lingis, "Animal Body, Human Face," 166.
23 Keller and Rubenstein, "Introduction: Tangled Matters," 2.
24 See Adams, *Sexual Politics of Meat*.
25 See Murphy, "Devouring the Human," 51–62.
26 DeConick, *Original Gospel of Thomas*, 66–7.
27 See Crislip, "Lion and Human," 597–8.
28 Ibid., 595–613.
29 Pliny, *Natural History* 6.195; Crislip, "Lion and Human," 604.
30 See Crislip, "Lion and Human," 598–603.
31 Spielman, "Playing Roman in Jerusalem," 1–24.
32 Cf. Strømmen, *Biblical Animality after Derrida*, 119–22, who situates the imagery of the Beast of Revelation in terms of animals in the arena.
33 See, for example, *Martyrdom of Perpetua* 19–21; *Acts of Paul and Thecla* 3.27, 33–4.
34 See remarks by Spittler, *Animals in the Apocryphal Acts of the Apostles*, 1–5.
35 Hopkins, *Death and Renewal*, 5. That the events of the Roman arena were scenes of human sacrifice is the thesis of Furtrell, *Blood in the Arena*, 169–210. See the Christianization of Roman human sacrifice with martyr traditions in Castelli, *Martyrdom and Memory*, 52–67.
36 Crislip, "Lion and Human," 595–613.
37 See Freud, "The Uncanny," 121–62.
38 Haraway, *Simians, Cyborgs, and Women*; Strømmen, *Biblical Animality after Derrida*, 4–6.

39 See Singer, *Animal Liberation*, 25–94.

40 Spittler, *Animals in the Apocryphal Acts of the Apostles*, 141–2, also reflects on the in-between categorization of dogs as neither fully wild nor fully domesticated; also Hobgood-Oster, *Dog's History of the World*, 33–58.

41 For spirit possession as ventriloquism in ancient sources, see Levison, *Filled with the Spirit*, 157–9.

42 See Erickson, "Toward a Negative Zootheological *Imago Dei*," 88–9.

43 Lingis, "Animal Body, Inhuman Face," 167.

44 Cohen, "Preface: In a Time of Monsters," x.

45 Halberstam, *Skin Shows*, 27.

46 For the cherubim as monstrous, see Hamori, *God's Monsters*, 41–73.

47 Cohen, "Monster Culture (Seven Theses)," 6–7; see also Atherton, "Introduction," x; Lada-Richards, "Foul Monster or Good Saviour?," 46–9; Halberstam, *Skin Shows*, 8; Hamori, *God's Monsters*, 3–4.

48 Halberstam, *Skin Shows*, 48.

49 Hamori, *God's Monsters*, 241–2.

50 Cohen addresses gender and monsterization in "Monster Culture (Seven Theses)," 9.

51 Cohen, "Monster Culture (Seven Theses)," 7.

52 Perhaps there is a resemblance because God too is monstrous; see Hamori, *God's Monsters*, 263–72; Mills, "Queering the Un/Godly," 116.

53 Stryker, "My Words to Victor Frankenstein," 83–96.

54 Ibid., 85.

55 In an intersecting manner, Hobgood-Oster has spoken of designer dogs as genetic "monsters," citing Mary Shelley's novel. For her the lesson is that creators have a responsibility for their creatures. Dr Frankenstein had a responsibility for his creation to help integrate it into society; he failed his obligation. Creators of breeds – her example is pit bulls – have a responsibility toward their breeds that they sometimes are able to uphold and sometimes not, often with, particularly in "pure breeds," genetic diseases. Hobgood-Oster, *Dog's History of the World*, 107–8, 123. Adams (*Sexual Politics of Meat*, 95–107) notes the monster is vegetarian.

56 Barad, "Transmaterialities," 392.

57 Ibid., 392.

58 Smith, *Womanist Sass and Talk Back*, 28–45.

59 Ibid., 30.

60 Ibid., 29. She associates "sass" with women, children, and especially women of colour.

61 On the relationship between *monstrum* and *monstrare*, see Cicero, *On the Nature of the Gods* 2.3.7; *On Divination* 1.93; for *monstra* and signs of the divine, see Augustine, *City of God*, 21.8; Stryker, "My Words to Victor Frankenstein," 86; Atherton, "Introduction," vii; Lada-Richards, "Foul Monster or Good Saviour?," 44n9. On the relationship between *monstrum* and *miraculum*, see Kritzman, "Representing the Monster," 172. As Hamori (*God's Monsters*, 9) writes, "Monsters have meaning; monsters raise questions; monsters make us think."

62 Stryker, "My Words to Victor Frankenstein," 86.

63 Barad, "Transmaterialities," 383.

64 Cohen, "Monster Culture (Seven Theses)," 12.

65 Crawley, *Blackpentecostal Breath*, 3; *Lonely Letters*, 88, 202.

66 See Crasnow, "'Becoming' Bodies," 49–62. Butler states, "Life histories are histories of becoming, and categories can sometimes act to freeze that process of becoming" (*Undoing Gender*, 80). Lada-Richards ("Foul Monster or Good Saviour?," 56) reflects on a monster as an unresolved or incomplete or failed transition between categories, things that are neither nor.

67 See Cohen, "Monster Culture (Seven Theses)," 20.

68 Erickson, "Irreverent Theology," 59; Stryker, "My Words to Victor Frankenstein," 85–6; cf. the use of racist propaganda in horror in Atherton, "Introduction," ix.

69 Lada-Richards, "Foul Monster or Good Saviour?," 49, 58, 66–7; Atherton, "Introduction," xv.

70 Halberstam, *Skin Shows*, 27.

71 Barad, "Transmaterialities," 410.

72 Stryker, "My Words to Victor Frankenstein," 86.

73 Stone, "A Posttransexual Manifesto," 299 (emphasis original).

74 Plato, *Timaeus* 48e; Rubenstein, *Worlds without End*, 236; Stewart, *Ordinary Affects*, 128–9.

Bibliography

Adams, Carol J. *The Sexual Politics of Meat: A Feminist-Vegetarian Critical Theory*. 25th anniversary ed. New York: Bloomsbury, 2015. First published 1990.

Adejumobi, Saheed Yinka. "Empire and Utopia: 'Resurrecting' Postcolonial Visions and Beyond in *Son of Man*." In *Son of Man: An African Jesus Film*, edited by Richard Walsh, Jeffrey L. Staley, and Adele Reinhartz, 69–87. Sheffield, UK: Sheffield Phoenix Press, 2013.

Ahmed, Sara. *The Cultural Politics of Emotion*. 2nd ed. Edinburgh: Edinburgh University Press, 2014.

Aichele, George. "Film as Betrayal: Some Thoughts on *Son of Man*." In *Son of Man: An African Jesus Film*, edited by Richard Walsh, Jeffrey L. Staley, and Adele Reinhartz, 206–16. Sheffield, UK: Sheffield Phoenix Press, 2013.

Atherton, Catherine. Introduction to *Monsters and Monstrosity in Greek and Roman Culture*, edited by Catherine Atherton, vii–xxxiv. Bari, IT: Levante Editori, 1998.

Avalos, Hector. *The Bad Jesus: The Ethics of New Testament Ethics*. Bible in the Modern World 68. Sheffield, UK: Sheffield Phoenix Press, 2015.

Barad, Karen. *Meeting the Universe Halfway: Quantum Physics and the Entanglement of Matter and Meaning*. Durham, NC: Duke University Press, 2007.

– "Transmaterialities: Trans*/Matter/Realities and Queer Political Imaginings." *GLQ* 21, no. 2–3 (2015): 387–422. https://doi.org/10.1215/10642684-2843239.

Barton, John. "Reading the Prophets from an Environmental Perspective." In *Ecological Hermeneutics: Biblical, Historical and Theological Perspec-*

tives, edited by David G. Horrell, Cherryl Hunt, Christopher Southgate, and Francesca Stavrakopoulou, 46–55. London: T&T Clark, 2010.

Bataille, Georges. *Theory of Religion*. Translated by Robert Hurley. New York: Zone Books, 1992.

Batten, Alicia J. "The Paradoxical Pearl: Signifying the Pearl East and West." In *Dressing Judeans and Christians in Late Antiquity*, edited by Kristi Upson-Saia, Carly Daniel-Hughes, and Alicia J. Batten, 233–50. Farnham, UK: Ashgate, 2014.

Bauckham, Richard. "Joining Creation's Praise." *Ecotheology* 7, no. 1 (July 2002): 45–59.

– "Reading the Synoptic Gospels Ecologically." In *Ecological Hermeneutics: Biblical, Historical and Theological Perspectives*, edited by David G. Horrell, Cherryl Hunt, Christopher Southgate, and Francesca Stavrakopoulou, 70–82. London: T&T Clark, 2010.

Baudrillard, Jean. *Simulacra and Simulation*. Translated by Sheila Faria Glaser. Ann Arbor, MI: University of Michigan Press, 1994.

Baugh, Lloyd. "The African Face of Jesus in Film: Two Texts, a New Tradition." In *Son of Man: An African Jesus Film*, edited by Richard Walsh, Jeffrey L. Staley, and Adele Reinhartz, 120–32. Sheffield, UK: Sheffield Phoenix Press, 2013.

Becker, Adam, and Annette Yoshiko Reed, eds. *The Ways that Never Parted: Jews and Christians in Late Antiquity and the Early Middle Ages*. Minneapolis: Fortress Press, 2007.

Bender, Courtney. *The New Metaphysicals: Spirituality and the American Religious Imagination*. Chicago: University of Chicago Press, 2010.

Bentham, Jeremy. *The Principles of Morals and Legislation*. Buffalo, NY: Prometheus Books, 1988.

Berkowitz, Beth. *Animals and Animality in the Babylonian Talmud*. Cambridge: Cambridge University Press, 2018.

Bernard, Andrew, trans. "The Life and Martyrdom of John the Baptist." In *New Testament Apocrypha: More Noncanonical Scriptures*, vol. 1, edited by Tony Burke and Brent Landau, 247–67. Grand Rapids, MI: Eerdmans, 2016.

Betz, Hans Dieter. *Essays on the Sermon on the Mount*. Translated by L.L. Welborn. Minneapolis: Fortress Press, 2009.

– "Jewish Magic in the Greek Magical Papyri (PGM VII.260–71)." In *Envisioning Magic: A Princeton Seminar and Symposium*, edited by Peter Schäfer and Hans G. Kippenberg, 45–63. Leiden, NL: Brill, 1997.

Birkeland, Janis. "Ecofeminism: Linking Theory and Practice." In *Ecofeminism: Women, Animals, Nature*, edited by Greta Gaard, 13–59. Philadelphia: Temple University Press, 1993.

Borowski, Oded. *Every Living Thing: Daily Use of Animals in Ancient Israel.* Tucson, AZ: AltaMira Press, 1998.

Bovon, François. "The Suspension of Time in Chapter 18 of *Protevangelium Jacobi*." In *The Future of Christianity: Essays in Honor of Helmut Koester*, edited by Birger A. Pearson, 393–405. Minneapolis: Fortress Press, 1991.

Broadie, Sarah. "Philosophical Introduction." In *Aristotle: Nicomachean Ethics*, edited by Sarah Broadie and Christopher Rowe, translated by Christopher Rowe, 9–91. New York: Oxford University Press, 2002.

Broadie, Sarah, and Christopher Rowe, eds. *Aristotle: Nicomachean Ethics.* Translated by Christopher Rowe. New York: Oxford University Press, 2002.

Brown, Peter. *Through the Eye of a Needle: Wealth, the Fall of Rome, and the Making of Christianity in the West, 350–550 AD*. Princeton, NJ: Princeton University Press, 2012.

Bulliet, Richard W. *The Camel and the Wheel.* Columbia University Press, 1990.

– *Hunters, Herders, and Hamburgers: The Past and Future of Human-Animal Relationships*. New York: Columbia University Press, 2005.

Burnside, Jonathan. "At Wisdom's Table: How Narrative Shapes the Biblical Food Laws and Their Social Function." *Journal of Biblical Literature* 134, no. 2 (2016): 223–45. https://doi.org/10.15699/jbl.1352.2016.3042.

Burrus, Virginia. *Ancient Christian Ecopoetics: Cosmologies, Saints, Things.* Philadelphia: University of Pennsylvania Press, 2018.

Butler, Judith. *Undoing Gender*. New York: Routledge, 2004.

Bynum, Caroline Walker. *Metamorphosis and Identity*. New York: Zone Books, 2001.

Calaway, Jaeda C. "Into Gospel Wilds: Divine, Demonic, and Animal." *The Bible & Critical Theory* 19, nos. 1–2 (2023): 1–19. https://bibleandcriticaltheory.com/vol-19-no-1-2-2023-jaeda-c-calaway/.

– *The Sabbath and the Sanctuary: Access to God in the Letter to the Hebrews and Its Priestly Context*. Tübingen, DE: Mohr Siebeck, 2013.

Carter, Warren. *What Are They Saying about Matthew's Sermon on the Mount?* Mahwah, NJ: Paulist Press, 1994.

Casson, Lionel. *Libraries in the Ancient World*. New Haven, CT: Yale University Press, 2001.

Chen, Mel Y. *Animacies: Biopolitics, Racial mattering, and Queer Affect*. Durham, NC: Duke University Press, 2012.

Cohen, Jeffrey Jerome. "Monster Culture (Seven Theses)." In *Monster Theory: Reading Culture*, edited by Jeffrey Jerome Cohen, 3–25. Minneapolis: University of Minnesota Press, 1996.

– "Preface: In a Time of Monsters." In *Monster Theory: Reading Culture*, edited by Jeffrey Jerome Cohen, vii–xiii. Minneapolis: University of Minnesota Press, 1996.

Coloe, Mary L. *God Dwells with Us: Temple Symbolism in the Fourth Gospel*. Collegeville, MN: Liturgical Press, 2001.

Cotter, Wendy J., CSJ. *The Christ of the Miracle Stories: Portrait through Encounter*. Ada, MI: Baker Academic, 2010.

Cottrill, Amy C. "A Reading of Ehud and Jael through the Lens of Affect Theory." *Biblical Interpretation* 22 (2014): 430–49. https://doi.org/10.1163/15685152-02245p04.

Craddock, Fred B. *Luke*. Louisville, KY: John Knox Press, 1990.

Crasnow, S.J. "'Becoming' Bodies: Affect Theory, Transgender Jews, and the Rejection of the Coherent Subject." *Crosscurrents* 71, no. 1 (March 2021): 49–62. https://doi.org/10.1353/cro.2021.0003.

Crawley, Ashon T. *Blackpentecostal Breath: The Aesthetics of Possibility*. New York: Fordham University Press, 2017.

– *The Lonely Letters*. Durham, NC: Duke University Press, 2020.

Crislip, Andrew. "Lion and Human in *Gospel of Thomas* Logion 7." *Journal of Biblical Literature* 126, no. 3 (2007): 595–613. https://doi.org/10.2307/27638454.

Crossan, John Dominic. *The Historical Jesus: The Life of a Mediterranean Jewish Peasant*. Edinburgh: T&T Clark, 1991.

– *Jesus: A Revolutionary Biography*. San Francisco: HarperSanFrancisco, 1994.

Daniel-Hughes, Carly. *The Salvation of the Flesh in Tertullian of Carthage: Dressing for the Resurrection*. London: Palgrave Macmillan, 2011.

Darwin, Charles. *The Descent of Man, and Selection in Relation to Sex*. Princeton, NJ: Princeton University Press, 1981. First published 1871 by J. Murray.

Davidson, James N. *Courtesans and Fishcakes: The Consuming Passions of Classical Athens*. Chicago: University of Chicago Press, 1997.

Davies, W.D., and Dale Allison. *The Gospel According to Saint Matthew*. Vol. 1. London: T&T Clark, 1988.

DeConick, April D. *The Original Gospel of Thomas in Translation: With a Commentary and New English Translation of the Complete Gospel*. London: T&T Clark, 2006.

– *Recovering the Original Gospel of Thomas: A History of the Gospel and Its Growth*. London: T&T Clark, 2005.

– *The Thirteenth Apostle: What the Gospel of Judas Really Says*. Rev. ed. London: Continuum, 2009.

– *Voices of the Mystics: Early Christian Discourse in the Gospels of John and Thomas and Other Ancient Christian Literature*. Sheffield, UK: Sheffield Academic Press, 2001.

Deleuze, Gilles, and Félix Guattari. *A Thousand Plateaus: Capitalism and Schizophrenia*. Translated by Brian Massumi. Minneapolis: University of Minnesota Press, 1987.

Dell, Katharine J. "The Significance of the Wisdom Tradition in the Ecological Debate." In *Ecological Hermeneutics: Biblical, Historical and Theological Perspectives*, edited by David G. Horrell, Cherryl Hunt, Christopher Southgate, and Francesca Stavrakopoulou, 56–69. London: T&T Clark, 2010.

Derrida, Jacques. *The Animal That Therefore I Am*. Edited by Marie-Louise Mallet. Translated by David Wills. Perspectives in Continental Philosophy. New York: Fordham University Press, 2008.

– *The Beast and the Sovereign*. 2 vols. Translated by Geoffrey Bennington. Chicago: University of Chicago Press, 2009–11.

Detienne, Marcel. "Culinary Practices and the Spirit of Sacrifice." In *The Cuisine of Sacrifice among the Greeks*, edited by Marcel Detienne and Jean-Pierre Vernant, 1–20. Translated by Paula Wissig. Chicago: University of Chicago Press, 1986.

Detienne, Marcel, and Jesper Svenbro. "The Feast of the Wolves, or the Impossible City." In *The Cuisine of Sacrifice among the Greeks*, edited by Marcel Detienne and Jean-Pierre Vernant, 148–63. Translated by Paula Wissig. Chicago: University of Chicago Press, 1986.

Deutsch, Celia. *Hidden Wisdom and the Easy Yoke: Wisdom, Torah and Discipleship in Matthew 11.25–30*. JSNTSS 18. Sheffield: JSOT Press, 1987.

Diamond, Irene, and Gloria Feman Orenstein, eds. *Reweaving the World: The Emergence of Ecofeminism*. Oakland, CA: Sierra Club Books, 1990.

Dixon, Edward P. "Descending Spirit and Descending Gods: A 'Greek'

Interpretation of the Spirit's 'Descent as a Dove' in Mark 1:10." *Journal of Biblical Literature* 128, no. 4 (2009): 759–80. https://doi.org/10.2307/25610218.

Donaldson, Sue, and Will Kymlicka. *Zoopolis: A Political Theory of Animal Rights*. New York: Oxford University Press, 2011.

Doniger, Wendy. "Epilogue: Making Animals Vanish." In *Animals and the Human Imagination: A Companion to Animal Studies*, edited by Aaron Gross and Anne Vallely, 348–53. New York: Columbia University Press, 2012.

Donovan, Josephine. "Animals Rights and Feminist Theory." In *Ecofeminism: Women, Animals, Nature*, edited by Greta Gaard, 167–94. Philadelphia: Temple University Press, 1993.

Douglas, Mary. "Deciphering a Meal." *Daedalus* 101, no. 1 (Winter 1972): 61–81. https://www.jstor.org/stable/20024058.

– *Purity and Danger: An Analysis of Concepts of Pollution and Taboo*. New York: Routledge, 2002. First published 1966.

Durkheim, Emile. *The Elementary Forms of Religious Life*. Translated by Karen E. Fields. Los Angeles: Free Press, 1995.

Edmondson, Jonathan, and Allison Keith, eds. *Roman Dress and the Fabrics of Roman Culture*. Toronto: University of Toronto Press, 2008.

Edwards, Douglas R. "The Social, Religious, and Political Aspects of Costume in Josephus." In *The World of Roman Costume*, edited by Judith Lynn Sebesta and Larissa Bonfante, 153–9. Madison: University of Wisconsin Press, 1994.

Ehrman, Bart, and Zlatko Plese, trans. *The Apocryphal Gospels: Texts and Translations*. New York: Oxford University Press, 2011.

Erickson, Jacob J. "The Apophatic Animal: Toward a Negative Zootheological Imago Dei." In *Divinanimality: Animal Theory, Creaturely Theology*, edited by Stephen D. Moore, 88–99. New York: Fordham University Press, 2014.

– "Irreverent Theology: On the Queer Ecology of Creation." In *Meaningful Flesh: Reflections on Religion and Nature for a Queer Planet*, edited by Whitney A. Bauman, 55–79. Santa Barbara: Punctum Books, 2018.

Everson, Stephen, ed. *Aristotle: The Politics and the Constitution of Athens*. Cambridge: Cambridge University Press, 1996.

Fernandez, James W. "Persuasions and Performance: Of the Beast in Every Body … And the Metaphors of Everyman." *Daedalus* 101, no. 1 (Winter 1972): 39–60. https://www.jstor.org/stable/20024057.

Finitsis, Antonios, ed. *Dress and Clothing in the Hebrew Bible: "For All Her Household Are Clothed in Crimson."* London: T&T Clark, 2019.

– *Dress Hermeneutics and the Hebrew Bible: "Let Your Garments Always Be Bright."* London: T&T Clark, 2022.

Finley, M.I. *The Ancient Economy*. Updated ed. Sather Classical Lectures, vol. 43. Berkeley: University of California Press, 1999. First published 1973.

Firmage, Edwin. "Zoology (Fauna)." In *The Anchor Bible Dictionary*, vol. 6 Si–Z, edited by David Noel Freedman, 1109–67. New York: Doubleday, 1992.

Fitzmyer, Joseph A., SJ. *The Gospel According to Luke (I–IX)*. Anchor Bible 28. New York: Doubleday, 1981.

Flannery, Frances. "Senators, Snowballs, and Scripture: The Bible and Climate Change." In *The Bible in Political Debate: What Does It Really Say?*, edited by Frances Flannery and Rodney A. Werline, 61–74. London: Bloomsbury, 2016.

Flesher, Paul V.M., and Robert Torry. "Filming Jesus: Between Authority and Heresy." *Journal of Religion & Film* 8, no. 1 (February 2004): article 14. https://doi.org/10.32873/uno.dc.jrf.08.01.14.

– *Film & Religion: An Introduction*. Nashville, TN: Abingdon Press, 2007.

Foucault, Michel. *Confessions of the Flesh: History of Sexuality, Volume 4*. Edited by Frédéric Gros. New York: Pantheon, 2021.

Freud, Sigmund. "The Uncanny." In *The Uncanny*, translated by David McLintock, 121–62. New York: Penguin, 2003.

Freyne, Seán. *The Jesus Movement and Its Expansion: Meaning and Mission*. Grand Rapids, MI: Eerdmans, 2014.

Furtrell, Alison. *Blood in the Arena: The Spectacle of Roman Power*. Austin: University of Texas Press, 1997.

Gaard, Greta, ed. *Ecofeminism: Women, Animals, Nature*. Philadelphia: Temple University Press, 1993.

Gaard, Greta. "Living Interconnections with Animals and Nature." In *Ecofeminism: Women, Animals, Nature*, edited by Greta Gaard, 1–12. Philadelphia: Temple University Press, 1993.

Gane, Roy E. *Cult and Character: Purification Offerings, Day of Atonement, and Theodicy*. Ann Arbor, MI: Eisenbrauns, 2005.

– "Privative Preposition מִן in Purification Offering Pericopes and the Changing Face of 'Dorian Gray.'" *Journal of Biblical Literature* 127, no. 2 (2008): 209–22. https://doi.org/10.2307/25610117.

Geertz, Clifford. "Deep Play: Notes on the Balinese Cockfight." In *The Interpretation of Cultures*, 412–53. New York: Basic Books, 2000. First published in *Daedalus* 101, no. 1 (Winter 1972): 1–37.

Georgoudi, Stella. "Sanctified Slaughter in Modern Greece: The 'Kourbánia' of the Saints." In *The Cuisine of Sacrifice among the Greeks*, edited by Marcel Detienne and Jean-Pierre Vernant, 183–203. Translated by Paula Wissig. Chicago: University of Chicago Press, 1986.

Giere, S.D. "'This Is My World'! *Son of Man (Jezile)* and Cross-Cultural Convergences of Bible and World." In *Son of Man: An African Jesus Film*, edited by Richard Walsh, Jeffrey L. Staley, and Adele Reinhartz, 23–33. Sheffield, UK: Sheffield Phoenix Press, 2013.

Gieschen, Charles. "The Lamb (Not the Man) on the Divine Throne." In *Israel's God and Rebecca's Children: Christology and Community in Early Judaism and Christianity: Essays in Honor of Larry W. Hurtado and Alan F. Segal*, edited by David B. Capes, April D. DeConick, Helen K. Bond, and Troy Miller, 227–43. Waco, TX: Baylor University Press, 2007.

Giffney, Noreen, and Myra J. Hird. "Queering the Non/Human." In *Queering the Non/Human*, edited by Noreen Giffney and Myra J. Hird, 1–16. London: Routledge, 2008.

Ginzburg, Carlo. *Ecstasies: Deciphering the Witches' Sabbath*. Translated by Raymond Rosenthal. New York: Penguin Books, 1991.

Girard, René. *Violence and the Sacred*. Translated by Patrick Gregory. Baltimore: Johns Hopkins University Press, 1977.

Gold, Barbara K., and John F. Donahue. *Roman Dining*. Special Issue of American Journal of Philology. Baltimore: Johns Hopkins University Press, 2005.

Goldman, Norma. "Roman Footwear." In *The World of Roman Costume*, edited by Judith Lynn Sebesta and Larissa Bonfante, 101–29. Madison: University of Wisconsin Press, 1994.

Goodacre, Mark. *The Case against Q: Studies in Markan Priority and the Synoptic Problem*. Norcross, GA: Trinity Press International, 2002.

Gruen, Lori. "Dismantling Oppression: An Analysis of the Connection Between Women and Animals." In *Ecofeminism: Women, Animals, Nature*, edited by Greta Gaard, 60–90. Philadelphia: Temple University Press, 1993.

Halberstam, Jack. "Animating Revolt/Revolting Animation: Penguin Love, Doll Sex and the Spectacle of the Queer Nonhuman." In *Queer-*

ing the Non/Human, edited by Noreen Giffney and Myra J. Hird, 265–81. London: Routledge, 2008.

– *The Queer Art of Failure*. Durham, NC: Duke University Press, 2011.

– *Skin Shows: Gothic Horror and the Technology of Monsters*. Durham, NC: Duke University Press, 1995.

– *Wild Things: The Disorder of Desire*. Durham, NC: Duke University Press, 2020.

Hamori, Esther. *God's Monsters: Vengeful Spirits, Deadly Angels, Hybrid Creatures, and Divine Hitmen of the Bible*. Minneapolis: Broadleaf Books, 2023.

Haraway, Donna J. "Foreword." In *Queering the Non/Human*, edited by Noreen Giffney and Myra J. Hird, xxiv–xxvi. London: Routledge, 2008.

– "A Game of Cat's Cradle: Science Studies, Feminist Theory, Cultural Studies." *Configurations* 1 (1994): 59–71. https://doi.org/10.1353/con.1994.0009.

– *Staying with the Trouble: Making Kin in the Chthulucene*. Durham, NC: Duke University Press, 2016.

– *When Species Meet*. Minneapolis: University of Minnesota Press, 2007.

Harrison, Peter. "Subduing the Earth: Genesis 1, Early Modern Science, and the Exploitation of Nature." *Journal of Religion* 79, no. 1 (1999): 86–109.

Hayward, Eva. "Spiderwomen." In *Trap Door: Trans Cultural Production and the Politics of Visibility*, edited by Reina Gossett, Eric A. Stanley, and Johanna Burton, 255–79. Cambridge, MA: MIT Press, 2017.

Healy, John, trans. *Pliny the Elder: Natural History: A Selection*. New York: Penguin, 1991, 2004.

Hird, Myra J. "Animal Trans." In *Queering the Non/Human*, edited by Noreen Giffney and Myra J. Hird, 227–47. London: Routledge, 2008.

Hobgood-Oster, Laura. *A Dog's History of the World: Canines and the Domestication of Humans*. Waco, TX: Baylor University Press, 2014.

– *Holy Dogs and Asses: Animals in the Christian Tradition*. Champaign: University of Illinois Press, 2008.

Hopkins, Keith. *Death and Renewal*. Cambridge: Cambridge University Press, 1983.

Horrell, David G. *The Bible and the Environment: Towards a Critical Ecological Biblical Theology*. Sheffield, UK: Equinox, 2010.

Horrell, David G., Cherryl Hunt, and Christopher Southgate. "Appeals to the Bible in Ecotheology and Environmental Ethics: A Typology of Hermeneutical Stances." *Studies in Christian Ethics* 21, no. 2 (2008): 219–38. https://doi.org/10.1177/0953946808094.

Horrell, David G., Cherryl Hunt, Christopher Southgate, and Francesca Stavrakopoulou, eds. *Ecological Hermeneutics: Biblical, Historical and Theological Perspectives*. London: T&T Clark, 2010.

Horsley, Richard A. *Jesus and Empire: The Kingdom of God and the New World Disorder*. Minneapolis: Fortress Press, 2003.

Hubert, Henri, and Marcel Mauss. *Sacrifice: Its Nature and Function*. Translated by W.D. Walls. Chicago: University of Chicago Press, 1964. Originally published as *Essai sur la nature et la function du sacrifice* (L'Année sociologique, 1898).

Johnson, Elizabeth A. *Ask the Beasts: Darwin and the God of Love*. London: Bloomsbury, 2014.

Johnston, Sarah Iles. "Rising to the Occasion: Theurgic Ascent in Its Cultural Milieu." In *Envisioning Magic: A Princeton Seminar and Symposium*, edited by Peter Schäfer and Hans G. Kippenberg, 165–94. Leiden, NL: Brill, 1997.

Kahl, Brigitte. "Reading Galatians and Empire at the Great Altar of Pergamon." *Union Theological Seminary Quarterly Review* 59 (2005): 21–43.

Kant, Immanuel. "What Is Enlightenment?" In *The Portable Enlightenment Reader*, edited by Isaac Kramnick, 1–7. New York: Penguin, 1995.

Kelhoffer, James A. *The Diet of John the Baptist: "Locusts and Wild Honey" in Synoptic and Patristic Interpretation*. WUNT 176. Tübingen, DE: Mohr Siebeck, 2005.

Keller, Catherine, and Mary-Jane Rubenstein, eds. *Entangled Worlds: Religion, Science, and New Materialisms*. New York: Fordham University Press, 2017.

Klawans, Jonathan. *Impurity and Sin in Ancient Judaism*. Oxford University Press, 2000.

– *Purity, Sacrifice, and the Temple: Symbolism and Supersessionism in the Study of Ancient Judaism*. New York: Oxford University Press, 2006.

– "Was Jesus' Last Supper a Seder?" *Bible Review* (October 2001). https://library.biblicalarchaeology.org/article/was-jesus-last-supper-a-seder/.

Klutz, Todd. *The Exorcism Stories in Luke-Acts: A Sociostylistic Reading*. Cambridge: Cambridge University Press, 2004.

Knowles, Michael P. "Serpents, Scribes, and Pharisees." *Journal of Biblical Literature* 133, no. 1 (2014): 165–79. https://doi.org/10.15699/jbibllite.133.1.165.

Knust, Jennifer. "Who's Afraid of Canaan's Curse? Genesis 9:18–29 and the Challenge of Reparative Reading." *Biblical Interpretation* 22 (2014): 388–413. https://hdl.handle.net/10161/26770.

Koosed, Jennifer L., ed. *The Bible and Posthumanism*. Atlanta: Society of Biblical Literature, 2014.

Koosed, Jennifer L. "Humanity at Its Limits." In *The Bible and Posthumanism*, edited by Jennifer Koosed, 3–12. Atlanta: Society of Biblical Literature, 2014.

– "Moses: The Face of Fear." *Biblical Interpretation* 22 (2014): 414–29. https://doi.org/10.1163/15685152-02245p03.

Kotrosits, Maia. *How Things Feel: Biblical Studies, Affect Theory, and the (Im)Personal*. Leiden, NL: Brill, 2016.

– *Rethinking Early Christian Identity: Affect, Violence, and Belonging*. Minneapolis: Fortress Press, 2015.

– "Seeing Is Feeling: Revelation's Enthroned Lamb and Ancient Visual Affects." *Biblical Interpretation* 22 (2014): 473–502. https://doi.org/10.17613/M64Z82.

Kritzman, Lawrence D. "Representing the Monster: Cognition, Cripples, and Other Limp Parts in Montaigne's 'Des Boyteux.'" In *Monster Theory: Reading Culture*, edited by Jeffrey Jerome Cohen, 168–82. Minneapolis: University of Minnesota Press, 1996.

Lada-Richards, Ismene. "'Foul Monster or Good Saviour'? Reflections on Ritual Monsters." In *Monsters and Monstrosity in Greek and Roman Culture*, edited by Catherine Atherton, 41–82. Bari, IT: Levante Editori, 1998.

LeDuff, Charlie. "At a Slaughterhouse, Some Things Never Die." In *Zoontologies: The Question of the Animal*, edited by Cary Wolfe, 183–97. Minneapolis: University of Minnesota Press, 2003.

Lerner, Anne Lapidus. "A Dogmatic Jesus." In *Soundings in the Religion of Jesus: Perspectives and Methods in Jewish and Christian Scholarship*, edited by Bruce Chilton, Anthony LeDonne, and Jacob Neusner, 47–57. Minneapolis: Fortress Press, 2012.

Levison, John R. *Filled with the Spirit*. Grand Rapids, MI: Eerdmans, 2009.

Lingis, Alphonso. "Animal Body, Inhuman Face." In *Zoonotologies: The*

Question of the Animal, edited by Cary Wolfe, 165–82. Minneapolis: University of Minnesota Press, 2003.

Linzey, Andrew. *Animal Theology*. Champaign: University of Illinois Press, 1994.

Lohr, Joel N. "A Jewish Teaching: Jesus, Gentiles, and the Sheep and the Goats (Matthew 25:31–46)." In *Soundings in the Religion of Jesus: Perspectives and Methods in Jewish and Christian Scholarship*, edited by Bruce Chilton, Anthony LeDonne, and Jacob Neusner, 29–45. Minneapolis: Fortress Press, 2012.

Loss, Scott R., Tom L. Will, and Peter P. Marra. "The Impact of Free-Ranging Domestic Cats on Wildlife in the United States." *Nature Communications* 4 (2013): article 1396. https://doi.org/10.1038/ncomms2380.

Magness, Jodi. *The Archaeology of Qumran and the Dead Sea Scrolls*. Grand Rapids, MI: Eerdmans, 2002.

– *Stone and Dung, Oil and Spit: Jewish Daily Life in the Time of Jesus*. Grand Rapids, MI: Eerdmans, 2011.

Massumi, Brian. *Parables for the Virtual: Movement, Affect, Sensation*. Durham, NC: Duke University Press, 2002.

McDonald, Tracy, and Daniel Vandersommers, eds. *Zoo Studies: A New Humanities*. Montreal: McGill-Queen's University Press, 2019.

McKay, Heather A. "Dress Deployed as an Agent of Deception in Hebrew Bible Narratives." In *Dress Hermeneutics and the Hebrew Bible: "Let Your Garments Always Be Bright,"* edited by Antonios Finitsis, 31–55. London: T&T Clark, 2022.

Metzger, Bruce M. *A Textual Commentary on the Greek New Testament*. 2nd ed. Stuttgart, DE: Deutsche Bibelgesellschaft, 1994.

Milburn, Josh. *Just Fodder: The Ethics of Feeding Animals*. Montreal: McGill-Queen's University Press, 2022.

Milgrom, Jacob. "Israel's Sanctuary: The Priestly 'Picture of Dorian Gray.'" *Revue Biblique* 83, no. 3 (1976): 390–9.

– "The Preposition מִן in the חטאת Pericopes." *Journal of Biblical Literature* 126, no. 1 (2007): 161–3. https://doi.org/10.2307/27638424.

Millar, Suzanna. "Species and Ethnicity in 1 Samuel 15: The Slaughter of Agag and Rejection of Saul." *The Bible & Critical Theory* 19, nos. 1–2 (2023): 1–22. https://bibleandcriticaltheory.com/vol-19-no-1-2-2023-suzanna-millar.

Miller, Patricia Cox. *In the Eye of the Animal: Zoological Imagination in Ancient Christianity*. Philadelphia: University of Pennsylvania Press, 2018.

Mills, Robert. "Queering the Un/Godly: Christ's Humanities and Medieval Sexualities." In *Queering the Non/Human*, edited by Noreen Giffney and Myra J. Hird, 111–35. London: Routledge, 2008.

Mitchell, Matthew W. "The Yoke Is Easy, but What of Its Meaning? A Methodological Reflection Masquerading as a Philological Discussion of Matthew 11:30." *Journal of Biblical Literature* 135, no. 2 (2016): 321–40. https://doi.org/10.15699/jbl.1352.2016.3087.

Montaigne, Michel de. "On Cruelty." In *Essays*, translated by J.M. Cohen, 174–90. London: Penguin, 1993.

Morgan, Jonathan. "Sacrifice in Leviticus: Eco-Friendly Ritual or Unholy Waste?" In *Ecological Hermeneutics: Biblical, Historical and Theological Perspectives*, edited by David G. Horrell, Cherryl Hunt, Christopher Southgate, and Francesca Stavrakopoulou, 32–45. London: T&T Clark, 2010.

Murphy, Erika. "Devouring the Human: Digestion of a Corporeal Soteriology." In *Divinanimality: Animal Theory, Creaturely Theology*, edited by Stephen D. Moore, 51–62. New York: Fordham University Press, 2014.

Nast, Heidi. "Critical Pet Studies?" *Antipode* 38, no. 5 (2006): 894–906. https://doi.org/10.1111/j.1467-8330.2006.00484.x.

Nickelsburg, George W.E., and James C. VanderKam. *1 Enoch: A New Translation*. Minneapolis: Fortress Press, 2004.

Nihan, Christophe. *From Priestly Torah to Pentateuch: A Study in the Composition of the Book of Leviticus*. Tübingen, DE: Mohr Siebeck, 2007.

Nilsen, Tina Dykesteen, and Anna Rebecca Solevåg. "Expanding Ecological Hermeneutics: The Case for Ecolonialism." *Journal of Biblical Literature* 135, no. 4 (2016): 665–83. https://doi.org/10.15699/jbl.1354.2016.3111.

Nkadimeng, Thabang, and Lloyd Baugh. "Strategies of Sound: Revolutionary Music and Song in *Son of Man*." In *Son of Man: An African Jesus Film*, edited by Richard Walsh, Jeffrey L. Staley, and Adele Reinhartz, 34–47. Sheffield, UK: Sheffield Phoenix Press, 2013.

Olson, Kelly. "The Appearance of a Young Roman Girl." In *Roman Dress and the Fabrics of Roman Culture*, edited by Jonathan Edmondson and Allison Keith, 139–57. Toronto: University of Toronto Press, 2008.

Orr, David W. "Armageddon Versus Extinction." *Conservation Biology* 19 (2005): 290–2. https://www.jstor.org/stable/3591239.

Pagels, Elaine, and Karen L. King. *Reading Judas: The Gospel of Judas and the Shaping of Christianity*. New York: Viking, 2007.

Parisi, Luciana. "The Nanoengineering of Desire." In *Queering the Non/Human*, edited by Noreen Giffney and Myra J. Hird, 283–309. London: Routledge, 2008.

Porter, Adam L. "Satanic but Not Satan: Signs of the Devilish in Contemporary Cinema." *Journal of Religion & Film* 17, no. 1 (April 2013): article 37. https://doi.org/10.32873/uno.dc.jrf.17.01.37.

– "Satanic Humans: Using Satanic Tropes to Guide and Misguide the Audience." *Journal of Religion & Film* 21, no. 1 (April 2017): article 40. https://doi.org/10.32873/uno.dc.jrf.21.01.40.

Punt, Jeremy. "'*Thula*' ('*Be Quiet*'): Agency in the *Son of Man*." In *Son of Man: An African Jesus Film*, edited by Richard Walsh, Jeffrey L. Staley, and Adele Reinhartz, 48–60. Sheffield, UK: Sheffield Phoenix Press, 2013.

Purcell, Nicholas. "The Way We Used to Eat: Diet, Community, and History at Rome." In *Roman Dining*, edited by Barbara K. Gold and John F. Donahue, 1–30. Special issue of *American Journal of Philology*. Baltimore: Johns Hopkins University Press, 2005.

Pyper, Hugh. "The Lion King: Yahweh as Sovereign Beast in Israel's Imaginary." In *The Bible and Posthumanism*, edited by Jennifer L. Koosed, 59–74. Atlanta: Society of Biblical Literature, 2014.

Reeve, C.D.C., trans. *Plato: Republic*. Indianapolis: Hackett Publishing, 2004.

Regan, Tom, ed. *Animal Sacrifices: Religious Perspectives on the Use of Animals in Science*. Philadelphia: Temple University Press, 1986.

– *The Case for Animal Rights*. Updated ed. Berkeley: University of California Press, 2004. First published 1983.

– *Defending Animal Rights*. Champaign: University of Illinois Press, 2001.

Rees, Susannah. "'Women Rule Over Them': Dressing for an Inverted World in Isaiah 3." In *Dress Hermeneutics and the Hebrew Bible: "Let Your Garments Always Be Bright,"* edited by Antonios Finitsis, 165–86. London: T&T Clark, 2022.

Reinhartz, Adele. *Bible and Cinema: An Introduction*. New York: Routledge, 2013.

Riley, Matthew T. "A Spiritual Democracy of All God's Creatures:

Ecotheology and the Animals of Lynn White Jr." In *Divinanimality: Animal Theory, Creaturely Theology*, edited by Stephen D. Moore, 241–60. New York: Fordham University Press, 2014.

Rogerson, John W. "The Creation Stories: Their Ecological Potential and Problems." In *Ecological Hermeneutics: Biblical, Historical and Theological Perspectives*, edited by David G. Horrell, Cherryl Hunt, Christopher Southgate, and Francesca Stavrakopoulou, 21–31. London: T&T Clark, 2010.

Rohrer-Walsh, P. Jennifer, and Richard Walsh. "Mary and the Mothers." In *Son of Man: An African Jesus Film*, edited by Richard Walsh, Jeffrey L. Staley, and Adele Reinhartz, 166–77. Sheffield, UK: Sheffield Phoenix Press, 2013.

Roughgarden, Joan. *Evolution's Rainbow: Diversity, Gender, and Sexuality in Nature and People*. 10th Anniversary ed. Berkeley: University of California Press, 2013. First published 2004.

Roussin, Lucille A. "Costume in Roman Palestine: Archaeological Remains and the Evidence from the Mishnah." In *The World of Roman Costume*, edited by Judith Lynn Sebesta and Larissa Bonfante, 182–90. Madison: University of Wisconsin Press, 1994.

Rowland, Christopher. *The Open Heaven: A Study of Apocalyptic in Judaism and Early Christianity*. Chestnut Ridge, NY: Crossroad, 1982.

Rubenstein, Mary-Jane. *Worlds without End: The Many Lives of the Multiverse*. New York: Columbia University Press, 2014.

Runions, Erin. *The Babylon Complex: Theopolitical Fantasies of War, Sex, and Sovereignty*. New York: Fordham University Press, 2014.

– "From Disgust to Humor: Rahab's Queer Affect." *Postscripts* 4, no. 1 (2008): 41–69. https://doi.org/10.1558/post.v4i1.41.

– "Queering the Beast: The Antichrists' Gay Wedding." In *Queering the Non/Human*, edited by Noreen Giffney and Myra J. Hird, 79–110. London: Routledge, 2008.

– "*Son of Man* and Resistance to U.S. Imperialism." In *Son of Man: An African Jesus Film*, edited by Richard Walsh, Jeffrey L. Staley, and Adele Reinhartz, 179–91. Sheffield, UK: Sheffield Phoenix Press, 2013.

Sanders, E.P., and Margaret Davies. *Studying the Synoptic Gospels*. Norwich, UK: SCM Press, Trinity Press International, 1989.

Schaberg, Jane. *The Resurrection of Mary Magdalene: Legends, Apocrypha, and the Christian Testament*. London: Continuum, 2004.

Schaefer, Donovan O. *The Evolution of Affect Theory*. Cambridge Elements: Histories of Emotions and Senses. Cambridge: Cambridge University Press, 2019.

– "Precopulatory Sexual Cannibalism and Other Accidents: Evolution, Material Trans Theory, and Natural Law." *Studies in Gender and Sexuality* 19, no. 1 (2018): 28–35. https://doi.org/10.1080/15240657.2018.1419685.

– *Religious Affects: Animality, Evolution, and Power*. Durham, NC: Duke University Press, 2015.

– "Visions of Contempt: Emotion and the Visual Culture of the Scopes Trial." *Material Religion* 18, no. 2 (2022): 250–76. https://doi.org/10.1080/17432200.2022.2048604.

Schüssler Fiorenza, Elizabeth. *In Memory of Her: A Feminist Theological Reconstruction of Christian Origins*. Tenth Anniversary ed. Chestnut Ridge, NY: Crossroad, 1994.

Sebesta, Judith Lynn, and Larissa Bonfante, eds. *The World of Roman Costume*. Madison: University of Wisconsin Press, 1994.

Sedgwick, Eve Kosofsky. *Touching Feeling: Affect, Pedagogy, Performativity*. Durham, NC: Duke University Press, 2003.

Seesengood, Robert Paul. "What Would Jesus Eat? Ethical Vegetarianism in Nascent Christianity." In *The Bible and Posthumanism*, edited by Jennifer L. Koosed, 227–46. Atlanta: Society of Biblical Literature, 2014.

Sherwood, Yvonne. "Cutting Up Life: Sacrifice as a Device for Clarifying – and Tormenting – Fundamental Distinctions between Human, Animals, and Divine." In *The Bible and Posthumanism*, edited by Jennifer L. Koosed, 247–97. Atlanta: Society of Biblical Literature, 2014.

Shinall, Myrick C., Jr. *Miracles and the Kingdom of God: Christology and Social Identity in Mark and Q*. Idaho Falls, ID: Lexington Books/Fortress Academic, 2018.

Singer, Peter. *Animal Liberation: The Definitive Classic of the Animal Movement*. Updated Edition. New York: HarperCollins, 2009.

Smith, Dennis E. *From Symposium to Eucharist: The Banquet in the Early Christian World*. Minneapolis, MN: Fortress Press, 2003.

Smith, Mitzi J. *Womanist Sass and Talk Back: Social (In)Justice, Intersectionality, and Biblical Interpretation*. Eugene, OR: Cascade Books, 2018.

Smith, William Robertson. *Lectures on the Religion of the Semites*. London: Adam and Charles Black, 1894.

Spielman, Loren R. "Playing Roman in Jerusalem: Jewish Attitudes toward Sport and Spectacle during the Second Temple Period." In *Jews in the Gym: Judaism, Sports, and Athletics*, edited by Leonard J. Greenspoon, 1–24. West Lafayette, IN: Purdue University Press, 2012.

Spittler, Janet E. *Animals in the Apocryphal Acts of the Apostles: The Wild Kingdom of Early Christian Literature*. Tübingen, DE: Mohr Siebeck, 2008.

Spoelstra, Joshua Joel. "Apotropaic Accessories: The People's Tassels and the High Priest's Rosette." In *Dress and Clothing in the Hebrew Bible: "For All Her Household Are Clothed in Crimson,"* edited by Antonios Finitsis, 63–86. London: T&T Clark, 2019.

Staley, Jeffrey. "What Hath New York City to Do with Khayelitsha? An Intertextual Reading of Two Jesus Films." In *Son of Man: An African Jesus Film*, edited by Richard Walsh, Jeffrey L. Staley, and Adele Reinhartz, 95–109. Sheffield, UK: Sheffield Phoenix Press, 2013.

Stewart, Kathleen. *Ordinary Affects*. Durham, NC: Duke University Press, 2007.

Stone, Ken. "The Dogs of Exodus and the Question of the Animal." In *Divinanimality: Animal Theory, Creaturely Theology*, edited by Stephen D. Moore, 36–50. New York: Fordham University Press, 2014.

– *Reading the Hebrew Bible with Animal Studies*. Stanford, CA: Stanford University Press, 2017.

Stone, Sandy. "The *Empire* Strikes Back: A Posttranssexual Manifesto." In *Body Guards: The Cultural Politics of Gender Ambiguity*, edited by Julia Epstein and Kristina Straub, 280–304. New York: Routledge, 1991.

Stratton, Kimberly B. "Magic, Abjection, and Gender in Roman Literature." In *Daughters of Hecate: Women & Magic in the Ancient World*, edited by Kimberly B. Stratton with Dayna S. Kalleres, 152–80. New York: Oxford University Press, 2014.

Strømmen, Hannah M. "Beastly Questions and Biblical Blame." In *The Bible and Posthumanism*, edited by Jennifer L. Koosed, 13–28. Atlanta: Society of Biblical Literature, 2014.

– *Biblical Animality after Jacques Derrida*. Atlanta: SBL Press, 2018.

Stryker, Susan. "My Words to Victor Frankenstein Above the Village of Chamounix - Performing Transgender Rage." *Kvinder, Køn & Forskning* 3–4 (2011): 83–96. https://doi.org/10.7146/kkf.v0i3-4.28037.

Tatum, W. Barnes. *Jesus at the Movies: A Guide to the First Hundred Years and Beyond*. 3rd ed. Temecula, CA: Polebridge Press, 2013.

– "*Son of Man*'s 'Son of Man': Becoming Human and Acting Humanely." In *Son of Man: An African Jesus Film*, edited by Richard Walsh, Jeffrey L. Staley, and Adele Reinhartz, 90–4. Sheffield, UK: Sheffield Phoenix Press, 2013.

Taussig, Hal. *In the Beginning Was the Meal: Social Experimentation & Early Christian Identity*. Minneapolis: Fortress Press, 2009.

Thiessen, Matthew. *Contesting Conversion: Genealogy, Circumcision, and Identity in Ancient Judaism and Christianity*. New York: Oxford University Press, 2018.

Tipton, Brian James. "A Backward Glance for a Queer Utopian Future: Genesis, Climate Change, and Hope as a Hermeneutic." *Biblical Interpretation* 28 (2020): 466–94. https://doi.org/10.1163/15685152-2804A005.

Truffaut, François, with Helen G. Scott. *Hitchcock*. Rev. ed. New York: Simon & Schuster, 1983.

Upson-Saia, Kristi. *Early Christian Dress: Gender, Virtue, and Authority*. New York: Routledge, 2011.

– "Hairiness and Holiness in the Early Christian Desert." In *Dressing Judeans and Christians in Late Antiquity*, edited by Kristi Upson-Saia, Carly Daniel-Hughes, and Alicia J. Batten, 155–72. Farnham, UK: Ashgate, 2014.

Upson-Saia, Kristi, Carly Daniel-Hughes, and Alicia J. Batten, eds. *Dressing Judeans and Christians in Antiquity*. Farnham, UK: Ashgate, 2014.

Vernant, Jean-Pierre. "At Man's Table: Hesiod's Foundation Myth of Sacrifice." In *The Cuisine of Sacrifice among the Greeks*, edited by Marcel Detienne and Jean-Pierre Vernant, 21–86. Translated by Paula Wissig. Chicago: University of Chicago Press, 1989.

Vuong, Lily C. *Gender and Purity in the Protoevangelium of James*. WUNT II 358. Tübingen, DE: Mohr Siebeck, 2013.

Waller, Alexis G. "Violent Spectacles and Public Feelings: Trauma and Affect in The Gospel of Mark and *The Thunder: Perfect Mind*." *Biblical Interpretation* 22, no. 4–5 (2014): 450–72. https://doi.org/10.1163/15685152-02245p05.

Warren, Meredith J.C. *Food and Transformation in Ancient Mediterranean Literature*. Atlanta: SBL Press, 2019.

– *My Flesh Is Meat Indeed: A Nonsacramental Reading of John 6:51–58*. Minneapolis: Fortress Press, 2015.

Walsh, Richard. "A Beautiful Corpse: Fiction and Hagiography in *Son of Man*." In *Son of Man: An African Jesus Film*, edited by Richard Walsh,

Jeffrey L. Staley, and Adele Reinhartz, 192–205. Sheffield, UK: Sheffield Phoenix Press, 2013.

Way, Kenneth C. "Donkey Domain: Zechariah 9:9 and Lexical Semantics." *Journal of Biblical Literature* 129, no. 1 (Spring 2010): 105–14. https://doi.org/10.2307/27821007.

Webster, Jane S. "Teaching *Son of Man*: A Dialogue with Biblical, Global, Film, and Theological Studies." In *Son of Man: An African Jesus Film*, edited by Richard Walsh, Jeffrey L. Staley, and Adele Reinhartz, 149–63. Sheffield, UK: Sheffield Phoenix Press, 2013.

West, Gerald O. "The *Son of Man* in South Africa?" In *Son of Man: An African Jesus Film*, edited by Richard Walsh, Jeffrey L. Staley, and Adele Reinhartz, 2–22. Sheffield, UK: Sheffield Phoenix Press, 2013.

White, Lynn, Jr. "Historical Roots of our Ecologic Crisis." *Science* 155 (1967): 1203–7. https://doi.org/10.1126/science.155.3767.1203.

Whitekettle, Richard. "A Study in Scarlet: The Physiology and Treatment of Blood, Breath, and Fish in Ancient Israel." *Journal of Biblical Literature* 135, no. 4 (2016): 685–704. https://doi.org/10.1353/jbl.2016.0042.

Wilkins, John. "Land and Sea: Italy and the Mediterranean in the Roman Discourse of Dining." In *Roman Dining*, edited by Barbara K. Gold and John F. Donahue, 31–47. Special issue of *American Journal of Philology*. Baltimore: Johns Hopkins University Press, 2005.

Wolfe, Cary. *Animal Rites: American Culture, the Discourse of Species, and Posthumanist Theory*. Chicago: University of Chicago Press, 2002.

– *Before the Law: Humans and Other Animals in a Biopolitical Frame*. Chicago: University of Chicago Press, 2013.

Wolfe, Cary, ed. *Zoontologies: The Question of the Animal*. Minneapolis: University of Minnesota Press, 2003.

Wright, Archie T. *Satan and the Problem of Evil: From the Bible to the Early Church Fathers*. Minneapolis: Fortress Press, 2022.

Zwick, Reinhold. "Between Chester and Capetown: Transformations of the Gospel in *Son of Man*." In *Son of Man: An African Jesus Film*, edited by Richard Walsh, Jeffrey L. Staley, and Adele Reinhartz, 110–19. Sheffield, UK: Sheffield Phoenix Press, 2013.

Index